Carceral Recovery

Carceral Recovery

Prisons, Drug Markets, and the New Pharmaceutical Self

Sanaullah Khan

LEXINGTON BOOKS
Lanham • Boulder • New York • London

Published by Lexington Books
An imprint of The Rowman & Littlefield Publishing Group, Inc.
4501 Forbes Boulevard, Suite 200, Lanham, Maryland 20706
www.rowman.com

86-90 Paul Street, London EC2A 4NE

British Library Cataloguing in Publication Information Available

Library of Congress Cataloging-in-Publication Data

Names: Khan, Sanaullah, author.
Title: Carceral recovery: prisons, drug markets, and the new pharmaceutical self / Sanaullah Khan.
Description: Lanham: Lexington Books, [2024] | Includes bibliographical references and index. | Summary: "Carceral Recovery is a medical anthropologist's account of demoralizing disciplinary and punitive approaches that continue to shape people's experience of recovery in an American city and makes a case for dis-entangling punitive approaches from the experience of substance use"—Provided by publisher.
Identifiers: LCCN 2023029184 | ISBN 9781666929096 (cloth) | ISBN 9781666929102 (ebook)
Subjects: MESH: Substance-Related Disorders—rehabilitation | Substance Abuse Treatment Centers—legislation & jurisprudence | Opiate Substitution Treatment | Medicalization | Social Control, Formal | Mental Health Recovery | Social Determinants of Health | United States
Classification: LCC HV5801 | NLM HV 5801 | DDC 362.29—dc23/eng/20230802
LC record available at https://lccn.loc.gov/2023029184

To my parents

Contents

Preface

This book was written in a rather unconventional manner. I wrote this book initially for a purely non-academic audience with the intention of making legible the lived realities of those suffering from the menace of substance use, by imbuing the non-fictional account with an anthropological flair. Frustrated that the book was not making a theoretical contribution, I wrote the entire manuscript again in a scholarly manner, finding useful literatures to integrate with my empirical findings based on existing academic conversations on substance use. As I worked with the data I gathered, my conviction that the book could contribute to interdisciplinary discussions on substance use and the problem of punitive attitudes increased. As a young graduate student in Baltimore, I could not detach myself from ordinary lives of young men and women living in poverty, subjected to public perceptions about not having the will to improve, moving between one disciplinary institute to another, completely unprepared for challenges of life. It is difficult to live for several years in the city and still be detached. Baltimore became my home but it was also my disappointment with the promise of American dream. Baltimore perhaps was much more "dangerous" than my hometown, Karachi, considered as one of the most "dangerous" cities of the world. I use inverted commas because ideas of danger are created through certain discursive practices that shape media representations. Karachi, of course, a metropolis in a "third world" country, the front-line state in the war on terror, *had* to be dangerous for western audiences. But to my surprise, life expectancy in certain neighborhoods of Baltimore is similar to that of many low-income countries, or perhaps even countries ravaged by war, including countries like Iraq, and so part of the project was to de-familiarize the western city without necessarily exoticizing it, as western scholars have done in much of the non-western world for many generations.

In classes, students talked about dispossession and urban renewal in the city. On campuses, students protested against police brutality. The challenge for me was to investigate how different institutions of the state policed, disciplined and punished marginalized groups and racialized minorities. One way to understand this was to look at the phenomenon of substance use. It is presented as a crime, but those who use drugs need to be disciplined and turned into good citizens, but in doing so, the state creates new psychological pressures, a topic I felt my book could contribute toward. When I shared some of my observations with a professor at Hopkins, he shared that Baltimore might have opened my "anthropological eye." It did. But I will also admit that as much as this book is about human suffering, it is also about my own extreme isolation during the pandemic. Writing allowed me to survive the isolation as I remained determined to convert my fieldnotes into larger, coherent arguments. The book was therefore also about my own transformation. During my five years in Baltimore, I experienced somewhat competing realities—realities of posh academic life and the realities of suffering. I began my graduate training in anthropology and later ventured into the world of global health and medicine, where scholars were increasingly talking about social determinants and health equities but also reinforcing the idea that it was the job of researchers in places like Johns Hopkins to save the world from the menacing problems of infections and illnesses. On the face of it, there was a concern for the social realities of illness, but "social" also became a fancy word that public health practitioners could also throw around to show that however scientific they were in their approaches, they still had a foot in social science, even when they did not give the latter its due importance.

This was also the time of my training in historical methods. I had the chance to go through archives in my spare time, but also as a student employee, where I learned about the historical legacies that shape the treatment of poverty and disease in contemporary Baltimore. Historical methods allowed me to understand "institutional memory" but also things that are otherwise erased or concealed in how history is told. I also had the chance to work on public health teams, including a program on expanding mental health support to low-income households in Baltimore. What I would often detect is the deep distrust many people shared toward how public health functions – many still had fears that the empathy of public health institutes was inherently of a selfish nature. To help others is to help oneself. My goals for the book are not extraordinary. It is to create awareness about punitive attitudes that do more harm than good in solving the problem of substance use. Perhaps for the academic, this might be too simple a premise, but the reason why a simple premise is more important is because I firmly believe that as scholars can write in ways that shape policy debates on the one hand, but also serve an educational role for a lay person on the other. The book then does not aim for the skies, but is for ordinary people—the ordinary Baltimorean, father, mother, doctor, scholar, student, and others.

Acknowledgments

I want to thank all my interlocutors. They all invested a great deal of faith in me to communicate their experiences in the best manner possible. Over the course of the past five years, we also became friends—as much as I became a central part of their lives, they had also become important in mine. I shared my own highs and lows with them. We talked extensively about politics, religion, love, marriage, heartbreak, family, and vulnerabilities. Some of them also gave valuable advice about family life and things to do and not to do based on their own experiences.

Resilience would be the one word I would use if I have to sum up my research and what I learned from my interlocutors. The reason why writing this book was transformational for myself was because looking at the resilience with which many of my interlocutors had dealt with stressful and extraordinary times led me to face my own challenges with somewhat greater calm than I would have otherwise. These friendships also helped sustain the isolation of COVID-19. I want to thank the addiction counselors who shared their experiences with me candidly and generously told me about their contributions in helping young men and women recover. I thank members of the Islamic community at Masjid-ul-Haqq for welcoming me and others with open arms.

I also want to thank my family for all the support they have continued to provide and my friends in Baltimore. The book is also a testament to my own distance from my family and the start of a new life with my wife after being apart for three years and successfully sustaining the test of time (and perhaps different time zones). I can't avoid thinking about my studio apartment at North Calvert in 2018 and 2019, my apartment in Hampden from 2019 to 2021, and then my time in Bolton Hill from 2021 to 2023 where writing and running became my two best ways to cope with almost every emotional and intellectual challenge. My parents, brothers, and their families, despite being away, provided constant support for me. When I recall writing this book, I can't help but think about the passing away of a beloved uncle and my grandmother. I thank them for being so special and kind. This book, I hope, also honors their lives.

List of Abbreviations

AIDS	Acquired Immunodeficiency Syndrome
US	United States
AMA	American Medical Association
GED	General Education Development
MAT	Medication-Assisted treatment
MMT	Methadone Maintenance Treatment
HIV	Human Immunodeficiency Virus
ARC	Addition Research Center
APWA	American Prison Writing Archive
BGF	Baltimore Guerrilla Family
DMI	Dead Man Incorporated
AB	Aryan Brotherhood
CINA	Children in Need of Assistance
DSS	Department of Social Services
EBDI	East Baltimore Development Initiative
BP	Blood pressure
PTSD	Post-traumatic Stress Disorder
ER	Emergency room
DEA	Drug Enforcement Authority
HIPAA	Health Insurance Portability and Accountability Act
NA	Narcotics Anonymous
OTP	Opioid Treatment Program
COVID	Coronavirus
ADHD	Attention Deficit Hyperactivity Disorder
VA	Veterans Affairs

Introduction

The last time Baltimore experienced major protests was at the death of Freddie Gray. While the institutions of the state, most notably the police, considered him to be a plain drug dealer, there were others who understood this problem of substance use as caused by structural conditions of poverty and inequality.[1] The twenty-five-year-old's death from a spinal injury while being in police custody made him a nationwide flashpoint in the debate over police brutality. Gray had attempted to find a job but had convictions for violent crimes, which is why he was turned down every time he applied. The structural problems overlapped with domestic violence. Gray's father Freddie Gray Sr. was largely absent when he was growing up. His mother, Gloria Darden, had gone into rehab for drug substance use, and his father had been prisoned periodically. In this context, there emerged new types of father-figures on the street life. One of them was Bailey, who said that Gray had once told him, "I am trying to do right. I don't want to go back out there [on the streets]. I am trying, but I cannot get a job. I have a record."[2] Gray's lawyer later said that while the police thought that he was acting as a lookout for transactions, he was only talking to people. Gray's arrests showed a pattern of unmarked cars observing him and his friends, and his return to the corner every time he was released was the center of attention. Upon a closer look into his life, it turned out that Freddie had learning issues and could not read or write properly because of learning disabilities caused by lead exposure. Sometimes court dates would confuse Gray, and he found it difficult to keep track of his court hearings. Videos of court proceedings showed him as a "largely passive, unengaging defendant." Smith, his lawyer, contended that for most men like Gray, "the corner [was] their social network."[3] Arguably, lead poisoning was one of the reasons why Gray persistently returned to drugs. Gray's case shows us that the stories of incarceration, substance use, and housing are linked. The corner is a site for interaction for men like Freddie, but it is also a site where the police routinely enter street life. It's also a site of socialization for men, not only to sell drugs but also simply to hang out and get to know people. However, these are also sites where gang violence easily erupts. It's also one where the police arbitrarily enter neighborhood lives to find collaborators or people who can report on the whereabouts of dealers, but for the most part, the purpose is simply to humiliate men, to make them stand against the walls as they are frisked and physically violated, as if their bodies are not entirely theirs, reminding us that there are important comparisons to be made between the ghetto and the slave plantation, as Waquant once argued.[4] The famous Baltimore writer, D. Watson, has also written about running a crack business, the loss of brotherly figures due to gang violence, experiences of pain and loss, new forms of aggression, and how supposedly "normal" people enter the drug ring to make ends meet in a broader socio-economic structure that marginalizes Black men and women.[5] While this type of racialized violence still takes place, there is a different type of biopolitics around the control and surveillance of drug use that has emerged in Baltimore. My argument in this book is that while housing, medicalization, and incarceration fundamentally create the conditions for substance use, increasingly individuals are being propelled into a new disciplinary apparatus of drug recovery where men experience competing pressures to create new lives and be propelled into older ones. While housing, prisons, and treatment centers co-produce substance use by creating the conditions for men and women to engage in violent behaviors and illegal economies, by using the concept of carceral recovery, I refer to the punitive approaches through which institutions engage with the problem of substance use. Instead of simply tracing the criminalization of substance use, as many scholars have considered in the past, my goal is to consider how punishment and punitive approaches in treatment clinics toward recovery make recovery increasingly difficult for many. Attempts made in the process of recovery are all silenced in favor of failures to comply, ignoring the factors that make it difficult for people suffering from substance use to undergo recovery. Fundamentally, the discipline experienced by those with substance abuse problems and in recovery corrodes self-worth and esteem, both beyond and inside households, and by doing so, discipline even creates the conditions for new drug dependencies. In exploring these aspects, the book makes a case for de-entangling carceral attitudes from experience of recovery—in other words, disentangling the *prison* or the *carceral* and its hangovers in a metaphorical sense from the experience of recovery. The book takes substance use as a social condition rather than a state simply marked by dependence. Housing consists of physical conditions and the social relations that constitute the household, which extend beyond the household as communities come under immense surveillance and policing, result in the entanglements between domestic spaces and prison, and shape trajectories of substance use. It is the excessive discipline and the specific socialities and interdependencies created as a result through which substance use and recovery need to be understood. These relationships go beyond the domestic and enter the prison. These relations are also generative of differences based on race and religion. It is within these same relations that the exchange of drugs takes place, and these same relations come to be marked by a different normativity or violent forms of behavior that generate violence—acting as lures to older habits and illicit use of drugs. These exchanges that sustain addictive habits take place at the wedge between goods considered legal and illegal, medicines or illicit drugs, prescribed or unprescribed, which is why medicalization and criminalization are central to the story I tell in this book. However, unlike existing scholarship, my goal is neither to consider the structural conditions that create drug dependence, nor is it to simply consider the criminalization of drug use—instead, my goal is to investigate how state's punishment and household discipline become enmeshed, giving the social relations a texture of suspicion and violence that makes recovery difficult. I employ carceral in a broader and more general sense. Prison attitudes even seep outside of disciplinary institutions such as the treatment center and the prison. As Todd Meyers argues, there is an afterlife of therapy that shows the excesses of treatment—something that remains unquantified where patients' experiences do not match up with the clinical frames of reference, representing a lag that cannot be accounted for in the process of treatment itself. Where my approach differs from his is that I consider the "afterlife" as the consequence of certain carceral structures.[6] The quality of excess that Meyers points out creates new intimacies, forms of relatedness, new antagonisms, and forms of compliance. This happens within the overall broader biopolitics of creating an addiction-free population, which entails putting people with substance use problems from illicit drugs to opioid substitution therapies such as methadone and buprenorphine and thus a new, and pharmaceuticalized, way to exert control—there is thus both a policing of substance use of illicit drugs and the disciplining of new medicalized selves. My goal in this book is to throw light on the longer processes of discipline within prisons given the fact that incarceration for drug-related charges has been a reality for many low-income and most Black households in Baltimore, as in much of the United States, but the story I tell does not end here —in fact, a new modality of control with traces of carceral attitudes is present even in the biopolitical regime of methadone maintenance. The transition from criminalization to medicalization is inherently fraught; this process remains difficult for many, especially given suspicions toward the client and their percieved lack of willingness to improve, which are reproduced in courts, prisons, and homes. Therefore suspicion and punishment are common experiences of substance use and recovery. What is also important to keep in mind is that this suspicion shapes the substance use experience as much as the recovery experience.

There is usually a tendency to view the experience of substance use either in domestic spaces alone, in the treatment center, or in prison, when in reality there is a continuous movement between these multiple sites. There appears to be a discussion about substance use and recovery experiences in silos. Moreover, there is either an emphasis on criminalization or simply on the creation of social conditions that generate substance use without focusing on the daily experiences of surveillance that shape how people engage with drug markets, strive to live "drug-free lives," and come under immense surveillance and sometimes even relapse. The major thrust of research has been focused on the medicalization of substance use, especially among historians. On the other hand, the preoccupation among sociologists has been to study the disciplining of abnormalities, which simplistically views substance use as a problem caused by structural changes. Scholars of social suffering have astutely noted how structural violence impacts patterns of social response and intimacy, including who to help and who to withhold help and support from in critical moments or times of distress, putting pressure on what constitutes "normal" behavior.[7] Global structural inequality also creates new forms of exclusion through the withholding of support for communities in distress, which has a direct impact on health and wellbeing. Meanwhile, global health institutes continue to pose disease as existing in far off lands when a critical epidemiology of exclusions within developed places would reveal that proportions of disease may even exist at higher rates in underprivileged and racially marginalized areas in the United States than in many parts of the developing world.[8] In recent days, there has been growing awareness about how improving housing conditions can result in better treatment and recovery outcomes among people struggling with substance use, especially in public health and epidemiological accounts. Still, an aspect that is crucially ignored in scientific and epidemiological accounts is the struggle, attempts to regain agency, and generate aspirations and to re-think one's life in conditions that are otherwise too constraining. The question for us then is: How do individuals struggle to overcome substance use while trying to live in constraining situations? What are the ways in which individuals articulate substance use in relation to longer histories of violence within their households and encounters with prison systems? How do individuals come together to transact in drugs, and how do they try to overcome their substance use despite several relapses? What are the ways in which individuals create long-term visions and interpret them in light of daily contingencies? These questions constitute the subject of this book. But to consider the complex intimacies and dependencies that shape the trajectories of substance use, it is important to first consider the social uses of medicine and the re-interpretation of medicine and drugs as legal or illegal.

A GENEALOGY OF MEDICALIZATION

The opioid crisis and its impact on social behavior is more profound than has been considered in the past, and this has to do with whether a drug is viewed as illicit or medical, or perhaps even both. Many drugs with medicinal uses may circulate in illegal drug markets, where their social meanings can be reinterpreted. Oxycontin is one example—initially proposed for pain reduction, it slowly made many users dependent on it. Its medical use was repurposed into something illegal. Investigative journalists have focused on courtroom dramas where the consequences of opioids such as OxyContin were debated, especially as the marketing of the drug had a direct impact on its illicit uses.[9] The same has been the case for many other drugs in the past. Some drugs considered illegal may come to be considered as medicinal, whereas other medicines can become illegal. These definitions have to do with the blurry lines between the white and the black market. Whereas pharmaceutical expansion may continue in the so-called white market, similar parallels of drug use and dependence may be increasingly penalized in black markets. This means that even when opioids are addictive and their effects are known, the blame for dependence and abuse is placed squarely on the shoulders of the patients as pharmaceutical companies continue to expand their supplies. According to Courtwright, the number of medical "addicts" using opium or morphine in the United States decreased from 1895 to 1935, whereas the rate of non-medical "addicts" using heroin continued to increase. He argues that eventually, non-medical substance use came to be considered as essentially an underworld phenomenon.[10] The distinction between medical and non-medical itself can be fairly blurry. But there are moral arguments about the weakness of will that are invoked to understand vulnerability to illicit drug use. Courtwright writes that initially substance use of opium was tied to inebriety:

> If the patient had inherited a neurotic tendency or predisposition to seek relief from every pain and discomfort or if he suffered from neurasthenia or some other nervous ailment, the pathologic impression was likely to be "more or less permanent," and repeated administration would intensify the impression into a morbid craving. Once the morbid craving or substance use was established, succeeding generations were especially vulnerable to inebriety.[11]

Compared to hereditary explanations, there were others who made the case that anyone could experience problems with substance use. Ernest S. Bishop presented the thesis that it was not as if inherent traits made a person an addict, but that "addicts were genuinely sick persons who ought not be denied the one substance, morphine, that could prevent a serious toxic reaction; and substance use was a disease that anyone, regardless of personality or heredity could contract.[12] Later, however, repeated relapse came to be interpreted as a problem of an "underlying personality disorder," where a person's rapid descent to substance use would be viewed as remaining "unchecked by the slightest ethical compunction."[13] However, by the 1930s, so-called psychopathic theories had begun to proliferate. According to these theories, an addicted person could "readily admit having fallen into substance use through associates and the pleasing effect that opium had upon them."[14] In this vein, Lawrence Kolb conclusively refuted the antitoxin theory, "knocking the scientific underpinnings from beneath the normal personality thesis."[15] In scientific discourses surrounding substance use, the person using drugs was no longer a "normal" person under the sway of bad company; instead, there was something inherently pathological about people who became substance users. The theme about the "dangerous individual" then came to dominate the medical debates about causes of substance use as the proportion of people consuming morphine for non-medical purposes continued to increase. What interests me here is how the category of the dangerous individual was constructed medically and legally. The construction of the dangerous and unstable individual in scientific discourse justifies new forms of control.

Like Courtwright, recently David Herzberg has drawn attention to the criminalization of black markets. He shows how barbiturates continued to be administered without much reluctance and how their addictive impacts continued to be neglected.[16] Barbiturates were increasingly advertised for everyday uses, such as sleeplessness. Sleeplessness was classified as a medical concern. As barbiturates were aggressively publicized, by the 1920s, the "drug habit" had become "drug addiction,"—a narrower and more terrifying concept applying to a specific set of drugs ("narcotics") and a specific type of drug user (poor, criminal).[17] On the other hand, barbiturates continued to be marketed, with the target population consisting invariably of white women. This was also the time of the experimentation with the so-called narcotic farms, first set up in 1929 but repealed in 1944, with farm establishments abrogated in 1975 with the advancement in medication treatment. The purpose of these farms was to ensure preventative custody and remedial care. The exclusionary logics to treat substance use had been still set into motion despite the abrogation of these farms, but with medication treatment, new contradictory logics of integration and exclusion were instituted.

Psychiatrists continued to reason that those consuming barbiturates were not themselves addictive but that barbiturates caused addiction among only those who were "mentally unstable," thus keeping the "white market" and its users bounded off from criticism. The Harrison Act, which sought to control narcotics trafficking, also excluded barbiturates. After 1943, barbiturates could no longer be sold without a prescription. The American Medical Association also began to raise awareness about dangers of self-prescribing.[18] According to Herzberg, there still remained a weaker control over white markets compared to stronger controls over black markets. Those who took advantage of easy accessibility and diverted drugs to the informal economy were mainly considered as culprits.[19] Overdoses continued to be blamed onto individuals rather than laws and structures that resulted in drug use. The moralizing tone was paradoxically accompanied by an indifference toward deaths caused by drug use. A close parallel to drug use was considered that of suicides caused by jumping from the Empire State, which also in some sense downplayed the immediacy of the problem. Harris Isbell, an American pharmacologist, stated that just because a drug caused addiction did not mean it had to be controlled using draconian state laws. It was reasoned that too strong a force of law would drive people to something else or perhaps even more dangerous drugs.[20] However, prescription controls were extended, and the Humphrey-Durham Amendment led to stricter pharmaceutical checks—a pharmacist giving prescription medicine without authorization of the physician could be prosecuted, according to the amendment. At the same time, narcotics continued to be met with greater force of law, as in the Boggs Act of 1956, which led to the toughening of penalties for non-prescribed medication.

Instead of focusing on any one category of narcotics or medically prescribed substance, my focus in this book is on understanding how drugs move between the formal and the informal economy, which creates new risks of non-compliance in treatment centers. However, it is still important to keep the insights from Herzberg and Courtwright in mind, as both use different histories to demonstrate the tightening control over narcotics and the classification of the person likely to engage in the black market as a dangerous and psychopathic individual, defined in some ways by his class and race. While Courtwright shows the expansion of the users of opium for non-medical purposes, Herzberg considers the tightening and the formalization of prescription-only drugs. What I will show ethnographically is how people traverse the boundaries between white and black markets, even if the boundaries between them are rigidly defined. Moreover, I will show how prescription-only drugs continue to expand alongside narcotics and enter the black market in the case of Baltimore, with people in treatment centers selling them for monetary benefits. Herzberg and Courtright's works are significant as starting points in the investigation because they show that the boundaries of what constitutes as white or black markets are not stable, and the contestation and recalibration of those boundaries invariably results in the criminalization of "non-medical" users. It is important to take up the theme of criminalization because the story of drug abuse is not complete without considering pharmacies, medical institutes, and carceral systems, which punish but also paradoxically create new pressures to undergo recovery, a form of biochemical control, namely through the use of methadone—shaping what can or cannot enter the body while also closely monitoring how much of something exists through routine assessments. However, this control is not uniform, and clients and those in recovery both make transgressions and conceal them, giving a picture of biopolitics, or perhaps *bio-chemico politics* that is far from complete. To consider people's experimentation and transgression while remaining within strict forms of discipline, it is useful to consider the materiality of the drug and the way it can be repurposed with new social meanings—from medicine to illegal and vice versa. A drug that is habit-forming can even become "medicinal" for a person with excruciating withdrawals. Thus, the materiality of the drug and the social ties it creates are important aspects to consider in the story of substance use. This also means that medicinal drugs can be combined with illicit ones, creating limit figures in the state's biopolitics of an addiction-free population.

OPIOID EPIDEMIC AND SOCIALITY

How then do people repurpose drugs or re-signify their meanings? Investigative journalists have been at the forefront of efforts to unravel the origins of the opioid crisis. Beth Macy's book *Dopesick* starts with the event of a dealer who used to run a trade ring and was caught by the police, leading to hundreds of people getting "dope sick" after the cutting off of the drug supply. When the ring had been eliminated, users headed to areas surrounding West Virginia to get their doses. OxyContin came to be widely used, specifically in Appalachia, where poverty had already been very rampant. People would first rub the coating of OxyContin and then reuse the remaining powder by snorting later.[21] Purdue Pharma, the makers of OxyContin, had envisaged that the slow-release delivery would, in fact, frustrate the abusers wanting a rush. OxyContin had been hailed as the most effective painkiller not only for stage four cancer patients but also for those who had sustained moderate injuries. OxyContin, however, also began to be paired with a "nerve pill" for a better experience among users.[22] When the use of OxyContin spread, instances of patients threatening doctors or even stealing prescriptions behind their doctors' backs began to increase. This epidemic deeply impacted sociality as users looked for opportunities to steal from others who had been prescribed with OxyContin by their physicians.

The story about the rise of Purdue Pharma and the Sackler Family—the founders of OxyContin—has been captured by Patrick Radden Keefe in the *Empire of Pain.* Keefe shows that the primary motivation of Arthur Sackler and his brothers was to find an alternative to the institutionalization of individuals in mental asylums. Arthur Sackler was committed to showing that mental illness could be understood as a response to neurochemical imbalances, which marked a shift from Freudian theories about personality and the unconscious as the basis of illness.[23] Beth Macy shows how the aggressive marketing of OxyContin by Purdue Pharma led a physician, Van Zee, to launch an official campaign to organize people against Purdue Pharma. Upon denial from the Purdue Pharma about the withdrawals of OxyContin, Van Zee said, "People aren't just stealing from their families breaking into their neighbors' homes just over blood-pressure pills."[24] Alan Spanos of Purdue Pharma suggested that it was important for patients to decide for themselves how many painkillers they could take without overdosing.[25] However, Van Zee continued to make calls to monitor marketing when incidences of violence and overdoses continued to increase. One person gunned down the manager of a Pay-less supermarket to find his next Oxy fix. It became common for people to be involved in "spot and steal" exercises in which they would spot an item during the day and return to steal it to buy their OxyContin doses. Once a person even killed a young man as he attempted to break into his house to steal his wife's prescription drugs that the latter had spotted in the kitchen through the window. In another case, a person got his own son arrested for stealing and buying OxyContin from the back market.[26] For me as an anthropologist, instances like these are not trivial, but facts that show how the epidemic had impacted sociality such that the home was no longer considered a safe place, a site bounded off from the wider community, but a site that was marked by violence as neighbors and even family members turned against each other in suspicion. Further, it shows how substance use—the use of drugs within a broader social structure—changed the way people interacted with each other.

In *Pain Killer,* Barry Meier gives a glimpse of the social context in Lee County where the epidemic had a deep impact on neighborliness and the overall sense of security,

> On the black market, OxyContin had a value of $1 per milligram, meaning that a 20-milligram-strength tablet sold for $20 and a 40-milligram tablet sold for $40. For people like Lindsay Myers, who had thousands of dollars in her bank account, finding the cash to buy Oxy wasn't a problem. Because most people didn't have that kind of money, crime accelerated alongside the abuse of

OxyContin. Addicts broke into houses and stole cash and televisions. In some cases, cancer and pain patients awoke to find bottles of OxyContin missing from their medicine cabinets. Forged, stolen, and worthless checks began to paper the region. So many of them were for $40—the street price of a 40-milligram Oxy—that cops would joke upon finding one: "We know where that forty dollars went." People eager to get the drug ran up huge debts on their credit cards, buying things they could quickly convert into cash. Those without credit lines shoplifted items like cigarette lighters or compact discs and sold those. In rural southwestern Virginia, chainsaws were popular targets.[27]

Barry Meier's emphasis is also on the politics of pain. He considers the work of Russell Portenoy, who was a proponent of providing patients with pain alleviation, even if this meant granting patients the autonomy to administer their doses.

Before long, other doctors were referring pain patients to Portenoy. As he learned about pain in many forms, he observed how difficult it was for patients to get help. One patient, a thirty-five-year-old Black man with sickle-cell anemia, told Portenoy that each time he suffered an attack he was forced to go to a hospital and endure hours of pain before a hospital emergency-room doctor would give him just a few painkillers. Portenoy wrote him a prescription for Percocet so he would have a ready supply at home. The man broke down and cried, telling Portenoy that no doctor had ever trusted him before.[28]

According to Portenoy, the high substance use rates noted by researchers in 1920s had skewed results as they only considered participants in the drug treatment programs, whereas if one looked at the experience of pain patients who received narcotics in medical settings, the addictive risks were outweighed by the benefits.[29] During the 1990s, spurred by leaders of the pain management movement, government authorities soon began calling for better care. In 1992, for example, a unit of the Public Health Service called the Agency for Health Care Policy issued new guidelines that urged hospitals to use powerful narcotics more aggressively to treat the type of acute pain experienced as a result of surgery.[30] Many doctors also looked unfavorably upon prescription oversight and considered it as an act of scaring doctors and not allowing them to provide care that the patients deserved.[31] Purdue Pharma intervened at precisely this moment when a growing need was felt to provide pain management by tabling their plans for OxyContin.

Pharmacies then began to be prosecuted for giving medicines without prescriptions, refilling prescriptions, or issuing them orally. The AMA opposed prescription surveillance but still supported restrictions on barbiturates. Later in 1948, the Supreme Court would uphold the FDA's authority to prosecute pharmacists. When prescription drugs began to be used non-therapeutically, law enforcement and public health institutes came together to police prescriptions and criminalize doctors, patients, and pharmacists. Nicholas Rasmussen has shown how the use of barbiturate goofballs provoked moral panic in the 1940s and a perception of loosening behavioral constraints.[32] It was thought that the impacts of barbiturates were corrosive socially, which led to calls for stricter inventory controls. I am particularly interested in tracking the social interpretations of prescriptions when they are increasingly surveilled. How do social actors such as the patient and his or her wider web of relationship determine the terms for opioid use? A point of entry into this question is provided by Marcia Meldrum, who helps us consider how the doctor's office itself becomes a gray market which gatekeeps the movement between the formal and the black market. She uses the example of a rheumatic patient who begged her physician for prescriptions.[33] Repeated attempts allowed the husband to take it as a sign of substance use rather than pain alleviation. Although initially she had been prescribed Oxycodone in combination with another substance, the rheumatologist, upon the insistence of the patient, gave a scrip for six Lortabs. Eventually the patient even became a "doctor shopper," that is, she went from one doctor to another just to get a prescription.[34] Her relations with her mother and husband continued to deteriorate. The patient's family, including the mother and the husband, were considered important by the physician for the successful discontinuation of the patient's use of opioids. Her medical condition further evolved. When she developed endometriosis, the doctor gave her a second prescription of Lortab. Her use of the prescription and regular visits to pharmacies in the hope of securing a scrip led to her being red-flagged in every pharmacy.[35] The husband increasingly thought he was trying to control Marie. Marie thought that the entire process even shaped her own self-image as a problem patient. She thought that everyone had started to treat her like a child or a criminal. Her self-esteem became so low that she even contemplated committing suicide. She thought that her presence was only a cause of pain for her family, until she met with a physician who gave her a prescription for painkillers, which surprised and demoralized her husband. However, she was asked by the doctor to record the pain and dosages in her daily journal so that the OxyContin intake could be reduced progressively.[36] Meldrum's important insight is that physicians and patients can both be exposed to stigma because of the use and the prescription of opioids, but they may still have different strategies related to pain management and remission, which cannot be fully appreciated if they continue to be stigmatized. The important takeaway is that the course of treatment and the management of withdrawals is crucially impacted by the webs of social relations around the patient, which I refer to as central aspects of *carceral recovery*, where successful pain management and reduction of opioid use cannot take place until the patient is provided enough autonomy.

If this does not happen, the care provided by family will only intensify tensions in social relations and prevent successful treatment outcomes. Taking up the example of Marie, how does one consider treatment in the case of individuals who have a history of incarceration? How do they negotiate the discipline of carceral and medical institutions? More specifically how do carceral attitudes toward substance use continue to persist and result in the undoing of recovery?

SUBSTANCE USE AND CARCERAL ATTITUDES

As shown in the case of Marie, people with substance use are put under various forms of discipline both within families and in other institutions—and experience a form of *carceral recovery*, where substance use takes place under conditions of strict disciplinary controls, degrading one's sense of self-worth. What I refer to as *carceral recovery* is when relapses are punished both by the state through its systems of surveillance and imprisonment and at home by relatives, undoing any gains made in recovery. Why is prison and incarceration generally more important to consider the story of substance use? The prison is relevant because many have had experience with incarceration. It is relevant also because the prison is actually the site where pharmaceutical experimentation takes place—where there is a constant tension between the principles of extending life through methadone and reducing life through heroin.[37] The distinction between illegal and the medicinal becomes blurred in the prison, especially in the smuggling of drugs. Carceral recovery also refers to the obligations created within prisons that extend even beyond. What does carceral recovery reveal about the structures of state authority and the webs of relations that many find it difficult to disentangle themselves from? To give one example of the complex relationships in which prisoners are entangled, let us now consider smuggling within Baltimore prisons. On September of 2019, almost twenty men—including an inmate, correction officers, and prison employees—were found smuggling drugs into a Maryland prison, in exchange for money and sex. The smuggling had taken place for two years before the investigation concluded its results. A person named McNeely had brought the packages into the correctional institute at Jessup, which were never checked for security, despite regulations that were meant to prevent such infiltrations. McNeely was caught when he was trying to drop off drugs at the prison library when he was seen in the possession of suboxone strips, heroin, fentanyl, cocaine, and K2, a form of synthetic marijuana. His collaborator, Alston, who had first been incarcerated on the account of his second-degree murder and weapons charge in 2017, only admitted to his involvement after McNeely had been caught getting the drugs into the prison.

When investigators tapped into telephonic conversations, they found that collaborators had even discussed the pay that was to be given to the correctional officer and the contract nurse who worked in the facility. The ring of twenty people involved individuals both outside and inside the prison. Bazemore, an inmate, admitted that he was collaborating with McNeely to smuggle drugs into the facility. Later, Bazemore even admitted that he had received the help of a correctional dietary officer, Patricia McDaniel. This is one in the series of other episodes in which the collaborators involved both the officers and the inmates and their networks of drug dealers outside of the prison. In June, a correctional officer at Eastern Correctional Institution in Somerset County pleaded guilty to charges of smuggling synthetic cannabinoids and buprenorphine into the prison. In 2016, up to eighty people were indicted in the state's largest corruption case, where inmates were accused of conspiring to sneak pornography and cell phones into prison. Later in January 2018, two guards in maximum-security detention in Jessup were accused of helping smuggle heroin, cocaine, and cellphones into the facility along with sixteen other people. The power of the gang members in the prison, such as those of the Black Guerilla Family, has become so rampant that they even conspired with the guards to ensure that they enjoyed all the pleasures of freedom. The inmates even ended up impregnating up to four guards.[38] The prison bureaucracy thus even serves as a grey zone in that it either facilitates many of these exchanges directly or turns a blind eye to them.

In the example above, we can see that it was through this network that inmates lured correctional officers into their plans and were successful in smuggling goods inside of the prisons. My point here is not simply to say that these officers were corrupt but to highlight the networks that inmates were able to deploy in which officers themselves participated. In one episode, David M. W. McCullers was initially found to be distributing drugs in a hotel. He was first caught and later found in the possession of drugs. The news report in *Baltimore Sun* and the charging documents, on which the former was based, did not discriminate between dealing outside or within the prison. The story goes, "On Friday McCullers was being taken to Carroll Hospital, along with two inmates who overdosed, when the paramedics transporting him saw him drop a baggie of suspected heroin, according to charging documents. A K-9 unit alerted the police about the presence of controlled dangerous substances in McCullers' cell, where police found part of a strip of suboxone, which is used to treat opioid substance use, and suspected crack cocaine, charging documents read."[39]

There are a few points to take from this: one is the presence of opioids found in the possession of the person, which showed the network of contacts the person might have drawn upon, including clients in treatment centers as well as participants within the informal drug market. Taking the inmates to the hospital testified to the deadly nature of the substance. One way in which the police could typically ascertain how widely drugs had been distributed in the prison was to see how many people overdosed and thereby belonged to the ring. The news report mentioned, "There were eleven men in the intake unit at the time of the overdoses, Warden Hardinger said. The women are kept separate from the men. While the unit was searched for drugs, the remaining inmates were removed from the area, checked by medical staff, searched, and questioned, he said. The dog was brought in from the Carroll County Sheriff's Office K-9 unit to aid in the search, according to Hardinger. One "suspicious substance" was found and will be tested, he said."[40] Thus, the prison and wider drug market are not as disconnected as one might think. They both have a dynamic relationship. The relationship between inmates in the prison is shaped by networks outside of the prison. The relationships between the inmates, in turn, shape how different gangs interact with one another on the streets. The rivalries and negotiations inside and outside influence one another, yet neither of the two can be taken as micro or macrocosm of the other. The second point to note is that inmates and prison administration share a dynamic and close relationship, in which the entire political economy of the prison could be understood through negotiations taking place between different actors, which is a different view than to assume that the prison is a panoptical-type institute where there is little interaction between the inmates and the correctional officers because of the individualizing role of the disciplinary gaze.[41] There is conflict as well as intimacy between the officers and inmates.

Some of my interlocutors went as far as to suggest that the rates of incarceration were broadly shaped by the imperative to let prisons maintain a relationship with the broader society. According to Jacob, whom I will introduce shortly, rates of incarceration and release were primarily based on a principle of efficiency, that is, firstly, how much capacity a prison had, and secondly, on a calculation at a particular time about who could be released or retained in order to ensure the entry of those who posed the greatest amount of risk to society. Individuals found to be involved in the drug market continued to re-join drug market having already completed prison sentences before, until they were reincarcerated. For Jacob, release was motivated by structural requirements to ensure that the prison did not overcrowd, and release was taken as an opportunity not only by an individual but by the larger group to re-establish ties with the outside world. In this sense, the release of an inmate in some cases even presupposes his or her eventual return to the prison, either through collaborations with the inmates or through incarceration on the grounds of drug possession or another crime.

The control over contraband was also viewed as discretionary. There are various limitations placed on how people interact with other inmates in prison. These interactions are often filtered for their content by the prison authorities. Letters and objects, such as gifts, are passed along the prison bureaucracy after they are screened for content.[42] The issue of objects being unable to pass was once raised when a female inmate from the Carroll County Detention Center found out that her letters were not being delivered to her boyfriend. Stacy Maczis, the female inmate, admitted that she had written an intimate letter to her boyfriend. She knew that her messages were being monitored but did not know how far she could go with the use of sexual content in the letters. The first letter that she had written to her boyfriend was sent successfully. The second letter, however, was flagged as sexually explicit and was not delivered. It was not returned to Stacy until several days later. The delay disturbed her because she thought that the letter had been floating around the prison during the period. Stacy later protested angrily, "Can you please send me the policy for what is allowed to be written? If you just send the policy, I will follow it."[43] Later, the warden George Hardinger described that all incoming mails except for legal mails were checked, but the primary concern was contraband and substance use treatment medication like suboxone. Even items such as photographs and drawings face restriction during delivery. He continued, "Inmates have gotten pretty creative and they will smuggle in drugs by concealing them in crayons. They can melt it and seal them as watermarks and other things. So we open it up, we look for anything that might be suspicious."[44]

The reason for the particular instance of unsuccessful delivery and censoring was its "pornographic content." Since the incident, Hardinger suggested that only one correctional officer was going through all the letters to ensure that there was only one standard criterion for delivery, gesturing to the fact that censorship and control were discretionary in the past. The reason why I mention this episode is to show how inmates continued to maintain relationships with each other, often times in very creative ways, and given the amount of written material exchanged on a regular basis, it was perfectly possible to have varying standards for what was permissible and what was disallowed at any given time. In any case, the complex political economy of the prison is shaped by the creative ways in which exchange takes place to overcome the restrictions placed on the delivery by the correctional officers. The subjective elements in evaluating what could and could not be sent also revealed gaps in prison administration's control over contraband. Although spatially distributed in different cells and areas in the correctional facility, inmates continue to draw upon existing knowledge about their friends in the prison to expand their networks.

The smuggling of drugs into the prison is based on the same enduring ties that continue to be mobilized even under restrictions over mobility and communication. In February of 2018, Nicholas Cole and Timothy Baker were charged with attempting to smuggle drugs into the prison. The news report in the *Baltimore Sun* described that the charges were based on "phone calls between Cole, Baker and a woman Jennifer Lee Drury, thirty-five, of the 7400 block of the Watersville Road, according to charging documents." The call was later intercepted by the prison authority. "The phone calls were recorded by the detention center and staff allegedly described Cole and Baker instructing Drury, who was not incarcerated at the time, on where to place drugs in a bathroom of DaVita Carroll County Dialysis Facility on Stoner Avenue in Westminster, according to charging documents. Cole was scheduled to receive treatment at the facility on Monday, according to the charging documents, and in the phone call, it was discussed that Drury should tape a condom filled with drugs to the toilet where Cole would recover them and smuggle them into the detention center. On Monday, the police waited for Drury to arrive and place the drugs in the toilet before recovering the drugs and arresting Drury. Police found fifteen sealed sublingual suboxone strips wrapped in a condom, according to charging documents. Suboxone is the name of the brand of narcotics medication often used to treat pain or substance use that is illegal to possess without a prescription."[45] Drury was asked for a prescription for suboxone in addition to other illicit drugs. For an opioid such as suboxone, the first response by the police would usually be to ask for a prescription. From the story, we can also get a sense of how a complex arrangement of communication takes place between those inside and beyond the prison. The communication is based on when and how the inmate leaves the facility and how this is coordinated with someone from outside. The communication can sometimes be intercepted, but other times the language and the creativity with which these actions are executed defy any possibility of interception. The other interesting thing is how objects are used to camouflage the movement of drugs. The use of social relations inside and outside the prison, modes of communication in codes, and creativity in camouflaging drugs in objects all contribute to the circulation of drugs. I have only documented a few cases in which this happened. There are plenty of cases like these in Baltimore, Maryland, and in the rest of the state. The reason why I have not limited myself to Baltimore correctional facility in my analysis is that the sources from Carroll County were easily accessible, and secondly, because a lot of the inmates or drug smugglers were residents of Baltimore. Besides, the proximity of these counties also means that there is a lot of trade and movement taking place between them. This is also a result of stricter surveillance in the city, which is why it is not surprising for the dealers to find customers in the surrounding counties. In August of 2014, Amanda Renee Jones of Charles Street, the Deputy State's Attorney Edward Coyne asked a confidential informant to contact her. The Deputy met with Jones and exchanged cash for a cigarette pack containing small bags of cocaine and heroin. The fact that Jones was enrolled in a GED program at the Carroll County Detention Center meant that she had "a lot of time to sit and gain insight."[46] It was added in the statement of facts that she was letting drug dealers live in her house. Her incarceration served as a turning point, as two of her associates had recently overdosed on heroin. The confession and the willingness to part with her ways were taken with suspicion by the judge, who suggested that she would have to complete the drug treatment program in the detention center to participate in the Drug Treatment Court if she wanted to modify her sentence.

Prisons are central to the story of substance use, not only because they present sites where those who have participated in drug-related crimes are incarcerated. Prisons are important as sites where drug abuse and activity takes place—as they are sites where individuals become entangled in carceral obligations, as I will discuss in chapter 2. Prisons are also important sites because their punitive behavior seeps into courts, treatment centers and families, especially in the new biopolitics of methadone treatment—in a metaphorical rather than a literal sense—because state perception toward substance use also shapes intimate responses, where the emphasis is on care rather than punishment. This is why in the ethnography I bring together prisons, courts, treatment centers, and homes to show how, despite a shift toward less punitive approaches to substance use, there is still a perception among families, clients and people suffering from substance use about being punished for violations—either for drug use or their inability to participate in treatment programs seriously. The disciplining and punitive approaches toward substance use also pervade the experience of recovery.

In cities like Baltimore, youth come under increasing surveillance by the police. As their households experience extreme precarity, they are made to engage in the drug economy to make ends meet, and often their livelihood is tied only to their survival in the violent and competitive drug market. I will explore this aspect in greater detail, but what is important to keep in mind here is that the surveillance of street life eventually results in the entry of the youth into juvenile prisons. This is the beginning of a lifetime of repeat incarcerations. While existing sociological work on institutions focuses only on discipline within institutions, this study expands how discipline is contested, negotiated and accepted at the levels of households and neighborhoods. The experiences of substance use and recovery carry traces of the carceral also because of the inherent nature of power that is exerted over many—one in which there is both active surveillance and oversight, coercion and force.

According to Erving Goffman, "total institutions" involve efforts by clients to compensate for their restrictive circumstances. A significant proportion of the interaction in such institutions is devoted to adjustment of the balance of power exercised by each actor. Guenther studied "shakedowns," which was a custodial tactic to locate and seize unauthorized possessions. Based on a study in a state penitentiary in Atlanta, he considered inmate deprivation and the staff responses to prisoners' compensations.[47] He draws upon the work of Gresham Sykes, who argues that imprisonment deteriorates the very foundation of an inmate's being and that the patterns of interaction among inmates signify widespread attempts to reestablish this lost identity. What I borrow from these discussions is that allowing a certain degree of freedom to socialize is part of the staff's attempt to monitor activity. Here, the idea of control is one that involves the granting of favors by the staff to the prisoners precisely to incriminate them. In the new biopolitics of substance use treatment, too, the state constructs new forms of autonomy. Sykes writes,

> To a large extent, the guard is dependent on inmates for the satisfactory performance of his duties, and like many figures of authority, the guard is evaluated in terms of the men he controls; a troublesome, noisy, dirty cellblock reflects on the guard's ability to handle prisoners and this forms an important component of the merit rating used as the basis for pay raises and promotions. A guard cannot rely on the direct application of force to achieve compliance, for he is one man against hundreds; and if he continually calls for additional help he becomes a major problem for the shorthanded prison administration. . . . The guard, then, is under pressure to achieve a smooth running cellblock by persuasion of rewards rather than by the threat of punishment or by force. . . . One is to make the best "offers" he can make in ignoring minor offenses or making sure that he never places himself in a position to discover infractions of the rules.[48]

According to Guenther, the management of inmates involves officers determining the implications of minor rule violations. This simultaneously also includes an avoidance to remind inmates about their infractions to blackmail or to exert psychological pressure. A second use of prisoners' compensation is to serve as a means to solicit information. This explains efforts such as "shaking down" inmates as a means to generate information such as movement of contrabands, where they are stored, and to whom they belong.[49] This reveals a much more general interrelationship between autonomy and punishment. Later in the ethnographic study, I will consider shakedowns in the case of an open-air drug market. For now, it is important to ask: how can we think about the entwinement of care and punishment in conditions of carcerality?

Given the shift toward treating substance use medically rather than through punishment, it is perhaps useful to consider how care and treatment carry traces of the carceral. It is useful to first consider what treatment in carceral settings looks like and then expand this to strictly medical settings to understand the competing pressures of punishment and cure from there. I would like to consider briefly what carcerality does to the treatment of illness and then expand it as an analytical framework beyond prisons. Lorna Rhodes describes how prison workers are trained to perceive prisoners in a maximum-security prison as manipulative.[50] Carolyn Sufrin has reflected on competing principles of care and discipline to "patient-prisoners."[51] She argues that care to female prisoners is situated within broader regimes of discipline, where nurses are often in an awkward position where they emphathize and treat prisoners only as patients, but often also experience the pressure to discipline them. In this process, nurses often also excuse patients for their infractions, such that there is simultaneously scolding and care.[52] According to Sufrin, the nurses' ethos of compassionate care does not contradict an ethos of punitive discipline but forms within it.[53] How can we expand this insight about the entanglement of discipline and care to consider the everyday experiences of substance use and treatment not just within the prisons but ethnographically among individuals moving between prisons households and street life?

In the past two decades, there has been a surge in literature around the expansive policing of populations. Ernest Drucker has persuasively argued for the need to employ epidemiological techniques for the study of incarceration, because of the magnitude of incarcerations in the United States, the persistence of trends, and the exponential increase in the population affected by them over the past few decades.[54] Drucker has even compared incarceration with AIDS and Cholera and has suggested the need to study the determinants that make repeat incarceration much more likely among certain populations compared to others, as 67 percent of discharged prisoners are expected to re-enter within three years of release. He suggests looking at incarceration through the lens of public health. Correctional officers' unions have played an important role in preventing the flow of money from the prison system to drug treatment. At the same time, the prison-industrial complex continues to bring new services, such as mandated drug treatments, under its auspices.[55]

According to Drucker, the prison has replaced social control over young males of noncoercive means involving family and community.[56] But interestingly, just as prisons turn noncoercive authority into coercive one, the coercive authority of prisons also extends to otherwise noncoercive sites, as I contend in this book. Prison behaviors are extended to noncoercive sites. It is also common for families to dissociate themselves from members with histories of drug abuse because their need for drugs continues to put a burden on meager household resources, but this is only one part of the story—the other part is that families also exercise new forms of control. Once incarcerated individuals are out of prison, the failure to comply with parole regulations, however minor, results in reimprisonment. Parole regulations are often associated with the failure to pass drug tests or violations of curfews. Over 65 percent of prisoners in New York State are re-incarcerated within three years of release, with 80 percent of these admissions being a consequence of administrative offenses. Drucker considers the Rockefeller drug laws of 1973 as the watershed moment in the history of drug laws in New York. Initially adopted in response to the rise in heroin use, these laws mandated an elaborate new set of lengthy sentences for many drug offences, which led to possession of a small amount of drugs being equated with violent crimes such as assault and robbery—with sentences even longer than those for manslaughter and homicide. Drucker writes,

> Possession or sale of even very small amounts of drugs could bring very long prison sentences, whose lengths were determined not by a judge or jury weighing all the evidence and extenuating circumstances but by mandatory sentencing policies in which the number of years in prison was instead strictly calculated based on the weight and type of drugs involved and the criminal history of the defendant. Progressively longer sentences for second and third offenses were mandated, and in some states led up to the infamous "three strikes" provision—life sentences for low-level felonies if there was a previous history of arrest and conviction.[57]

As a result of the drug laws, people in possession of ordinary drugs were often targeted. At the same time, people would often be caught for "predicate offenses," resulting in the extension of sentences to keep the system filled. At the same time, operations conducted against New York's feeder groups resembled military operations such as counterinsurgency operations in Iraq and Vietnam, which allowed the police to work their way up the chain of drug supply.[58] I was often told about similar operations by my interlocutors during my research in Baltimore. Many individuals interviewed experienced competing pressures of selling hard drugs to pay off loans to their dealers, but at the same time they could also be asked to side with the law enforcement by being their eyes and ears, a tension they negotiated by engaging strictly in benzodiazepine and methadone trade instead of narcotics trade for illicit drugs like heroin. Individuals also provided help to others who had overdosed, especially when the latter feared acquaintances reporting overdoses to the emergency services. Fresh perspectives are required to consider the hesitancy and compliance with evidence-based treatment in conditions of intense policing.

Another important feature of the discussions around drug use is that they continue to treat Medication-Assisted Treatment (MAT) as stigmatized. Much of the discourse around addition and the prisons in the early 2000s was focused on the inability of prison administration to manage withdrawal systems. Venters, like Sufrin, is mindful of the tension between the imperatives to discipline drug users and provide care to them as "patients" justifications for punishment among persons involved in both health and the criminal justice systems.[59] Like Drucker, Venters talks about the contrasting opinions of correctional officers compared to physicians. Venters shows the ways in which the impacts of incarceration are progressively erased in correctional health.[60] He shows how a prisoner, Mercado, was denied insulin and was believed to be suffering from withdrawals of drugs and alcohol when he was in fact suffering from diabetic ketoacidosis.[61] Another prisoner, Angel Remirez, experienced seizures and hallucinations but was treated with benzodiazepines. He saw people throwing knives at him and swung a punch at an officer, for which he was beaten by several correctional officers in turn. He was later dropped at the medical clinic, where the impact of beating was not fully captured. Venters also thinks that there is a trend in drug courts to insist on ineffective abstinence. By the time Venters was writing, Sheriffs and commissioners still did not approve of methadone and buprenorphine. Venters further suggests that withdrawal symptoms continue to be labelled as "excited delirium," which is a non-specific term that erases the impacts of incarceration on the prisoner, when in reality incarceration itself was a risk factor in the health of prisoners.[62] Compared to scholarly research from the early 2000s, in this book I remain mindful of the fact that methadone maintenance treatment has proliferated in many cities in the United States and that there is a new emerging nexus between drug use and punishment, which is mediated by treatment. As my research taught me, in a city like Baltimore, methadone and buprenorphine have been made increasingly accessible both within and outside the prison—these centers touted themselves for the autonomy they provided to their clients. The question was to consider the specific challenges faced by those enrolled in substance use treatment centers in completing their programs as they traversed the boundaries between the clinics and the black markets once outside the prison, and not so much about the lack of opportunities to enroll in methadone treatment centers.

NEW POLITICS OF TREATMENT

Compared to almost two decades ago, methadone use has now become commonplace, but there is still a hangover of the old days, a form of inertia that makes punitive action the only way to engage with those suffering from substance use. In this new politics, there are new marginal figures, namely people who do not ascribe the state's imagination of a new drug-free population, who do not take up new medical notions of recovery, and treatment centers, even when for many "clients" and "addicts," the difference between illicit and medical can be minimal, especially when there are persisting lures of the illicit, even when they have self-medicalized and become docile subjects.

In San Francisco, as Kelly Rae Knight tells us, hotels act as brothels by creating pressure on women to engage in the drug-sex economy as they simultaneously experience substance use and the pressure of paying their daily rents, for which they engage in prostitution.[63] Kimberly Sue has shown how drug treatment and carceral regimes are closely tied with one another as families send members who have fallen prey to substance use to drug treatment programs situated in prisons. She highlights the difficulties experienced by individuals when they leave their treatment programs and face the possibility of relapsing due to their return to older social networks of friends and acquaintances. These persons see their admission to the programs as a series of repetitive failures.[64] Such ethnographies allow us to consider disciplinary control and punitive action over the lives of ex-prisoners beyond prisons. I now want to briefly consider the case of a person, the bare and killable life, who stood outside the imagination of the new "responsible" methadone user to consider the tensions between two competing principles of substance use and recovery as signified by the two figures of the "addict" and the "client" in the new biopolitics of creating addiction-free populations.

"Don't come back to my country!" shouted Nephew, a Black homeless male possibly in his 50s with a hunched and unsteady gait, as I walked into the supermarket. I had heard something like this on television, but never in real life. I was in a complete state of shock. I remember taking a few minutes to gather myself and get the bottle of milk. I left and saw Nephew say, "Alright, take care." It was almost as if he knew that his words had pierced through my skin. I replied nonchalantly, "Yes, thank you!" my head was bowed down as I walked from in front of the nearby pub back to my home. I walked slowly, letting these words resound in my ears, convinced that I did not hear the words incorrectly. He would often also order me to get food on my way into the supermarket, saying, "Get me a turkey sandwich, extra mayonnaise and no lettuce!" I often refused, like I had done a few times before. He took a few steps toward me to instill some fear and be able to exact his daily meal. He had also done this before. I stood in my place firmly, knowing how dangerous this could have been in any place where there was not a constant flow of pedestrians to monitor threats. The corner was protected from public gaze but had a constant flow of people entering or leaving the pub or the Korean restaurant. His threatening gait also made me rethink the extent to which I could interact with him casually. One day he told me while being draped in blankets on a freezing morning, "I came out of prison after thirty-four years." He had been released earlier that year. I had seen him on several occasions, sometimes on the city circulator or walking around the city.

I had learned in my graduate training, particularly in lectures on power and psychiatry, about the construction of the "abnormal" or "pathological" individual.[65] In brief encounters as well as in engagement over many months with individuals who had become homeless, I realized that the category of the abnormal individual not could simply be considered to be a product of institutions of psychiatry and those designated specifically as delinquents but was also shaped by how one interacted once he or she was outside of those institutions. According to Foucault,

> By situating the crime in infracriminal and parapathological series, a kind of region of juridical indiscernibility is established around the author of the offense. With his irregularities, his lack of intelligence, his failures, and his unflagging and infinite desires, a series of elements are constituted concerning which the question of responsibility can no longer be posed, or simply cannot arise, since ultimately, according to these descriptions, the subject is responsible for everything and nothing. He is a juridically indiscernible personality over whom, in the terms of its own laws and texts, justice has no jurisdiction.[66]

The question was, once outside, in the absence of any direct disciplinary control, was a person ready to reclaim himself or herself and strive toward improvement and recovery? Pehraps there was no secondary "normalization" after leaving the prison, as in the case of others who joined methadone treatment centers, who would be under the pressure to emulate the figure of the ideal drug-free client, who visited the treatment center regularly. Unenrolled and unsupervised, the "addict" compared to the "client" was a constant source of frustration for the state.

During March 2020, the streets became much quieter during the coronavirus pandemic, with students in the city returning to their homes. I knew that Nephew edged on some form of verbal abuse in his encounters with me. For the past few days, I had been avoiding going home from in front of the pub because I knew I would find him there. Whenever I had to visit the supermarket, I would often take the alley to return to my apartment instead of from in front of him. However, this time he caught me by surprise. He had already come close to me in a threatening manner and jokingly said that he was going to steal my bike. This time, however, he came in front of me and said, "Hey friend." After he noticed that I had ignored him, he came close and shouted, "Don't you dare ignore me, I am going to beat the shit out of you, you *fa**ot*!" I stepped away and then continued walking. However, in a few seconds, I found myself sweating and walking aimlessly into a restaurant to catch some air to breath and to figure out what had just happened. When I was returning to the campus, I saw Nephew across the road this time. I saw him with his back toward me as he walked away through the zebra crossing. After this night, I was alerted to some of the pressures exerted by homeless people on bystanders for survival, of which I had become a part, too.

Jacob, who remained an important interlocutor throughout the ethnography, had on several occasions asked me to let him know if I needed any help or felt danger from anyone. I once asked Jacob if he knew Nephew in our meeting in 2020. I asked, "Do you know Nephew?" He replied,

> Stay away from him! He is a heroin addict. I have told him several times to join the programs, but he does not take it seriously. Do you know how heroin substance use takes place here? There is a network of addicts and whenever anyone finds out that the person has died due to overdose, they try to track the dealer. People have some idea about their tolerance, so they reduce the dose but get a better hit.

Compared to Jacob, a methadone user, Nephew was still a "heroin addict." I was struck by this example because it demonstrated how substance use was perceived by individuals like Jacob as tied to death. Knowledge about drugs and their lethality spread and even shaped consumption—there was a lure of death instead of life, as was the case among clients in methadone maintenance treatment (MMT). Jacob knew that Nephew had been in prison on and off and wanted me to stay away from him because of his aggressive and predatory behavior. Whenever Nephew would need his dose, his behavior would become even more aggressive, Jacob told me, and this was perhaps confirmed by his recent attitude toward me, in which he was fairly conversational at one point but then became more threatening with time, where ridicule turned into an overt form of aggression, after which I had completely broken my ties with him.

For many days, I continued to avoid him. I heard him say, "Oh friend!" as if he had felt bad for what he did, but I knew I could not take his aggression anymore and that the police, although physically present, could not do anything unless his acts turned into serious physical aggression. I told Jacob that I would let him know if I needed any help. By this time, when we were passing the bench where Nephew would normally be sitting with his head dropped low, he asked, "Do you want me to go and talk to him?" I refused sternly, "No! Thanks for your help. I will let you know when I need help. If you go and talk to him, it might make him even more aggressive." He nodded, and we continued our walk. I felt comforted by it. Jacob had slowly made himself that figure who could help me out in the streets. But I still wanted to avoid relying on his help, and I could not do that without disturbing the web of relationships that defined street life among the homeless in a few blocks in central Baltimore. Jacob exclaimed, "This area is mine." This showed that even though he had not been on the streets, the fact that he had made himself such an important part of the place he once occupied meant that he still had some control over who occupied which position on the block. While he did not use any force, he could still threaten to use it to get things done. According to Jacob, some people were not afraid to give up their own lives in a petty fight. Jacob said that these people had simply lost their will to live, all they needed was their dose of heroin, and if they didn't get it, they could easily become aggressive, and for them, it would not even matter if they ended up in the prison again. Jacob continued,

> These people have served time numerous times, and their life appeared to be revolving around incarceration, and when they were out, they didn't have any hope or will to improve their circumstances, even when there are treatment centers around every corner.

Compared to the life-loving MMT client (in this case also white), Nephew, a racial other, was viewed as a lover of death—someone who could potentially one day even be found dead while struggling to find his next hit, or by getting into a fight with someone in order to get food. The move from death-loving addict to live-loving client is an important one as I will show in this book.

By 2018, the number of deaths due to drug overdose had exceeded 2000 in Baltimore, which was higher than deaths due to homicide.[67] There are different types of drugs that contribute to rates of overdose. Although the overall deaths related to overdose and other opioid-related causes have dropped over the past few years across Maryland, fatality due to cocaine continues to increase. In addition, on the streets, many continue to consume different mixtures of medically prescribed drugs and illicit drugs such as fentanyl, known colloquially as speedball. Fentanyl appears in an illicit version in a mixture with cocaine, which allows the drug to have a competitive edge over other drugs. The mixture of synthetic opiates with cocaine shows how much the drug market can adapt to restrictions in drug markets as well as the ease of accessing opioid prescriptions. Drug-related abuse continued to be treated as homicide or as predicate crimes.[68] Mostly drug possession appears in charging documents only as by-products of possessing dangerous firearms. The use of "homicide" for drug-related crimes blurred the distinction between perpetrator and the victim. In this vein, the City Councilman Brandon Scott in 2017 lamented that while the city knows when there is murder, given open-source data provided by websites such as Baltimore Homicide by the *Baltimore Sun*, there was little knowledge about drug overdose because of the delay in reaching the scene of the crime, which results in drug overdose being tackled through the broad category of homicide, which shows why there has been a persistence in criminalizing substance use and drug-related activities.[69] The figure of the violent and dangerous "addict," though in some sense distinct, also haunts the image of the "client" in recovery, just as the latter tried to distinguish himself/herself from the latter.

METHODOLOGY

I use a combination of methods in this book. In addition to ethnographic and qualitative methods, I conducted archival research in drug-related cases in Maryland in the past two decades to understand how courts adjudicated drug-related crimes (chapter 2), as well as archival research among prison archives (chapter 3). I triangulate research in prison archives with interviews with four men who had experienced incarceration in the past on the account of drug-related charges to understand how drugs shaped violence within prisons. I also conducted research in archives consisting of scientific papers and conference documents to understand the intrusiveness of public health initiatives in Baltimore since the early twentieth century (chapter 1).

This study is based on five years of ethnographic research in Baltimore. I conducted interviews with my primary interlocutor, Jacob, and tracked his movement between treatment centers, his household and the streets as well as his past experiences of incarceration, over five years. I also captured my interactions with Jacob in the presence of his friends and acquaintances. I also conducted household visits in another household in North Baltimore over six months during 2020, which I describe in chapter 6. During my visit to households, I tracked conflicts with roommates and partners, and the way they shaped experiences of substance use. I conducted interviews with four clients (in pairs) who had become homeless, as well as three interlocutors who had become homeless but were not enrolled in treatment centers. I also recruited five clients from the treatment center in 2020 and conducted interviews telephonically to understand their experiences of recovery and illness trajectories. I combine this qualitative data with in-person visits to treatment center including an ethnographic observation of open-air drug markets. Before each interview, I received oral consent from participants. I made notes during my conversations with the interlocutors. I ensured that none of the participants were under distress or under the influence of substances when they were interviewed. They also shared their experiences of withdrawals and incarceration retrospectively. This was specifically borne out of my ethical commitment that researchers have an unequal relation with vulnerable populations, where there is a potential for exploitation for the purpose of collecting data. I have realized that one has to be ethical and suspend one's role as a researcher at certain moments to fully empathize with interlocuters who are humans with lives, feelings and vulnerabilities, even when public discourses present them as having lost their will to live and to improve. I went into this research fully understanding the vulnerable position of my interlocutors, as even during recovery many had precarious living conditions and worried about successfully completing their programs, finding jobs, a place to stay, and reuniting with families. I remained mindful of emotionally intense moments when my interlocutors shared their experiences of drug use, illness and family troubles, and in moments of heightened emotional intensity. I often tried to create a space for conversation while also suspending my role as an interviewer seeking data to let my interlocutors share their full range of feelings without worrying about the constraints of the research.

My decision to occasionally rely only on the contents of my conversations with my interlocuters instead of thick descriptions about domestic spaces and physical appearances (during household visits) was also to help my interlocutors maintain a right to privacy—as we as researchers coming from a position of privilege try to maintain—instead of objectifying their suffering for the purpose of research,[70] a critique that has been levelled onto anthropologists studying substance use (and rightly so!). Some have critiqued scholars for disregarding the power relations that render the homeless voiceless in the same way as the anthropologist's description of the so-called "primitive" cultures did in the past.[71] Being receptive to this critique, it is necessary to keep in mind that the relations between the researcher and the participant are mostly unequal, imposing newer demands on the researcher to respect personal space even when the homeless appear to be lacking any semblance of a "private life" as was the case among those situated in households. Geographically, the research was conducted in three neighborhoods in central Baltimore as well as one neighborhood in Old West Baltimore Historic District, where I conducted interviews, participated in prayers and congregations, and met with participants—mostly Black—to make sense of their experiences of substance use, incarceration, and turn to religion.

OUTLINE OF CHAPTERS

The first three chapters are about institutions of the state, including courts, prisons, and public health and the ways in which they create specific types of discipline, subjectivities and psychological pressures that act as obstacles in the process of recovery. In the fifth and the sixth chapters, I consider carceral attitudes combined with autonomy to consider the new biopolitics of treatment in Baltimore, a move away from coercive ways of disciplining and controlling substance use to one shaped by autonomy, but one that is still shaped by the specter of carceral attitudes, which influences both how family members treat each other and also how substance use counselors treat clients.

Chapter 1 considers the intrusive histories of public health in Baltimore, which have shaped attitudes toward the poor and the marginalized in the city. I track how benevolence and humanitarian ethics have been invoked in uplifting the lives of the poor with a moralistic tone, which has resulted in intensifying suspicions toward the medical institutes of the city. I consider the implications this has had since the 1980s following the "HIV scare" and the fear of poor health practices among mostly racialized minorities. Then in chapter 2, I consider the need to look at substance use trajectories through carceral experiences—namely the ways in which drug exchange within prisons makes recovery as well as incarceration-free lives difficult for many, using the concept of carceral obligations. In chapter 3, I consider how courts pick up the language of treatment to modulate sentencing and decide parental rights. I consider the struggles of couples to recombine with their loved ones and the ways in which emotional ambivalence is flattened out as courts decide whether parents with histories of drug abuse are "responsible" enough or not. Here, "responsiblization" refers to compliance in methadone treatment centers.

From chapter 4 onward, I consider the politics of recovery and treatment rather than substance use. I consider the attempts by people who have become homeless to employ frameworks of medicalization to de-stigmatize substance use, and the ways in which being compliant in treatment centers provides opportunities to de-stigmatize their conditions, even when symptoms of recovery are confused as signs of substance use. Then in chapter 5, I consider the nexus between treatment centers and open-air drug market to consider the lure of illicit drugs for people undergoing recovery. Finally, in chapter 6, I consider new tensions between people based on different degrees of compliance, namely, between people in recovery and people who are unable to overcome the use of illicit drugs, resulting in new forms of discipline and violence within households. By doing so, I consider the competing pressures of drug use and recovery in Baltimore. By considering the centrifugal effects of treatment among populations with different perceptions and sensibilities toward recovery, I consider the experience of discipline that comes to define the experience of substance use for many in streets, households and institutions of the state, referring to the experience as a type of *carceral recovery*. Perhaps by considering these disciplinary pressures, the book will be able to make a case to re-envision recovery and its relationship with discipline for more humane and empathetic approaches toward people suffering from the menace of substance use.

NOTES

1. Names of all participants have been anonymized. Only the names of individuals in publicly available archives including case law, journal articles and newspapers have been retained. No patient records have been used for the research.
2. Catherine Rentz, "Freddie Gray Remembered as Jokester who Struggled to Leave Drug Trade," *Baltimore Sun* (Nov 2015).
3. Ibid.
4. Loic Wacquant, "From Slavery to Mass Incarceration: Re-thinking the 'race question' in the US," *Race, Law and Society,* ed. Ian Haney Lopez (Routledge, 2007); Loic Wacquant, "Deadly Symbiosis: When Ghetto and Prison Meet and Mesh," *Punishment and Society* 3, No. 1 (2001): 95–134.

5. D. Watkins, *Cook Up: A Crack Rock Memoir* (Grand Central Publishing, 2017).

6. Todd Meyers, *The Clinic and Elsewhere: Substance Use, Adolescents, and the Afterlife of Therapy* (Seattle: University of Washington Press, 2013).

7. Arthur Kleinman, Veena Das & Margaret Lock, *Social Suffering* (Berkeley: University of California Press, 1997).

8. Paul Farmer, "Social Inequalities and Emerging Infectious Diseases," *Emerging infectious diseases* 2, No. 4 (1996): 259–269. doi:10.3201/eid0204.960402; Paul Farmer, "An Anthropology of Structural Violence," 45, No. 3 (2004): 305–325.

9. Patrick Radden Keefe, *Empire of Pain: The Secret History of the Sackler Dynasty* (Doubleday, 2021).

10. David T. Courtwright, *Dark Paradise: A History of Opiate Substance use in America* (Harvard University Press, 2001), 123.

11. Ibid., 124.

12. Ibid., 129.

13. Ibid., 130.

14. Ibid., 131.

15. Ibid., 133.

16. David Herzberg, *White Market Drugs: Big Pharma and the Hidden History of Substance Use in America* (The University of Chicago Press, 2020).

17. Ibid., 127.

18. Ibid., 136.

19. Ibid., 146.

20. Ibid., 148.

21. Beth Macy, *Dopesick: Dealers, Doctors, and the Drug Company that Addicted America* (Little, Brown & Co., 2018), 22.

22. Ibid., 38.

23. Patrick Radden Keefe, *Empire of Pain: The Secret History of the Sackler Dynasty* (Doubleday, 2021).

24. Beth Macy, *Dopesick: Dealers, Doctors, and the Drug Company that Addicted America* (Little, Brown & Co., 2018), 48.

25. Ibid., 50.

26. ibid., 51.

27. Barry Meier, *Pain Killer: An Empire of Deceit and the Origin of America's Opioid Epidemic* (Penguin Random House, 2018), 19.

28. Ibid., 30.

29. Ibid., 32.

30. Ibid., 35.

31. Ibid., 37.

32. Nicolas Rasmussen, "Goofball Panic: Barbiturates, "Dangerous" and Addictive Drugs, and the Regulation of Medicine in Postwar America," in *Prescribed*, eds. Greene and Watkins (The Jacobs Hopkins University Press, 2012).

33. Marcia L. Maldrum, "The Prescription as Stigma: Opioid Pain Relievers and the Long Walk to the Pharmacy Counter," in *Prescribed*, eds. Greene and Watkins (The Jacobs Hopkins University Press, 2012).

34. Ibid., 193.
35. Ibid., 194.
36. Ibid., 196.
37. For more on such experimentation, consider the case of Megan and Cedric in Todd Meyers' ethnography who use illicit opiates alongside buprenorphine, showing that they are committed to recovery on their own terms. See Todd Meyers, *The Clinic and Elsewhere: Substance use, Adolescents, and the Afterlife of Therapy* (Seattle: University of Washington Press, 2013). 81.
38. Phil David, "Prison Exterminator, Two Others Admit to Role in Smuggling Drugs in Jessup Prison," *Baltimore Sun* (September 18, 2019).
39. The drug economy is shaped by death itself. Markets continues to emerge around deaths due to overdose as death also testifies to the potency of the drug in circulation. As much as epidemiological data attempts to prevent death, the clusters of deadly batches continue to create an economy of users who are vying for even more potent forms. Mary Grace Keller, "Baltimore man charged with giving drugs to inmates who overdosed at Carroll County Detention Center," *Baltimore Sun* (March 10, 2020). Later in the book, I will show how the combination of methadone and illicit drugs involve "beating" the former through a higher intake, thus putting the life of the consumer in great jeopardy.
40. Ibid.
41. For the emergence of the modern prison as a site of continuous surveillance and discipline, see Michel Foucault, *Discipline and Punish: the Birth of the Prison* (Vintage Books, 1995). Such an idea of discipline has also been used by proponents of forensic architecture to think about use of infrastructure to discipline populations, see Eyal Weizman, *Hollow Land: Israel's Architecture of Occupation* (Verso, 2017). Historians have begun considering the experience of patients from the first-person, i.e., from below. This historiographical shift can also be applicable to prisoners and more generally understanding experiences of people within disciplinary infrastructures from below. See Roy Porter, "The Patient's View: Doing Medical History from Below." *Theory and Society* 14 (1985): 175–98.
42. I find a parallel to the exchange of information in prisons in the recent publication of letters by the British Library. These letters were sent by Indian soldiers during WWI. In these letters they attempted to bypass censors to communicate with their families and comrades back home and on the war fronts and described the realities of war through the use of metaphors. See, Santanu Das, "The Indian sepoy in the First World War," *The British Library.*
43. Jon Kelvey, "Sexy Letters vs. Jailhouse Censors," *Baltimore Sun* (November 21, 2019).
44. Ibid.
45. Jon Kelvey, "Mount Airy Woman Charged with Attempting to Smuggle Drugs into Jail," *Baltimore Sun* (June 30, 2018).
46. Heather Cobun, "Woman Enters Plea for Selling Fake Drugs to Undercover Deputy," *Baltimore Sun* (August 19, 2014).
47. Anthony L. Guenther, "Compensations in a Total Institution: The Forms and Functions of Contraband," *Crime & Delinquency* (1975).

48. Ibid.

49. See Erving Goffman, "On the Characteristics of Total Institutions," *Asylums: Essays on the Social Situation of Mental Patients and Other Inmates* (1962): 1–124; Gresham M. Sykes, *The Society of Captives: A Study of a Maximum Security Prison* (Princeton University Press, 1958), 63–83; Gresham M. Sykes, *Crime and Society* (New York Random House, 1967), 175–6.

50. Lorna A. Rhodes, *Total Confinement: Madness and Reason in the Maximum Security Prison* (University of California Press, 2004).

51. Angela Garcia (2010) uses the concept of "patient-prisoner" in her work on substance use and loss in rural New Mexico. For Garcia, the patient-prisoner is the subject who gets produced by juridical, medical, and carceral regimes that govern the drug addict through the dual logics of recovery and punishment. See Angela Garcia, *The Pastoral Clinic: Substance use and Dispossession along the Rio Grande* (University of California Press, 2010).

52. Carolyn Sufrin, *Jailcare: Finding the Safety Net for Women behind the Bars* (University of California Press, 2017), 88.

53. Ibid., 116.

54. Ernest Drucker, *A Plague of Prisons: The Epidemiology of Mass Incarceration in America* (the New Press, 2013).

55. Ibid., 46.

56. Ibid., 47.

57. Ibid., 51.

58. Ibid., 57.

59. Homer Venters, *Life and Death in Rikers Island* (Jacobs Hopkins University Press, 2019), 17.

60. Ibid., 20.

61. Ibid., 31.

62. Ibid., 37.

63. See Kelly Ray Knight, *Addicted, Pregnant, Poor* (Duke University Press, 2015).

64. See Kimberly Sue, *Getting Wrecked: Women, Incarceration and the American Opioid Crisis* (University of California Press, 2019).

65. According to Kurt Goldstein, a preeminent German psychiatrist, pathology is the shrinking of one's response, an attempt by the defective organism to have order. For him this is also for the purpose of avoiding any "catastrophic reactions" for which the only route is to reduce or restrict the milieu. Kurt Goldstein defines catastrophic reactions as the opposite of "ordered" reaction. Such reactions are inadequate, "disordered, inconstant, inconsistent and embedded in physical and mental shock." This response is usually not proportionate to the requirements of the situation and represents an excess or deficiency, which becomes a mark of a person's lack of normativity. See, Kurt Goldstein, *The Organism* (Zone Book, 2000), 49 & 56. Moreover, Canguilhem following Goldstein, considered pathology to be the lack of normativity of an organism, i.e. the inability to establish norms in a range of environments. See Georges Canguilhem. *The Normal and the Pathological* (New York: Zone Books. 1991).

66. M. Foucault, *Abnormal: Lectures at the College de France, 1974-1975* (Picador, 2003), 21.

67. National Institute of Drug Abuse, "Maryland: Opioid- Involved Deaths and Related Harms."

68. McKenna Oxenden, "Baltimore Guerilla Family Member Gang Member Sentenced to Life in Prison," *Baltimore Sun* (June, 2019).

69. Luke Broadwater and Ian Dunkun, "'Neighborhoods Are Crying Out': Baltimore Has Highest Homicide Rates in US Big Cities," *Baltimore Sun* (September, 2018). For crime statistics in Baltimore, visit https://homicides.news.baltimoresun.com/

70. Mary Madden, "Braving Homelessness on the Ethnographic Street with Irene Glasser and Rae Bridgman," *Critique of Anthropology* 23, No. 3 (2003): 289 304. doi: 10.1177/0308275X030233003

71. M. Madden, "Braving Homelessness on the Ethnographic Street with Irene Glasser and Rae Bridgman," *Critique of Anthropology* 23, No. 3 (2003): 289–304. doi: 10.1177/0308275X030233003

Chapter 1

Public Health and Discipline

Before we consider the question of substance use, it is important to ask a more general question about the ways in which public health discourses have been perceived in Baltimore, especially among the poor and racialized minorities. Scholars have previously commented on the ways in which lending practices create specific racial cartographies in many cities of the United States.[1] In Baltimore, like any other city, only a few meters can make a difference in the racial composition of a neighborhood. In American history, racial segregation initially took place through legacies of the Jim Crow and the slave plantation, but these cartographies continue to be reanimated through the ghetto and the prison-industrial complex.[2] There is a close relationship between the prison and the ghetto in that the prison takes over "the spatial racial containment and gerrymandering that perpetuated the exclusion and marginalization of the African-Americans."[3] According to Wacquant, "the prison enacts and replicates the ghetto's main mechanisms of ethnoracial control, which are stigma, control, territorial confinement, and institutional encasement."[4] Thus, a ghetto and the prison may be invoked interchangeably in resembling their modalities of control and their ethnoracial composition. It is interesting to consider how disciplinary apparatuses, in their capillary form, pervade both the institution of the prison and beyond it in the ghettos.

From 2018–2021, I collected notices about armed robberies within areas of central Baltimore. I found that a total of ninety-seven armed robberies took place in only three or four main neighorhoods of central Baltimore. In many of the cases, it was impossible to catch the culprit. This number does not include incidences in East and West Baltimore. These acts of violence are invariably linked with social vulnerabilities, of which substance use is one symptom. Policy debates continue to show that policing does not reduce violence in drug markets, where the disruption of drug markets paradoxically enhances street violence, as shown in a systematic review by Werb and colleagues.[5] These violent episodes occur at sites of geographical and cartographic racial divisions persisting in many cities of America, including Baltimore. American Community Survey data from 2012–2016 shows the concentration of Black residents in both West and East Baltimore, with areas in the north, such as Towson, having very few Black residents.[6] American Community Survey data from 2012–2016 also shows that neighborhoods in West Baltimore have poverty rates of more than 35 percent, except for the small pockets of white neighborhoods east and west of Charles Street. Incidentally, neighborhoods in the vicinity of Johns Hopkins University are also experiencing the highest construction, rehab and demolition volume per household, as per the American Community Survey data.[7] These areas also require more permits for renovation which increases their real estate value. In some areas of North and East Baltimore, home prices have been increasing steadily compared to neighborhoods further away. Even as prices increase, lending levels for commercial real estate have continued to be much lower for neighborhoods with above 50 percent Black population. Areas with higher percentages of Black populations, such as Sandtown-Winchester, meanwhile, also have the highest rates of unemployment, with main areas of rioting after Freddie Grey's death also taking place at the borders of the Charles Street, which incidentally also separates Black and white populations.[8] These are structural factors that must be kept in mind because racialized boundaries have been reinscribed in the provision of care to poor neighbourhoods in Baltimore. This has been accompanied by a moralizing tone in public health systems of the city, where poor health is not simply viewed as a product of the lack access to healthcare but as a product of moral qualities like vice, poor ethics, and the inability to take care of oneself, justifying the use of force, which results in public health to be approach as punitive rather than caring and empathetic.

Since the early twentieth century, Baltimore-based psychiatrists understood mental disorders partly as inherited but also as products of social circumstances, in which there were no controls over indulgence. The brain was viewed as if it had already been predisposed to illness in specific social circumstances, and chemicals like alcohol or drugs could only activate existing, yet concealed morbidities, resulting in delirium and convulsions. Meanwhile, psychiatric problems, to some extent, were viewed as indistinguishable from the range of infections and public health problems caused by poor living conditions as well as habits. This chapter will explore how Baltimore-based psychiatrists and physicians historically treated moral vices among the population as foremost reason for poor health. In doing so, they employed ideas about morality and vices that have been the cause of resistance among specific social groups in the twentieth century. From the earliest days of the newly established hospitals and the establishment of a public health system in Baltimore, two moral ideas were viewed as central to the process of treatment in hospitals. One was of healing and compassion to be guided by Christian ethics, where the hospital was to be the center of civilization, and where medical practice was posited as a "true anthropology."[9] Secondly, institutionalization was deemed necessary for those from poor backgrounds and considered longer for "colored" patients because their condition could result in relapse due to poor hygiene, but also because their households represented a type of normativity from which only the hospital could truly provide an escape.

The chapter will first show how medical surveillance was extended to the control of the youth in order to monitor disorders and disturbances in domestic spaces and to provide preventative care through collaborations between hospitals, social services, and schools. Then the chapter shows how hereditary ideas became central to psychiatric discourses, where one can find a curious combination of environmentalist ideas about disease used to justify medical intervention among racialized populations. The chapter then asks how the growing interest in mental hygiene resulted in populations and mental disorders being rigorously classified, in which delinquency and mental illness come to be conflated, and despite a higher occurrence of mental illness among white populations, Black populations continue to be treated as delinquent. I then consider how this context is ripe for public health discourses to take up a language whereby failure to remain healthy gets treated as a sign of moral weakness. Finally, I ask how longstanding histories of segregation and excessive intervention result in growing skepticism toward public health initiatives among African-American populations, where so-called care comes to be perceived as violent by the white "medical establishment." I borrow the word "medical establishment" from the description provided by one of my interlocutors to reflect on skepticism toward medicine within Black populations in Baltimore. In making the case for peer support instead of psychiatric treatment to low-income communities, this addiction counselor said, "People are deeply distrustful of the white medical establishment—they see psychiatrists as part of the same establishment, and this explains why they look down upon psychiatric care. Peer support is useful because it reduces this gap, especially when the mentor is from the same racial background—they are able to instantly connect with communities."

Baltimore was historically a major railroad city. By 1860, Baltimore had a greater number of freed slaves than any other city. African-American populations were generally distributed around the city, but especially close to the Basin and west of the Basin toward the B&O railways. Yet segregation through legal and implicit means meant that white people lived on the streets and Black populations in alleyways. Baltimore's Black population grew dramatically during the Civil War. In Baltimore, capital flows further shaped the segregation of neighborhoods. In 1911, the city council passed the first housing segregation ordinance in the country directed at Black people.[10] When a similar Kentucky ordinance was struck down by the Supreme Court in 1917, then Mayor of Baltimore, James H. Preston, ordered housing inspectors to instead cite anyone who rented or sold property to Black people in predominantly white areas for code violations, by using the rationale of public safety and health,

> [T]he evil effects of the unhealthy state of the negro race are not confined within their own numbers . . . Regardless of our efforts to maintain [a] sanitary and healthful environment for ourselves and families the insidious influence of slum conditions is carried into our very midst to defile and destroy.[11]

In 1930, the Federal Housing Administration prevented Black people from moving into white neighborhoods.[12] Such laws had a particularly severe impact on health and wellbeing of Black populations. Meanwhile, as this segregation continued, the poor health was also compounded by intrusive approaches to public health, creating distrust among populations, an aspect that has also been observed in histories of public health in other parts of the world as well.[13]

Tuberculosis was one of the bigger problems by the beginning of the twentieth century, with official reports suggesting its greater prevalence among "negroes" than the white population. The immediacy of providing care to African-American communities was touted as a form of self-defense in order to gain support for public health initiatives from the white populations, who were reluctant to expend resources for their care and treatment. In an introductory address at a conference in 1915, Governor Goldsborough stated, "We must see, even from a selfish viewpoint, that we never hope to make any progress against the disease amongst the white race so long as we allow negro to be the center of infection."[14] He then goes on to say, "Wherever you go, you will find at one point or another, in some way or another, come into contact everyday of your life with the negro race," suggesting that segregation alone was not enough to keep the disease at bay. Then he also goes on to say that the "negroes" were much more susceptible to tuberculosis than those who were white.[15] He brought attention of the audience then to the appallingly low number of beds for Black communities, with a total of 902 people dying, to make a claim about how the "colored problem" had remained unaddressed.[16] He adds that the provision of care had to be seen as a problem of public health and not charity alone. With a curious mix of indifference or neglect and a shared obligation to the Black community, he reminds the audience about the population being forced to come to the United States due to their conditions back home, completely ignoring to mention the historical legacies of slavery, and suggests the need to take care of them as a form of moral responsibility. By this time of course, there is also a great inflow of African-American populations settling in parts of the city. There was also a great deal of discussion about Baltimore's "colored" districts being overcrowded. The seriousness of the lack of care was signaled by Theodore Janeway complaining about one patient coming to the hospital and being transferred to Bayview. He rhetorically asks how hospitals could be made attractive so that patients could come voluntarily without the use of force, given suspicion among poor communities toward them.[17] Martin Sloan, superintendent of Eudowood Sanitorium in Towson, even went on to ask the audience to picture a scene of a "Black [person], who has just been told he has tuberculosis, but with hospital treatment his life probably could be prolonged many years and be useful, and in reply to his inquiry for such hospital facilities he is told there are none."[18] Many speakers at the presentation therefore highlighted the need to have a greater number of beds and talked about the urgency of expanding care in a context where it is greatly viewed as intrusive by African-American communities.

DISCIPLINING THE YOUTH

By the turn of the century, there were new types of surveillance to which the medical institutes contributed. Medical judgments about orphans were entwined with perceptions about predisposition to illness. This way, racial knowledge slowly entered medical discourses. Although the Colored Orphan Asylum in Baltimore was closed in 1924 when orphans had reached the age of maturity, it had a long history of raising Black children in the manner of white nuclear families. It is important to consider that the wards of the asylum were placed under the strict surveillance of the social service department, which regularly communicated with families and schools. The social service department, in other words, was the intermediate agency between the schools and the physicians. In the annual report of 1914, the superintendent of Johns Hopkins Hospital mentioned the importance of the social service department, suggesting that as time goes on, it was expected "to be of still greater assistance in helping the public schools to solve the tremendous problem of dealing with the many *retarded* and *defective* children found in their classrooms."[19] In some cases, there was a close cooperation between families and the school. In one case, a mother was determined to put her kid to work. The case summarized in the report mentions, "The mental examination showed a retardation of three years, and he was recommended to a special class."[20] The boy showed marked improvements in manual work. The social services convinced the mother, who readily agreed to leave the boy in school as long as advised to do so.[21] Meanwhile, the Juvenile Court also continued to send in many children for examination at the Johns Hopkins Hospital, while also demanding the cooperation of the orphan asylum and the hospital staff to help with these cases.

Among some students who had been disorderly, the hospital worked with social services to get them admitted to institutes to harness their manual skills, with the assistant superintendent also playing a role in getting the student readmitted if they discontinued while also evaluating progress.[22] We can thus notice two important things here—one is that the child was constructed as disorderly at home, and second that the only way for him to be disciplined for the juvenile court was for him to engage in manual labor or mechanical work. Thus recovery was related to making the masculine body ready for work in a factory.[23] The juvenile court arbitrated the child's behavior with the help of parents by assessing their willingness to change. It was a matter of disciplining the child to become obedient both within the family and outside of it in the broader society.

Evidence shows that the social service department by this time was also conducting home investigations. In one such investigation, they found a child, a girl of fifteen, who had "marked mental deficiency," and had a stammer. There were ten children in the home altogether. Initially, the parent was reluctant, but then her cooperation was secured. The superintendent's report mentions, "The fifteen-year-old girl was brought to the clinic, examined, and the State Training School for feeble-minded recommended, but the father refused to commit her. Recently his consent has been won. Several home visits have been made, the mother instructed, tea and coffee have been eliminated from the children's diet, and regular habits, as to sleep, etc., secured."[24] Yet at the same time, there was also an anxiety about not doing enough in terms of institutionalizing such teenagers and children and the need to expand further expand institutional care.

Other cases show not only a growing control over children but also the responsibility taken by the orphan asylum in reintroducing these boys and girls back in the community. One young woman experienced epilepsy and was kept in a home for those with epilepsy. She found herself without any support. The Johns Hopkins Superintendent's report mentions, "her relatives were angry at her being discharged and would take little responsibility in regard to her."[25] It was brought to the attention of the orphan asylum that she had been working in uncongenial conditions. The report further mentioned "the great challenge in her case was to secure the right environment and suitable occupation."[26] She was later placed provisionally in the care of a family. Later, she was brought back to Baltimore and placed in boarding, where she showed aptitude for needle work. The report mentioned that her family was being convinced about supporting her so she could become fully independent. Note how such measures are not only used to increase self-sufficiency but also keep the girl under constant surveillance to ensure that she showed keenness to learn.

Often, the problem was not only the inability to learn but also the inability to control sexual desires. One girl with tuberculosis, aged twenty-three, was brought to the clinic and was diagnosed with psychoneurosis. The report mentioned, "Her principal trouble was insomnia, accompanied by sexual imaginations. She was very rigid and would talk little with the doctor. She was turned over to the Social Service Department, and soon a friendly relation was established. The patient was taught to understand her own nature and the principles of sex-control." In most cases, there was resistance against the efforts of the social service. In less than three months, she reported sleeping "splendidly." Yet another girl, seventeen, brought in by a worker from an outside agency, thought that she might have been "mentally defective" when she was about to be discharged from the Florence Crittenton Home. She had an illegitimate child six months old, "and the agency was most anxious to know what was best to be done with her. Examination showed no mental retardation, and an investigation led to the conclusion that the patient was the victim of a *vicious environment*, rather than a moral defect."[27] The superintendent's report mentions that she was placed in a *good* home, where the people are much interested in her, to make a case for her improvement. Control over children was based on taking them out of environments that were deemed as causing pathologies and putting them in safe homes, under the protection of caring "white" parents, and disciplining them in the mold of white nuclear families. The superintendent continued,

> Though there has been difficulty in getting her back to the clinic dispensary, she has been visited a number of times by a worker and instructed, and her *maternal love aroused*. She visits her baby weekly in the nursery where he has been placed, and is most anxious to succeed for his sake.[28]

The environmentalist paradigm, which could possibly offset strictly racial explanations of illness, was instead used to reinforce ideas of disorder based on racial difference, with recovery as the assumption of white norms. The problem was constructed as her inability to take care of her child, and recovery was viewed as the woman's development of affection, which was previously missing. These examples were used to argue for the expansion of social services, which could play a vital role in "helping to make diagnosis complete and medical treatment more effective."[29] The Johns Hopkins Colored Orphan Asylum stopped functioning as its own facility in 1914, when the Board of Trustees decided to convert the buildings into a convalescent home for African-American children. The Board of Trustees and the Committee on the Colored Orphan Asylum argued that "a much greater service would be rendered to the colored race" by converting the Colored Orphan Asylum into a convalescent home for Black children "than by operating this institution entirely as an orphan's home."[30] The reason why I have provided these examples is to show that while an explicit mention about race was missing, at least in the earlier days of the asylum, the children over whom control was exerted were mostly "colored." They were often accompanied by juvenile officers, and from a very young age, experienced conditions of incarceration in the name of helping them become better students and productive members of society. Thus, young children in Baltimore being exposed to carceral regimes since an early age has a long history.

PSYCHIATRY AND THE "PSYCHOPATHIC" INDIVIDUAL

Ideas of moral defect as a cause of illness had already been in swing. One paper by J. K. Baudry was particularly graphic in recording the evil effects of "addiction," stating, "The most alarming poisonous effects of the drug are debasing and enslavement of the will, a general demoralization which is as diabolical as it is indescribable, and which tends rapidly toward depravity and to the development of everything that is degrading and ignoble in human nature."[31] One of the physicians at Johns Hopkins, William Halsted, while experimenting with the effects of cocaine, had himself become addicted. Halsted was rescued by William H. Welch, who in 1885 put him away for a year in a hospital in Providence, Rhode Island.[32] Unfortunately, a similar chance to redeem oneself would not be provided to many less privileged Black residents of Baltimore.

Henry M. Hurd was the first superintendent of the Johns Hopkins Hospital. His intuitiveness led him to distinguish between psychiatric cases of different types, which led him to empirically define categories of paranoia and delusions as based on the fear of persecution and delusions of exaltation.[33] A psychiatrist by training, his theories were firmly situated in the environmentalist paradigm about chemicals activating illnesses among men and women already predisposed to illness.[34] He based his analysis on the upbringing of children in communities. The perception of neglect toward children led him to make a case for better care for the mentally ill. The fear toward institutional care was already there, as he wrote about the poor condition of asylums,

> The records all make it evident that the friends of the insane had a strong feeling against sending them to the country almshouses. The reason given for asking state aid in many instances is the wish to keep an insane relative at home, it being generally thought that those who were feeble, helpless and deranged were better cared for out of the almshouse than in it.[35]

In Owings Mills, the Rosewood Training School had placed a particular emphasis on caring for children. Richard Gundry, then superintendent of the Spring Grove State Hospital, in several reports called the attention of the state to the great need of doing something for the care and training of "feeble-minded children."[36] Important here is the perception that the feeble minded had not been "feeble" biologically, but their social conditions had made them incapable to live independent lives without supervision, as it was noted,

> In most cases they require training specially adapted to their condition, or they will become a burden upon their friends or the community; but by receiving kind and painstaking care and tuition at the hand of the competent, experienced persons many of them become partly self-supporting under proper supervision.[37]

The main problem was perceived to be developmental—mainly related to poor influences and the lack of authority in the lives of the children. One former resident psychiatrist at Johns Hopkins in 1916 wrote, "There seems to be little doubt that the vast majority of those unfortunate individuals who use drugs to excess are constitutionally unstable, poorly balanced, and psychopathic."[38] A statement like this shows that those who were addicted were perceived as troubled even before the act of consumption, in that for them the only resort from the difficulties of life was to turn to substance use. The psychiatrist differentiated these cases from those who "are a few, especially those addicted to opium and morphine, who, on the other hand, to start with may be fairly sound constitutionally but due to painful disorders have had a narcotic prescribed to them and find themselves unable to live without it." He differentiates the two from a third category of those who use heroin and "are the lowest of the low, and if anything, are vicious and more degenerate than those addicted to other forms of drug habituation."[39] The age of those engaging in heroin consumption, he reasoned, was also lower, displacing the cause from ease of accessing drugs to developmental flaws in the child. He said that the age of the user of heroin varied from eighteen to twenty-eight, compared to morphine, which, according to him, is consumed by those who are at least in their 30s.[40] The resident quoted several cases of substance use who had been taking thirty to forty doses daily by sniffing. However, substance use was only understood through longer histories of disease, as in one case where a patient showed that he had a "history of truancy at school, of gonorrhea in 1912, and of smoking twenty to thirty Piedmont cigarettes daily."[41]

By this time, the question of substance use management or long-term support for heroin users—as is found today—of course had not been there. Another patient stated that he took up to fifty tablets a day and suffered from auditory and visual hallucinations. As mentioned above, the question about the effect of the drug on the mind was central. Even this patient was thought to have completely recovered and had given up on his cravings, which would previously make him desperate "to steal or do violence if only he could obtain a further supply of the drug." The consumption was viewed as clouding will and the ability to differentiate between right and wrong. At this time, most patients with substance use were provided with the Towns-Lambert treatment, also known as the Belladona treatment. The Belladona treatment, has also been referred to as a type of purgative, used a combination of belladona, hyoscyamus, and xanthoxylum. This was followed by giving castor oil to clear the intestinal tract.[42] In almost all cases, patients' substance use problems were accompanied by problems of delirium. The problem of substance use was also tied to other habits, such as smoking. Even at this time, there was a perception about patients who were serious about recovery and others who lacked the same seriousness. Patients who did not recover were considered undisciplined, and continued to receive supplies of heroin and morphine during treatment.[43] This study acknowledges the limitation in following up with patients while suggesting the need to extricate individuals from the so-called baleful environment, which was interpreted as the cause of their illness, as suggested in one study, "after they had been freed from the drug, they should be taken in hand by philanthropic and aftercare associations, so that a definite attempt might be made to break the old environmental influences, and thus a lasting and a permanent benefit might result."[44] Thus, the physician calls for strictly legal measures governing the consumption of narcotics for complete elimination of habits to be secured.[45]

Meanwhile, cases of syphilis had also begun to be reported in large numbers in hospitals like Johns Hopkins. Convulsions were attributed as the result of epilepsies, to which, in the eyes of physicians, promiscuity and lack of self-restraint contributed. These convulsions were also attributed to the presence of toxic substances. At the same time, hereditary factors continued to be viewed as predominant causes, as Daniel Stuart, a neurologist at Johns Hopkins University wrote,

> A majority of cases in the series came from definitely neuropathic families, there was a higher percentage of mental deteriorates among such cases than those coming from untainted stocks, measured by intelligence tests, the deteriorates in the former group graded lower than those in the group having clear family histories.[46]

While by this time race was not categorically mentioned as the cause of degeneracy, it was implicit that most of the sick, or from the so-called "tainted" race, were Black. I would like to briefly mention that insanity by this time continued to be viewed as a problem of morals, and Henry Hurd even considered insanity as a product of evil, causing immense burden on families.[47] Hurd, even occasionally conflated biology with social circumstances[48] and goes on to say that a major clinical problem arises due to the lack of knowledge about the hereditary nature of vices,[49]

> It is desirable that the public should be instructed as to the character of heredity, until the knowledge becomes universal that every individual born into the world inherits the sum total of the vices and virtues, faults and perfections, strength and weaknesses, of remote ancestors, plus special morbid conditions or otherwise which existed among his immediate progenitors. In the question of marriage, education and occupation the consideration of heredity seems forgotten or wholly ignored by the majority of people. People with neurotic heredities marry; they bring neurotic children into the world; they educate them faultily and in such a manner as to add to their neurotic inheritance; they allow them to choose unsuitable employments; and finally their children develop in their turn insanity.

Then he goes on to say that it is not enough for the neurotic person to receive education, he also needs to remain under discipline,

> It is not sufficient for neurotic persons to acquire knowledge alone; they should acquire with it a discipline which will help them to overcome the morbid and vagrant tendencies which spring from a neurotic organization. They should be trained to use their mental powers judiciously, to strengthen their wills and to build up their physical energies.[50]

Important here is the continual reliance on discipline as pre-requisite for recovery. Then Hurd turns to the importance of schools in detecting these pathologies and laments that these pathologies often remain undetected by teachers. According to Hurd, the neurotic person's formation of idle, pleasure-seeking, or dissolute habits are the most dangerous.[51] By making this claim, he considers substance use through ideas of moral weakness and a lack of self-restraint, which in combination with a person's habits developed overtime, result in adverse effects on his mind that become generative of "insanity."

By this time, the diagnosis of "imbecility" had come to dominate psychiatric discourse on illness. Hurd argued that people with imbecility were unobservable until plagued by companions. He wrote,

> If carefully guarded at home from the persecutions of vicious and unfeeling persons, they frequently go through life quiet, harmless and not unuseful members of society. If plagued by their companions they become irritable and violent and often require the seclusion and restraint of an asylum, for no other reason than the fact that they had attempted to live among semi-savages.[52]

Here, familial discipline is viewed as a safeguard against mental pathologies compared to those who live without any restraint. In fact, in another paper, Hurd even compared mental states of childhood with those of primitive people lacking the ability to make logical associations, a belief that had developed deep roots in psychoanalytic thinking of the early twentieth century.[53] Hurd writes about the so-called primitive mind,

> The primitive mind is imaginative, unreasoning, full of superstition, credulous and the creature of desire and of impulse. His intellectual processes are automatic, spontaneous, instinctive and his conclusions are not elaborated by thought or by painstaking inquiry.[54]

Then Hurd goes on to compare the rites of passage for the so-called savage child before he turns into a warrior, such as hunger, lack of sleep, and so on. and compare this with the condition of morbid mental states of children who are not fed properly or do not receive the required amount of sleep.[55] For Hurd, the unruly child was a central point of interrogation, a child who could no longer be disciplined, and who easily gave into his urges that led to moral vices. It is then no surprise that for Hurd, psychiatric morbidity, as in the context of substance use, was actually a result of being wrongly educated about meanings of hallucinatory experience, as he would later suggest. Not only would the patient, according to Hurd, not understand his or her illness or interpret conditions correctly, but also those around him, which made the role of the psychiatrist important. Consider what he writes,

> The ability to recognize delusions is often absent even in assured convalescence, because many patients have been wrongly educated, or entertain false beliefs, like a faith in spiritualism, witchcraft or other unseen agencies, and are unable to be judge of evidence. With these, morbid religious sentiments are not recognized to be morbid, and are not struggled against because they correspond closely with former religious beliefs, which are held from force of habit.[56]

According to Hurd, the patient's "normal personality is abnormal to everyone else, and this view must be accepted when a judgment is formed as to his recovery."[57] In one case, the futility of releasing an alcoholic, Jack Mathew, who initially got injured fighting the Indians in January 1877, was moved from one asylum to another after being caught by the police, as he returned to his old habits, led Hurd to write frustratingly for the need to give indefinite care to individuals who did not recover so that they did not become a burden on the society.[58]

Drawing from his experience as a superintendent at the Eastern Michigan Asylum, he talked about the occurrence of periodic insanity among children and said that often the same person who provided care became the chief antagonist for the child in question. He added,

> It is a matter of experience that periodic insanity usually develops gradual perversions of feelings towards those who care for them during their successive attacks of mental disturbances. Every attack leaves as its memento in the patient's mind a grudge against someone, until finally the accumulation of grudges renders him a very trying and uncomfortable person.[59]

Talking about the need to incorporate empiricism and observation in science, he argued in a presidential address that the same principles that had been applied to previously distinguish confounding conditions such as typhoid and typhus to be used in the understanding of insanity.[60] Hurd knew that mental illness could not be "weighed and measured" and it was "evanescent and fleeting" and could not be "reduced to grams or grains or measured by instruments of precision."[61]

EPIDEMIOLOGY OF MENTAL HEALTH

I would now like to consider the evolution of psychiatric diagnoses at Johns Hopkins Hospital. The change in psychiatric classification is useful; it shows their arbitrary nature as well as, interestingly, the fact that diagnostic categories coalesced into each other in interesting ways. These classifications were part of the growing interest in public mental hygiene, which entailed placing populations into discrete categories.[62] Once viewed critically, these categories show how blame for illness was placed differentially on communities. The purpose behind giving a brief history of these classifications is therefore to also show the role played by expanding psychiatric services in the screening of populations defined by race.[63] There were several entries with cases of opium poisoning and alcohol overdoses. In some cases, patients became suicidal after opium poisoning, and in others, they were treated and improved.

Adolf Meyer joins Johns Hopkins Hospital in 1909 and starts working on the opening of the new Phipps Psychiatric Clinic. By this time, Eugene Bleuer's diagnosis of dementia praecox had been absorbed in clinical practice at the Johns Hopkins Hospital with the opening of the Phipps Psychiatric Clinic in 1913. Meyer expanded on Bleuler's optimistic outlook for schizophrenia. He viewed mental illness as a reaction to lifelong habits and conflicts leading to mental breakdown.[64] While one group of patients was referred to as having dementia praecox, another group had "allied dementia praecox" or "dementia paralytica."[65] This is also the time when there is an increasing differentiation between diagnosis of neurological and psychiatric illnesses. Physicians begin to make a distinction between psychasthenia and neurasthenia for the first time. Further distinctions include "undifferentiated depression," "manic depressed psychosis," "manic depressive insanity," and "simple depression."[66] The increasing frequency of psychiatric diagnoses showed the increasing importance of understanding mental illness by 1914.[67] Logbooks from the period also contain cases of "constitutional inferiority," which was in once case also used alongside antisocial personality disorder.[68]

After the opening of the Phipps Psychiatric Clinic in 1913, it takes a year or so for the clinic to take responsibility of psychiatric cases from the medical department. Children with epilepsies began to be treated in the psychiatric wards, whereas neurasthenia continued to be treated in the medical ward. There were new adjectives used for psychiatric conditions such as senile psychosis. For example, some were diagnosed with "imbecility" and began to be treated in the psychiatric ward. Often, states such as the "paranoid state" were used as diagnostic markers. The diagnosis of constitutional inferiority was retained, and the condition began to be treated psychiatrically. Constitutional inferiority also began to be used interchangeably with psychopathic inferiority.[69]

Logbooks eventually also describe the movement of patients to the psychiatric ward. Psychiatric disorders undergo further classification into manic-depressive reactive type (including an assessment about whether or not the person was in the manic phase), schizophrenic reactive type, and schizophrenic paranoid reactive type.[70] Meyer proposed a system of reaction types that were not diagnoses but a structural analysis of abnormal responses of "frequently recurring acquaintances."[71] The various reaction-types were not seen as necessarily exclusive of each other in one patient and could exist in combinations. The complex (emotionally active experience) was not the cause of the disease but was the cause of the symptoms or their becoming manifest.[72] Patients who were "schizophrenic reactive type" could also demonstrate depressive features. The reaction-types continue to increase, such that there are types that bring together symptoms from different diagnostic categories like depression, paranoia, and schizophrenia. Further, there was a temporal classification as well. The patients were classified based on whether they were under the manic phase as well as how they behaved in the phase. In some cases, a diagnosis of manic excitement was given. Neurasthenia begins to increasingly be treated in the psychiatry department. Psychiatric disorders continue to be clumped, as in the case of psychoneurotic depression, or "depression of anxiety features."[73]

Meyer can be credited as being the first to consider mental illness as a problem of adaptation and "not some mysterious devil in disguise."[74] While there was a great potential for the undoing of racial bias present in Hurd's psychiatry, the focus on adaptation yielded a different outcome in that it exposed the sick person's body to new disciplinary pressures so that the adaptive malfunction could be corrected.[75] In 1903, Meyer wrote about the need to use observation to detect developing abnormalities that had not turned into insanity yet.[76] As he had recounted in his presidential address,

> I had not till last week considered how during my early medical training while assisting my uncle in vacations and free time, I myself was often called as physician to a small institution that really was a small cotton mill in which about a hundred or less demented women were employed and cared for; and I had to see

them occasionally for their inter-current diseases. I knew they were abnormal; but I do not even remember thinking of them as insane; they simply were "not all there" but could work in this factory poorhouse.[77]

He too had sometimes relied on hereditary history and the frequency of mental illness as an etiological factors in the experience of illness.[78] Yet in other cases, he also denied heredity factors as playing a role.[79]

During this period, patients' drug problems are mentioned alongside the drugs they were dependent on. The column for diagnosis shows that transition of users from one type of drug to another, as in the case of heroine to cocaine. Although Baltimore-based psychiatrists, especially like Adolf Meyer, played a central role in thinking about mental illnesses in relation to reactions and thus played a major role in the move away from strictly genetic understandings of mental illness, which had been prevalent at the time, medical institutes were also creating caricatures about "normal" social behavior based on family relations. Meyer wrote,

> At the very outset of the problem rather different to the physician from what it appears to the layman. The layman, and I am afraid most lawyers, consider insanity as a condition characterizing a more or less subdivision of humanity, which is, or should be fenced in by asylum walls.[80]

Here Meyer reversed Hurd's understanding of illness, suggesting that "insanity is not a disease in the sense in which tuberculosis or leprosy are diseases, but it is a condition to which a number of totally different diseases may lead."[81] However, just as there is a move toward a more social understandings of illness, these were accompanied, inadvertently, by moral arguments about the family of the mentally ill, the addict, or the promiscuous.

There was a shift from earlier understandings of substance use in psychiatric debates, in which hereditary factors were considered as central to the transmission of habits. Henry Hurd, who was also a superintendent of the Johns Hopkins Hospital had famously written about alcoholism as linked to hereditary which resulted in the production of insanity. He went to great lengths to compare the inheritance of alcoholism to the inheritance of physical traits.[82] He wrote,

> Physical characteristics are transmitted by parents to their children. The expression and distinctive features of the countenance, the color of the hair and eyes, the complexion, the texture of the skin, the physical stature, the gait and general bearing of the father or mother are reproduced in their children. The same is equally true of mental characteristics. They are notably matters of inheritance. Diseased bodily states are also inherited. Gouty, rheumatic and tubercular parents beget children whose constitutions are impaired by the inherited taint in the blood.[83]

He used tuberculosis as the closest parallel and wrote, "If a person predisposed to tubercular disease does not live prudently in accordance with hygienic laws, avoiding excesses, unhealthy occupations, unhealthful climates or undue exposures to the weather, there is every reason to anticipate that he too will develop a similar disease."[84] Then he goes on to say,

> A similar law governs in diseases of the mind or of the nervous system. They are peculiarly transmissible because they affect the most complex part of the human mechanism and tissues which are at all times easily disordered. If a child inherits a defective nervous-organization, the tendency of his growth as he develops is towards a condition of disease; or in other words, the divergence from a healthy standard is wider and wider as the body develops and matures.

He then adds,

> The sensitiveness of the nervous system is due to the fact that its structure is more unstable than that of any other bodily tissue, and hence destructive changes occur more rapidly in it than in other less highly organized structures. If therefore a child inherits a defect of the nervous system whether from the insanity, inebriety, or nervous exhaustion of his parents, he is much more liable to develop actual disease than if he had inherited a tendency to bodily disease merely. The same is true of mental defects. The eccentricity or violent temper of a father is reproduced as actual insanity in his son. The feeble-minded mother has an idiot child. Highly nervous parents beget children whose lives are clouded by the forebodings of insanity. The children of insane parents inherit a capacity for the development of mental disease. These and similar degenerations can be predicted with comparative certainty when the morbid characteristics of parents are fully known.[85]

He talked about drunkenness as a form of transient insanity. He argued that the stages of drunkenness have a close parallel with insanity in that the early stage is marked by mild excitement, which is followed by mental aberration, which in turn is followed by stupor and profound insensibility. Not only does chronic alcoholism disrupt the mental vigor of the individual, it also has an effect on moral faculties, Hurd suggests, in that the person displays "moral perversion and loses his sense of justice, of honor, and of right and wrong. No inheritance can be worse than vicious propensities, and no qualities are surer to be transmitted to children."[86] Given such understandings of a changing normativity in which children are raised, it was no surprise that the primary target for medical intervention was children to separate them from social conditions causing them to develop illness.

These disciplinary efforts extend and diffuse beyond psychiatry and are made possible with the collusion of the police and the social service. Schooling has a central role to play in the detection of such pathologies among children.

Children and their fantasies was a topic of central importance for Meyer, which he also interpreted as a factor caused by excessive socialization with older adults, which prevented youthful instincts.[87] For Meyer, behavior within the classroom could also say something about imminent insanity.[88] In fact, Meyer had been a vocal proponent of the expansion of psychiatry to the doors of the classrooms, suggesting the need to delegate some responsibilities for detecting moral and mental problems to the school.[89] Meyer suggested the psychiatrist's sphere of study was supposed to be "patient" as a person as well as their activities and total behavior.[90] In fact, Adolf Meyer also departed from existing theories about psychotherapy by suggesting that talking or thinking alone did not shape pathology and treatment, but equally important was the *doing of things*.[91] Thus, treatment involved bringing about a change in behavior and habit, according to Meyer. Along with bringing a change in habit, as mentioned above, he recommended the need for psychiatrists to develop the craft of detecting abnormality before the emergence of insanity, which was the bedrock of the mental hygiene movement.[92]

The idea of mental hygiene spearheaded by Meyer led to the use of typologies of "reactions" such as "psychotic," "post-psychotic," and "social problems," including "behavior problems in children," "alcoholism," "addiction," and even "marital problems" and "problems with social agency."[93] This was followed by a secondary classification into "psychopathic" and "maladjusted." Results from the Eastern Health District showed that despite the higher rates of illness, "delinquency" was still presented as higher among Black populations than their white counterparts, showing that while softer forms of surveillance and preventative care was for white populations, much more brute forms could be employed for Black populations based on the presentation of epidemiological data.[94] With the increasing emphasis on socio-psychiatry, Henry Stack Sullivan forcefully made the case that psychiatry was not an impossible study of individuals suffering mental disorders. Instead, it had to be focused on "disordered interpersonal relations nucleating more or less clearly in a specific person," as he drew upon his clinical notes from Sheppard and Enoch Pratt Hospital, Baltimore.[95] Then he goes on to critique psychiatrists, whose focus was often on the individual alone. Bringing together his interest in psychoanalysis with Meyerian adaptive theories, he then went on to say,

> The theoretic implications of this very distinction of social versus personal recovery might long since have turned the attention of research personnel on the processes concerned. A study of "social recoveries" in one of our large mental hospitals some years ago taught me that patients were often released from care because they had learned not to manifest symptoms to the environing persons; in other words, had integrated enough of the personal environment to realize the prejudice opposed to their delusions. It seemed almost as if they grew wise

> enough to be tolerant of the imbecility surrounding them, having finally discovered that it was stupidity and not malice. They could then secure satisfaction from contact with others, while discharging a part of their cravings by psychotic means. The path to social recovery—so often a necessary preliminary to thoroughgoing treatment thus seemed to be along the line of really sympathetic environment.[96]

Yet even as these breakthroughs were made by Meyer and Sullivan, a social argument also entailed making specific assumptions about behavior, which, however well-intentioned, only reinforced the moralism of public health efforts. Even the strides made by Meyer to complicate the hereditary basis of illness were undone, especially as George Everett Partridge published a series of studies postulating the "delinquent type" common among males who drank or resorted to drugs or stealing based on observational studies in the Sheppard and Enoch Pratt Hospital in Baltimore. He also pointed to the difficulty of differentiating cultural and personality patterns and thought that it was possible for a group as a whole to become pathological. He even went as far as to hypothesize that the thorough and adequate investigation of the individual consciousness in its pathological manifestations yields precisely the background needed for the study of "group consciousness"—that is, for the development of scientific socio-pathology.[97]

PROBLEMS OF MORALITY

Due to the construction of substance use as a moral problem, proponents of control advocated for strict supervision and control.[98] In one conference on drug control, it was argued that even private treatment centers were to be under strict supervision and control by the public authorities entrusted with the enforcement of anti-narcotic laws.[99] Here it was also reasoned that, without restraint and control, habit-forming narcotic drugs could be self-administered, which was completely contrary to public policy.[100] By this time, there were also calls to prevent the spread of adulterated drugs.[101] Clinical epidemiology explored the chemical composition of methadone and how it behaved or metabolized in the liver.[102] This was also a time when hospital services closely evaluated the effects of barbiturates on mood changes, such as becoming quiet or depressed.[103] By the 1950s, methadone had also emerged as a replacement for morphine and its impacts were being compared with those of morphine-based compounds.[104] Meanwhile, as there were stricter checks imposed on the use of drugs, scientific discourses continued to understand substance use mainly through criminal behaviors. Some scientific studies continued to develop comparisons and departures between alcoholism and the use of other substances:

> There has existed in the minds of most people a feeling that the drug addict is degenerate but that the alcohol addict is stubborn, immoral and contrary. This is reflected in the common attitude that a drug addict is so enmeshed in his habit that he cannot extricate himself but that the alcohol addict could stop drinking if he wished to do so.[105]

Moral arguments were possible by using ideas of deterioration in habits, whereas others even suggested that the person with substance use was also originally unstable. Kolb has also pointed out that "much of the moral deterioration attributed to narcotics in the past was not deterioration but an original nervous instability and moral obliquity."[106] In creating parallels between drug and alcohol use, researchers reasoned,

> Many of the cases associated with the use of drugs were also intemperate in the use of alcohol and might validly have been classified as well among the alcoholic psychoses. The intemperate use of alcohol is a serious complication of addiction with and without psychosis and may be an important precipitating factor in causing readmissions to mental hospitals in a large number of cases of this type.[107]

Substance use by this time was treated largely through the lens of underlying pathological problems, with specific triggers and social conditions creating the need to consume drugs or alcohol,[108] especially in a situation where a person had little inhibitions about committing a crime and intervention was required to change habits. Lawrence Kolbs had commented on the movement of people from one city to another to seek treatment. He noted, "We have seen addicts in Washington and Atlanta who have been on the register of the New York and other clinics. Patients have come to us within a few weeks after leaving a hospital in Philadelphia, and patients from Baltimore have told of other addicts in that city who went to Philadelphia for treatment."[109] The passing of the Harrison law resulted in cocaine users turning to morphine or heroin while discontinuing cocaine altogether, as Kolbs noted.[110]

Psychotherapy by the 1930s would rapidly be incorporated in the treatment of schizophrenia, especially with the coming of Harry Stack Sullivan to Shepard Pratt in Baltimore. This is also the period when psychiatrists were experimenting with psychoanalytic explanations about drug use. Robert Lindner, a well-known Baltimore psychiatrist, maintained that the youth had abandoned solitude and individuality in favor of pack-running and predatory assembly.[111] While his work was remarkable in shedding light on the relationship between psychoanalysis and politics, he interpreted neurosis too rigidly through a Freudian framework, which was in fashion in the 1940s, using dreams about landscapes in Baltimore to equate the loss of speech with erectile disfunction, and leakage of semen with secrets about communism.[112]

A slight downward trend in substance use was noted around 1950s, but Public Health Service officials did not accept it as definite.

In 1950, admissions for substance use related problems totaled 4,564 while the 1951 total, based on a projection of actual cases received in the early months was estimated at 4,200. It was observed that in recent months there had not been a single application for hospitalization for substance use from one of the eight worst problem cities.[113] Meanwhile, there were also growing calls for a change in attitude toward people suffering from substance use in some isolated academic circles.[114] Still, there remained a big gap between such lone voices and policy. Some of Kolb's conclusions in relation to narcotics and crime were that both heroin and morphine in large doses changed drunken, fighting psychopaths into sober, cowardly, unaggressive idlers. He suggested it was the use of drugs itself that could cause criminality. Cocaine, up to a certain point, made criminals more efficient as criminals, he would suggest. Beyond this point, cocaine could bring on a state of fear or paranoia during which the person with substance use could murder a supposed pursuer, Kolb further added.[115]

Meanwhile, behavioral factors based on one's social background continued to shape moralistic impulses in drug control policy and scientific discourses. Minority groups other than Black families would also be scapegoated for lack of care and treatment. For example, an analysis of data on drug use among Jewish populations in Baltimore indicated that they shared with their non-Jewish counterparts the "same general weakness and lack of ego strength which is characterized by immaturity, dependency, and passivity." Like Black families suffering from the havoc of substance use, Jewish individuals were viewed as resorting to drugs to resolve certain psychological needs.[116] However, by the 1960s, there had been a move away from strictly psychoanalytic understandings and calls for the establishment of methadone maintenance programs as well as the expansion of group therapy as the means of drug treatment.

Even by this time, the blame for substance use continued to be placed directly on the shoulders of those suffering from it. Harris Isbell, director of the Addiction Research Center, United States Public Health Service Hospital, Lexington, Kentucky, said:

> The majority of addicts don't want to be normal; they want to be what they call "high" they want to be "loaded." If you provide them with drugs by this single-shot mechanism at five trips a day, that is just enough to keep the addict going and he will go out and get more so that he can get high.[117]

Not only would the "addict" raise his dosage, according to Isbell, but he would then require a variety of drugs to compliment his dosage. He further added that those with problems with substance use got their doses from the so-called narcotic bars, but would then go out and buy more on the illicit market.[118]

The Baltimore Drug Addiction Clinic began to contact people suffering from substance use in prisons for the daily urine testing program. After volunteering, they were followed up daily in a clinic in downtown Baltimore with active parole supervision and some group psychotherapy. Positive urine tests are initially used to discuss the patients' problems. Continued drug consumption could lead to a return to prison. People suffering from substance use are now increasingly dependent upon treatment centers to prove their intentions in front of law enforcement agencies. Among medical circles, there were calls for a long-acting complex so that patients with problems of substance use would no longer be required to remain dependent on their programs. A cyclazocine-like drug with a much longer duration of action (three days to two weeks) could provide a solution to patients, as they would have to come to the clinic less frequently.[119] Thus, the clinical epidemiology of drug treatment became central to thinking about the best way to treat people while also making them drug-free and autonomous. Still, there was also a competing trend toward a punitive attitude toward substance use, where punishment was perceived as the only effective solution.

The relationship between crime and substance use remained central to scientific discourses and imagination.[120] By now, the fact that individuals, most Black men, were engaged in dangerous behavior for the thrill of it could be backed by theories such as that of Lindesmith's, according to which substance use had a relationship with euphoria. Euphoria remained latent even despite the need to prevent withdrawals, according to the theory. This theory proposed a typology between hardcore, weekender and lind addicts,[121] and suggested that the reason for repeated consumption of drugs was not simply to avoid withdrawals, as had been suggested before, but to feel a renewed sense of euphoria. Such a perspective could then lead drug use to not only be taken as a problem of dependence but also gratification, a danger thought to have been limited to Black neighborhoods previously but slowly also moving into predominantly white areas, alerting the state authorities of the need to take prompt action. By 1951, Judge Sherbow commented on the spread of drugs to "better" class neighborhoods and lamented that only when the drug-addiction problem "hit some people in the upper economic groups" that something had to be done about it. He also lamented the lack of facilities to treat substance use, causing many to travel all the way to the Lexington Hospital in Kentucky for treatment.[122] Racial geographies thus remained central to the perception of danger and risk and also shaped the mobilization of resources. By 1970s, many began to critique methadone maintenance, saying that it was replacing one form of substance use with another. One writer advocating for group therapy suggested, "There is a realization that the methadone gimmick, with its 'fill'er up' gas station philosophy, is no answer for the underlying causes of drug addiction."[123] Just as people remained critical of methadone maintenance, there was also a great deal of reluctance toward funding Baltimore's treatment programs by the office of economic opportunity.[124] By 1969, there was an outcry around methadone making its way to illegal markets, with estimates suggesting the presence of between 3,000 and 10,000 people suffering from hardcore addiction.[125] By 1973, Baltimore-based psychiatrists even began to differentiate affective disorders (depressed and manic types) from personality disorders with drug abuse, which inadvertently separated the language of trauma and mental illness from drug dependence, as if the two could easily be separated.

FEAR AND PUBLIC HEALTH IN THE ERA OF AIDS

The relationship between crime and substance use was further consolidated in the 1980s with the outbreak of HIV.[126] The Addiction Research Center (ARC) became part of the National Institute on Drug Abuse, which was moved from Lexington to Baltimore, Maryland, in 1979. The ARC became one of the largest facilities in the United States devoted to studying substance use and drug abuse.[127] Meanwhile, public health campaigns continued to invoke the picture of lascivious couples having sex without any restraint, with one campaign poster showing a man and woman having sex openly in the street.[128] Just as there had been a belief about AIDS transmission only among gay men, another caricature used was that of men and women engaging in dangerous behavior due to uncontrolled sexual appetites, behaviors whose racialization has a long history, as I have shown above.

By the 1980s, there was a growing concern to counter drug abuse and the spread of AIDS, with public health warnings excluding specific populations such as Haitians as particularly vulnerable.[129]Yet even as there was an inclusion of mental health as an important agenda for public health and a growing support for "health-based drug policies," there was still resistance toward the implementation of a needle exchange program,[130] with the chairman on the governor's advisory body, Richard Jacobson, stating as an excuse that such a program would be "very offensive for the general population."[131] By 1990, the responsibility to change the domestic settings viewed as generative of substance use was also outsourced to private players, such as the Family Life Center, which began to offer support to kids up to fifth grade in case they had problems with substance use at home.[132] AIDS reanimated the enduring relationship between morality and health by posing the disease as specifically impacting a racial other who is unable to keep up with notions of citizenship and self-care, thus chronically relapsing into conditions of disease and illness.

Mark Smith, Associate Director of AIDS services at Johns Hopkins Hospital, suggested, "AIDS is one of many scourges affecting African-American communities, intertwined with poor education, drug dependence, inadequate care and general malaise."[133] On the one hand, the Black population had been marginalized from the delivery of adequate services, and on the other, words like *malaise* made it appear as if there was something inherent in a way of life that attracted illness. Then, of course, there was another problem related to deep-seated suspicions toward the "white medical establishment" which further intensified suspicions about medicine.[134] By 1988, methadone maintenance was viewed as the best way to reduce the risk of AIDS transmission.[135] The suspicion toward a racial other was also redirected toward suspicion among sexual partners, about whether they had been loyal or not. Women discussed in ethnographic studies pointed out that they would be careful about initiating condom use in their sexual practices because their partners associated such practices with being "sexually loose."[136] The moralistic tone of public health now also implicates how household members view each other, with self-care being perceived as a sign of infidelity.

In an NCAIDS hearing on the frequency of AIDS, Commissioner Dalton's speech suggested the state of Black communities, "If we are talking about gay men and AIDS, we are talking about Black men . . . if we are talking about I.V drugs and AIDS we are talking about African-American communities."[137] Dalton's speech also shows the great extent to which Black community internalized ideas about their susceptibility to AIDS as a matter of biology rather than social conditions. Dalton then reaches out to point out a sense of commonality across race, "African-Americans are especially fond of invoking our commonality, Blacks and whites together . . . at moments when we are internally feeling most separate." When a professor of medicine at Johns Hopkins, Mark Smith, speaks, he admits that the Black population had been alienated from the system but also commented on the increasing suspicion of the community toward health programs, stating that they were "somewhat cynical about the motives of those who arrive in their communities to help them." He says that the Tuskegee syphilis experiments still haunted them and led to suspicions about the medical establishment's "ethical even-handedness." He considers drug use to be the biggest cause of the rapid spread of AIDS. He then shows that just as there was suspicion toward the Black community, there was also suspicion within the Black community toward the drug user, which prevented the community from mobilizing around the problem of drug use. He says,

> Traditional leadership in the Black community has not become more mobilized to deal with AIDS in part because people who use intravenous drugs are not the sort of citizens the leadership would like to hold up as needy recipients of

> community or governmental assistance, particularly when they see so many other perhaps more "deserving" people whose lives are constantly under assault.[138]

Moreover, he says that being targeted and blamed for the virus by virtue of their race further intensified suspicion about government involvement in the creation of the virus as a form of biological warfare, where diagnostic testing only meant detection and isolation rather than actual care.[139] Talking about the "guinea-pig syndrome," he says,

> When I arrived in Baltimore two years ago, I started actually hearing stories from a number of people who had grown up in the vicinity of Johns Hopkins Hospital. That their parents had told them not to be out on the street after dark because if they were, those people from Johns Hopkins would snatch them off the street and experiment on them in the basement of the hospital at night.[140]

He goes on to describe that the reputation of a place like Hopkins was not as good in the neighborhood as it was with the National Institute of Health, and says this in response to growing demands within the medical community for experimental medicine. In the context of the disregard for Black population's health, he rhetorically asks, "I believe many people, perhaps in their heart of hearts, ask the question: are they [medical and public health authorities] interested in the spread of AIDS because they are concerned about us [the Black community] or are they interested in us because they are concerned about the spread of AIDS?" Thus, the perception of public health efforts continued to be plagued by perceptions of self-interest rather than the actual needs of communities.

CONCLUSION

The reason why I have turned to public health discourses in Baltimore is to consider the moralistic language through which poor health was linked with the problem of vices, which were perceived to be transmitted within families if not properly disciplined. Using the discussion of mental illness, substance use and infectious diseases, I have considered not only the justifications for intervening in low-income communities in Baltimore but also the forms of suspicion that have shaped how low-income, racialized communities in Baltimore perceive and relate with healthcare institutions. Though occasionally I talk about psychiatric or public health institutions more generally, the purpose was to explore how scientific discourses justified certain forms of control as a pre-requisite for recovery—these related to formal forms of control through institutional care but also informal forms within domestic spaces and in communities. This discussion will foreground the relevance of prisons in the substance use landscape of the city. I use the centrality of discipline for public health institutes and extend the analysis to now directly consider carceral authority and the different types of subjectivities they create among individuals suffering from substance use. I also go beyond public health to the policing of communities, the experiences and intimacies that shape incarceration on the account of drug-related crimes, as well as the enduring traumas of incarceration and drug-related dependencies—or new forms of carceral obligations—even after completing many years in prison. Having considered how scientific discourses made a case for disciplining those with mental illness and substance use, I would now like to turn to the experience of incarceration in contemporary Baltimore and ask how punishment rather than care has remained a primary modality of engaging with the problem of substance use, which then provides the foundations to consider people's experience of recovery as shaped by similar punitive attitudes.

NOTES

1. Katherine Rankin, "A Critical Geography of Poverty Finance," *Third World Quarterly* 3, No. 4 (2013): 547–68.
2. Loic Waquant, "Creating the Neoliberal State: Workfare, Prisonfare, and Social Insecurity," *Sociological Forum* 25, No. 2 (2010): 197–220. Loic Wacquant. "The New 'Peculiar Institution': On the Prison as Surrogate Ghetto," *Theoretical Criminology* 4, No. 3 (2000): 377–389. doi: 10.1177/1362480600004003007; Loic Wacquant, "Deadly Symbiosis: When Ghetto and Prison Meet and Mesh," *Punishment & Society* 3, No. 1 (2001): 95 133. doi: 10.1177/14624740122228276
3. Eduardo Mendieta, "Plantations, Ghettos, Prisons: US Racial Geographies," *Philosophy & Geography* 7, No. 1 (2004): 53. doi: 10.1080/1090377042000196010
4. Loic Wacquant, "From Slavery to Mass Incarceration," *New Left Review* 13 (2002): 50.
5. Dan Werb, Greg Rowell, Gordon Guyatt, Thomas Kerr, Julio Montaner, and Evan Wood, "Effect of Drug Law Enforcement on Drug Market Violence: A Systematic Review," *International Journal of Drug Policy* 22, No. 2 (2011): 87–94.
6. "The Black Butterfly: Racial Segregation and Investment Patterns in Baltimore." https://apps.urban.org/features/baltimore-investment-flows/
7. Ibid.
8. Ibid.
9. "Report of the Superintendent of the Johns Hopkins Hospital," (1889).
10. Baltimore, MD., Ordinance 692 (May 15, 1911).
11. Preston, James, "What Can Be Done to Improve the Living Conditions of Baltimore's Negro Population?" *Baltimore Mun.* 1, No. 1 (March 16, 1917).
12. "U.S. Comm'n on Civil Rights, Understanding Fair Housing 4-5" (Clearinghouse Pub. No. 42, 1973).

13. Ira Klein, "Plague, Policy and Popular Unrest in British India," *Modern Asian Studies* 22, No. 4 (1988): 723–55. doi: 10.1017/S0026749X00015729.

14. "The Negro tuberculosis problem in Maryland: whose problem?" *Maryland Association for the Prevention and Relief of Tuberculosis* (1915).

15. Ibid.

16. By this time medical services employ the word "colored" rather than Black or African-American.

17. "The Negro tuberculosis problem in Maryland: whose problem?" *Maryland Association for the Prevention and Relief of Tuberculosis* (1915).

18. Ibid.

19. Report of the Superintendent of the Johns Hopkins Hospital (1914).

20. Ibid.

21. Ibid.

22. Ibid.

23. See Heather R. Perry, *Recycling the Disabled: Army, Medicine and Modernity in WWI Germany* (Manchester: Manchester University Press, 2014); Beth Linker, *War's Waste: Rehabilitation in World War I America* (Chicago: University of Chicago Press, 2011).

24. Report of the Superintendent of the Johns Hopkins Hospital (1914).

25. Ibid.

26. Ibid.

27. Ibid.

28. Ibid.

29. Ibid.

30. Johns Hopkins Hospital, Colored Orphan Asylum Logbook, 1875-1923.

31. The Kansas City Medical Index-Lancet, Volume 7 (1889), 58.

32. W.R. Bett, "William Steward Halsted (1852-1922) Cocaine Pioneer and addict," *British Journal of Substance use to Alcohol & Other Drugs*, 49 (1952): 53–9. doi: 10.1111/j.1360-0443.1952.tb04225.x

33. Henry M. Hurd, "Paranoia," *Journal of Insanity* (April 1886).

34. For more on environmentalism in public health see, Raquel A. G. Reyes, "Environmentalist Thinking and the Question of Disease Causation in Late Spanish Philippines," *Journal of the History of Medicine and Allied Sciences* 69, no. 4 (October 2014): 554–579, doi: 10.1093/jhmas/jrt030; Julyan G. Peard, "Tropical Medicine in Nineteenth-Century Brazil: The Case of the 'Escola Tropicalista Bahiana,' 1860–1890," in *Warm Climates and Western Medicine* (Leiden, The Netherlands: Brill, 1996); Samiparna Samantha, "Unseen Enemy: The English, Disease, and Medicine in Colonial Bengal, 1617-1847," *The Historian* 78, No. 4 (winter 2016): 792.

35. Henry M. Hurd, *The Institutional Care of the Insane in United States and Canada 1843-1927* (1916), 511.

36. Ibid.

37. Henry M. Hurd, *The Institutional Care of the Insane in United States and Canada 1843-1927* (1916), 574.

38. D.K. Henderson, "The Treatment of Drug Substance Use," *Glasgow Medical Journal* 85, No. 3 (March 1916): 190–202.

39. Ibid.
40. Ibid.
41. Ibid.
42. C.S. Bluemel, "Morphine Habit," *The Journal of Nervous and Mental Disease* 51, No. 1 (1920): 105–6.
43. Henderson, "The Treatment of Drug Substance Use."
44. Ibid.
45. Ibid. 202.
46. "Epilepsy, and Certain Types of Epileptiform Attacks," *JAMA* 75, No. 14 (1920): 932–3. doi: 10.1001/jama.1920.02620400026008, 932.
47. He also says, "The evils which follow insanity in the individual, and the heavy public and private burdens entailed by it upon every community, are well known. Next to alcoholism, insanity is probably the most potent cause of pauperism and dependence. Wherever insanity develops in a family of moderate means and the State does not interfere to lift the burden of support, wholly or in part, the tendency of that family is to poverty. Every person who has had only moderate experience in the care of the insane can call to mind instances where the expense of attempting to care for one insane member of a family who suffered from chronic insanity has eventually proved the financial undoing of the whole family, and has brought its members to poverty, if not to the almshouse." Hurd M. Hurd, "How can Psychiatry assist Preventive Medicine?" *Am J Public Hygiene*. 18 No. 3 (1908): 273–8.
48. For an understanding about scientific discourses and their conflation of racial and social difference prevalent in early 20th century see Franz Boas, "The Mind of Primitive Man," *The Journal of American Folklore* 14, No. 52 (1901): 1–11. doi: 10.2307/533099.
49. Henry M. Hurd, "How can Psychiatry assist Preventive Medicine?" *American Journal of Public Hygiene* 18, No. 3 (Aug 1908): 273–8.
50. Ibid.
51. Ibid., 276.
52. Henry M. Hurd, "Imbecility with Insanity," *American Journal of Psychiatry* 45, No. 2 (1888): 263.
53. Ibid. also see Kevin Groark, "Freud among the Boasians: Psychoanalytic Influence and Ambivalence in American Anthropology," *Current Anthropology* 60, No. 4 (2019): 559–88.
54. Henry M. Hurd, "Some Mental Disorders of Childhood and Youth" (1894), 282.
55. Ibid.
56. Henry M. Hurd, "The Data of Recovery from Insanity," *American Journal of Psychiatry* 43, No. 2 (1886): 246.
57. Ibid.
58. Henry M. Hurd, "A Case of Inebriety with Insanity: With Remarks," (1889).
59. Henry M. Hurd, "The Treatment of Periodic Insanity," *American Journal of Psychiatry* 39 No. 2 (1882): 179.
60. Henry M. Hurd, "The Teaching of Psychiatry," *American Journal of Insanity* LVI, No. 2 (1899): 220.

61. Given the influenza epidemic of the early twentieth century and the periodic outbreaks of typhoid, Hurd had also written in detail about delusions accompanied by illnesses like pneumonia, such as a patient who recovered, and was "confused, suspicious, lacking in ability to fix her attention and with definite delusions about her husband… she believed that her husband, during her illness, had improper relations with the nurse in her presence." Other cases were of melancholia developing from convalescence from typhoid fever. ibid., 221.

62. Bernard M. Cohen and Ruth E. Fairbank, "Statistical Contributions from the Mental Hygiene Study of the Eastern Health District of Baltimore," *Human Biology* 11, No. 1 (Feb 1939): 112.

63. The Johns Hopkins admission logbooks from 1889 to 1900 shows the emergence of psychiatric disorders. The logbooks show the differentiation of neurasthenia further into nervous neurasthenia, nervous dysphasia, sexual neurasthenia (mostly among men) and neurasthenia along with movable kidneys and nervous dyspepsia along with hyper-acidity. Physicians also differentiated between different types of hysteria e.g., simple hysteria, hysteria (child crowing) and hysteria due to contracted pelvis. Logbooks from 1900 to 1950 also show the emergence of psychiatric and neurological nosology as diagnosis such as neurasthenia undergo further differentiation. JHH Patient Records, Admissions and Discharges—Oct 4, 1899—Nov 29, 1900 (113540).

64. He felt that schizophrenia was the natural result of a life history that could be clearly traced to various physical, social, and psychological factors in the patient's past. While both had different prognoses about schizophrenia, both shared the identical view that schizophrenia could be traced back to a biological illness.

65. JHH Patient Records, Admissions and Discharges—December 1913–September 1914

66. Ibid. This is also the period where disparate categories begin to be clumped together, as in "psychoneurosis neurasthenia."

67. Ibid.

68. Even after psychiatric diagnoses become complex, patients continue to be diagnosed with "hysteria." By this time, even psychoneurosis and neurasthenia continued to be treated in the medical ward, yet there is also a push to treat neurasthenia and epilepsy psychiatrically, especially as new diagnoses such as "idiopathic epilepsy" emerged.

69. Ibid.

70. JHH Patient Records, Admissions and Discharges—February 4, 1918-September 1918 (308346)

71. JHH Patient Records, Admissions and Discharges—February 4, 1918-September 1918; Adolf Meyer, "The Problems of Mental Reaction-Type, Mental Causes and Diseases," *Psychological Bulletin* 5, No. 8 (1908): 245–261. doi: 10.1037/h0072906

72. Adolf Meyer, "The Problems of Mental Reaction-Type, Mental Causes and Diseases," *Psychological Bulletin* 5, No. 8 (1908): 245–61. doi: 10.1037/h0072906

73. Even as psychiatric nosology becomes sophisticated, diagnosis of hysteria is retained, as in "hysterical reaction type" patients. There are new diagnostic

anxieties presented by convulsions which were identified as "unexplained." JHH Patient Records, Admissions and Discharges—Sep 1, 1920–May 6, 1921 (113543).

74. Adolf Meyer, "The Philosophy of Occupational Therapy," *Archives of Occupational Therapy* 1, No. 1 (February 1922): 1–10.

75. Ibid.

76. Jacob Bowlby, "The Adolf Meyer Lecture: Childhood Mourning and Its Implications for Psychiatry," *American Journal of Psychiatry* 11, No. 6 (1961): 481–98.

77. Adolf Meyer, "Presidential Address," *American Journal of Psychiatry* 85, No. 1 (1928): 20.

78. Adolf Meyer, "The Anatomical Facts and Clinical Varieties of Traumatic Insanity," *American Journal of Insanity* LX, No. 3 (1904).

79. Adolf Meyer, "The Dynamic Interpretation of Dementia Praecox," *American Journal of Psychiatry* 21, No. 3 (1910): 388. In some of the cases he presented was the centrality of masturbation in the emergence of symptoms as in the case of one patient who had "impure thoughts, confessed about having long indulged in masturbation," and said that she felt overwhelming guilt and ashamed at having looked at men and said, "I thought they saw what I had done in my eyes." ibid. 389.

80. Adolf Meyer, "The Problems of the Physician Concerning the Criminal Insane and Borderland Cases," *JAMA* LIV, No. 24 (1910): 1930–5.

81. Ibid.

82. Henry M. Hurd, "The Hereditary Influence of Alcoholic Indulgence upon the Production of Insanity," *Sanitary Convention* (Michigan, 1883).

83. Ibid.

84. Ibid.

85. Ibid.

86. Ibid.

87. Adolf Meyer, "An Attempt at Analysis of the Neurotic Constitution," *American Journal of Psychology* 14, no. ¾ (1903): 98.

88. Adolf Meyer, "What Do Histories of Cases of Insanity Teach Us Concerning Preventative Mental Hygiene During the Years of School Life?" *The Psychological Clinic* 2, No. 4 (1908).

89. Adolf Meyer, "Mental and Moral Health in a Constructive School Programs," in *Suggestions of Modern Science Concerning Education*, eds. Herbert Jennings, Jacob B. Watson, Adolf Meyer, and William Thomas (New York: MacMillan Co, 1917).

90. Ibid.

91. Adolf Meyer, "The Role of Mental Factors in Psychiatry," *American Journal of Psychiatry* 65, No. 1 (2006): 46.

92. Adolf Meyer, "The Mental Hygiene Movement," *Canadian Medical Association Journal* 8, No. 7 (1918): 632.

93. Ibid.

94. Bernard M. Cohen and Ruth E. Fairbank, "Statistical Contributions from the Mental Hygiene Study of the Eastern Health District of Baltimore," *Human Biology* (Baltimore) 11, No. 1 (1939).

95. Harry Stack Sullivan, "Socio-Psychiatric Research: Its Implications for Schizophrenia Problem and for Mental Hygiene," New York City. Presented in abstract at the eighty-sixth annual meeting of The American Psychiatric Association, Washington, D. C., May (1930).

96. Ibid.

97. George E. Partridge, "A Study of 50 Cases of Psychopathic Personality; Psychopathic Personalities Among Boys in a Training School for Delinquents; Psychotic Reaction in the Psychopath," (1932); George E. Partridge, "Psychopathic Personality and Personality," *The American Journal of Psychiatry* 6, No. 85 (May 1929): 1053–5.

98. "Proceedings of an annual meeting of the National Drug Trade conference held at the Hotel Emerson, Baltimore," January 4 (1918) In Pursuance of a call of the president upon the written request of five delegates.

99. Ibid.

100. Ibid.

101. F.W. Nitardy, "Notes on Early Drug Legislation," *Journal of Pharmaceutical Sciences* 23 (1934): 1122–7. doi: 10.1002/jps.3080231113

102. D.D. Bonnycastle and C.W. Delia, "Effect of Hepatectomy upon the Analgetic Action of 1 Methadone," *Proceedings of the Society for Experimental Biology and Medicine* 74 No. 3 (1950): 589–91. doi:10.3181/00379727-74-17983

103. H. Isbell, S. Altschul, C.H. Kornetsky, A.J. Eisenman, H.G. Flanary, and H.F. Fraser, "Chronic Barbiturate Intoxication: An Experimental Study," *Archives of Neurology and Psychiatry* 64, No. 1 (1950): 1–28. doi: 10.1001/archneurpsyc.1950.02310250007001

104. J. A. Schuldiner, "Identification of Amidone," *Analytical Chemistry* 21, No. 2 (1949): 298–300. doi: 10.1021/ac60026a017

105. Merrill Moore, Alice F. Raymond, and Mildred G. Gray, "Alcoholism and the Use of Drugs; A Review of 841 Cases Diagnosed "With Psychosis Due to Drugs and Other Exogenous Toxins" or "Without Psychosis: Drug Substance Use," *Quarterly Journal of Studies on Alcohol* 2 No. 3 (1941): 496–504.

106. Ibid.

107. Lawrence Kolb, "Pleasure and deterioration from narcotics substance use," United States Public Health Service Hygienic Laboratory, Washington DC, Reprint No. 211, the National Committee for Mental Hygiene, Inc., New York City (1925).

108. Robert V. Seliger & Victoria Cranford, "Psychiatric Orientation of the Alcoholic Criminal," *JAMA* 129, No. 6 (1945).

109. Lawrence Kolb and A.G. Du Mez, "The Prevalence and Trend of Drug Substance Use in the United States and Factors Influencing It," *Public Health Reports* (1896-1970) 39, No. 21 (May 23, 1924): 1179–204.

110. Ibid.

111. Jacob E. Owen, "How Delinquent Are Our Juveniles?" *The Educational Forum*, 21 No. 2 (1957): 203–6. doi: 10.1080/00131725709341085

112. Robert Lindner, *The Fifty-Minute Hour* (The Other Press, 2013).

113. Frank Cassino, "Control of Narcotic Substance use," *American Journal of Psychotherapy* 7 No. 1 (1953): 164.

114. Edward J. Donovan, "Two Years of the Presidency of the New York Academy of Medicine," Address of the Retiring President, *Bulletin of the New York Academy of Medicine* 33, No. 4 (1957).

115. Walter Adams, Norbert Glasser & Leonidas H. Berry, "The Narcotic Problem in an Urban Community," *Journal of the National Medical Association* 45, No. 1 (1953): 52.

116. J.R. Rosenbloom, "Notes on Jewish Drug Addicts," *Psychological Reports* 5, No. 3 (1959), 769–772. doi: 10.2466/pr0.1959.5.3.769

117. H. J. Anslinger, "Narcotic Substance Use as Seen by the Law-Enforcement Officer," *Federal Probation* 21, No. 2 (June 1957): 34–41.

118. H. J. Anslinger, "Narcotic Substance Use as Seen by the Law-Enforcement Officer," *Federal Probation* 21, No. 2 (June 1957): 34–41.

119. Jonathan O. Cole, "Report on the Treatment of Drug Substance Use," (1966). https://www.ojp.gov/pdffiles1/Digitization/135534NCJRS.pdf#page=144

120. Louis S. Harris, "Impact of Heroin Substance Use Upon Criminality (from Problems of Drug Dependence)," Proceedings of the 41st Annual Scientific Meeting (1979) https://www.ojp.gov/ncjrs/virtual-library/abstracts/impact-heroin-substance use-upon-criminality-problems-drug-dependence

121. W.E. Mcauliffe, *A Test of Lindesmith's Theory of Opiate Substance Use* (Available from Dissertations & Theses at Johns Hopkins University, 1973).

122. "Dope Habit Widespread, Judge Says: No Section of the City Free of Drugs," *The Sun* (Oct 14, 1951): 30.

123. Blake Carolyn Stinchcomb, "Debate and Discussion: Methadone: Treatment, or a Worse Substance Use?" *The Sun* (1976, Jan 31).

124. S. J. Lynton, "OEO Turns Town Narcotics Plan: Refuses to Give Funds for Substance Use Treatment," *The Sun* (Jul 1, 1967).

125. F. P. McGehan, "Baltimore's Drug Scene-I: Silent Disease Infects Rich, Poor," *The Sun* (1969, Jun 24).

126. J.C. Ball, L. Rosen, E.G. Friedman, and D.N. Nurco, "The Impact of Heroin Substance Use on Criminality," Committee on Problems of Drug Dependence (1981).

127. Researchers at the ARC in Baltimore used new noninvasive imaging techniques, such as positron emission tomography (PET scanning) to produce imaging of the parts of the brain impacted by drugs. The PET scan of a former opioid dependent under the influence of morphine showed decreased brain activity through lighter tones in the scan compared to activity in the same parts of the brain under the placebo (no drug) "Images from the History of Public Health Service," https://www.nlm.nih.gov/exhibition/phs_history/images.dir/134.gif

128. Harm Reduction/Clean needles, AIDS Posters & Stories of Public Health https://www.nlm.nih.gov/exhibition/aids-posters/digitalgallery_theme_6.html

129. Ibid.

130. D. Simon, "Politics and Drugs: Preventing AIDS by Having Drug Users Exchange Needles, as Has Been Suggested in Kurt L. Schmoke's Baltimore, May Work but the Politicians Don't Seem to Want to Find Out," *The Sun* (1990, Apr 15).

131. "Officials Shun AIDS Report," Baltimore Evening Sun (1991) https://collections.nlm.nih.gov/catalog/nlm:nlmuid-101763264X163-doc

132. “Pupils in Families with Drugs Get Aid,” *The Sun* (1990, Dec 23).

133. Jonathan Bor, “Blacks’ Mistrust of Doctors Slows AIDS Treatment,” *Baltimore Sun* (1990).

134. Ibid.

135. Ibid.

136. T. L. Whitehead, “Urban Low-Income African American Men, HIV/AIDS, and Gender Identity,” *Medical Anthropology Quarterly* 11 (1997): 411–47. doi: 10.1525/maq.1997.11.4.411

137. “NCAIDS Hearing on HIV Disease in African American Communities,” transcript, Baltimore, Maryland.

138. Ibid.

139. Ibid.

140. Ibid.

Chapter 2

Carceral Obligations and the Prison of the Mind

Having considered how scientific and public health discourses led to problems of health to be viewed from the lens of moral weakness as a means of justifying the use of discipline, I now want to turn to prisons and the subjectivities they create among individuals suffering from substance use. The reason why I turn from historical public health approaches to substance use to prisons is because since the 1980s, there has been an aggressive crackdown on drug use in much of the United States. Of course, the move to criminalize drug use has a longer history as I have considered in the introduction, and also has to do with Reagan-era policies, scientific discourses in some sense, provide a justification for repressive measures in the absence of evidence-based substitution therapies. In this chapter, I move to prison experiences to investigate the element of "discipline" that shapes experiences of substance use within prisons but also among those who leave prisons. Perhaps this discipline is exerted in more acute forms in prisons, but a close analysis of the intersecting experiences of drug use and incarceration will also help contextualize the sustained relation between force and compliance in later chapters on the experience of recovery, and also show how there is something inherent about the nature of carceral authority that makes recovery difficult for many, especially as they leave the prison unprepared for life outside—and mostly even turn to the use of illicit drugs even when they do enter treatment programs, therefore risk non-compliance. The question then is about how incarceration and carceral authority create new drug-related dependencies and obligations that make recovery difficult for many. In this chapter, I start with an analysis of archival material that reveals how prisoners refer to carceral authority as inherently racist but also differentiate between themselves and others based on whether the inmate had the will to live. I then ask how gang-rivalries entering prison worlds leave severe psychic impacts. I would like to consider the concept of carceral obligations, whereby the prisoner and the drug dealer are involved in a complex web of relations, dependencies and interdependencies, which makes recovery difficult, and sometimes even impossible, given the amount of violence these relations entail. I then ask how incarceration also provides opportunities for reflection, where maturity is construed as the ability to dissociate oneself from conflict and gang rivalry, even after release from the prison. I make this argument not to demonstrate the positive effects of incarceration, but simply to consider moments of reflection that allow people to disentangle themselves from webs of contestations and dependencies. Yet I also ask how the prison habit extends to life outside prisons. I argue that the complex psychological experiences of prisoners are shaped as much by obligations of exchange among prisoners as by collusion between states and prisoners. I ask what psychic effects these networks, conflicts, and intimacies create such that the prisoner feels morally and psychologically imprisoned even after release. Therefore, in the first part of the chapter, I consider the experiences of incarceration whereas in the second half I consider the problems with adjusting to life outside of prisons, including the extension of prison behaviors in streetlife, as well as the enduring psychological traumas that increase the possibilities of relapse, especially among those on parole.

The return to the prison after release was in some sense inevitable, also because it was difficult to disentangle oneself from the exchange of the drug economy once outside the prison. But this also created new forms of care. During one of my conversations, Jacob told me about how prison taught him to help others. This included helping others find their next hit, given how ideas about drug-related sickness and care are reconfigured due to the severity of withdrawals. He also said that he would help others when they had overdosed. He described, "I know many people panhandle even after having roofs over their heads." These people mainly ask for money to buy drugs, according to Jacob. Many others were involved in getting a portion of drugs for themselves by buying drugs and selling them others. This was referred to in street slang as "copping." One person, Jimmy, whom I also interviewed, according to Jacob, provided a good example. Jimmy had once become homeless, and Jacob had known him from his time in prison. Jacob knew Jimmy's copping skills as he explained, "They [people like Jimmy] draw upon their connections from dangerous hoods and after providing drugs to their client, kept a portion for themselves as a tip."

One can see how the texture of relations is not simply one of exchange in the sense of a person eliciting favors, but also one in which the dealer seeks an opportunity to provide for someone else as a means to get access to drugs for his or her own consumption.[1] Copping introduced individuals to new forms of risks of street violence as well as the risks of getting caught. Jacob told me that in central Baltimore, over the years, the drug market had expanded to several blocks, even despite heavy surveillance. He said that there were inherent dangers brought on by the drug market. There were two main types of dangers—one was the violence that erupted due to the inability of buyers to pay and clear their dues to dealers, who had in turn accrued debts to their dealers. The second was the possibility that the dealers themselves were involved in getting their clients robbed. Jacob said, "There was a dealer who used to get people robbed after selling drugs to them." These were all dangers inherent in the drug market. Overall, the drug market had become much more dangerous over the past years. In a report on substance abuse in Baltimore written in 1994, Agar and Murdoch provided a snippet from their interviews with a participant about copping, which I find useful and illustrative. It is illustrative in showing how since the 1990s, drug trade has become a lot more visible on the streets. Drug exchange was previously based on a relationship of trust between the buyer and the seller. Under conditions of policing, the possibility of defrauding or inflicting violence on the buyer or the seller was much greater. One of the participants of the study by Agar and Murdoch stated,

> Oh yeah, copping's real quick now. But it used to be, I mean, I remember years ago when it would be you would go to one corner and give the money up front. And you'd go to one corner and give the runner the money. And then he'd send you to another corner. And then you'd go sit there and then somebody completely different might come by. I mean you might be sitting there in your car with your window down and out of nowhere—boom, bag of dope comes flying in the window. And you happen to look around and see someone come scooting by on a bicycle. And that's how it used to be then. And I said you had to trust them because you had to give the money up front. But now you just pull up in the car. And as soon as you pull up, they'll say how many and you hold up two fingers. You hand them the money and they hand you the stuff—boom you're out of there. Yeah it's a lot faster now, it's just in and out.[2]

Thus, copping under conditions of intense surveillance entails new risks of getting into violence encounters with sellers and other stakeholders—especially as drug trade moves to new and less visible sites while also becoming dispersed through the city, and especially in different parts of Baltimore. There is also an erosion of trust between sellers and clients. While before incarceration many men talk about their experiences of running wild, the tense webs of relations from the outside world continue to impact them psychologically in prison in such a way that many find it impossible to dissociate themselves from the ongoing gang violence within prisons. I now ask how obligations and exchange of drugs enter everyday life in prisons and create conflict and rivalry as well as new opportunities for relations among the officers and prisoners. I want to briefly move to the prison context to consider how prisoners created distinctions between those who still had the ability to reflect and improve lives versus those whose involvement in involve had taken their ability to reflect on the enduring rivalries that continue to propel them into more violence.

CARCERAL AUTHORITY

For a lot of men who have grown up in low-income neighborhoods of Baltimore, drug use was mainly driven by the need for thrill and a sense of adrenaline rush—many still gradually began to dissociate themselves from these patterns of aggression. Just as carceral authority was perceived as ethnocial, this authority also had the effect of creating distinctions between those who lost the ability to reflect and others for whom drug use had led to habits in a way that individuals could no longer dissociate themselves from them. This distinction will remain salient in other chapters as well. I analyzed letters written by prisoners about their experiences in Baltimore prisons.[3] One of the prisoners, Andre Elliott, described his experience in incarceration by viewing it directly as a form of racism by the state,

> The State of Maryland Judicial System is categorically infected with unrepentant racism. The laws are enforced unequally, the courts are inherently racist, and the prison population illustrates the disproportionate number of Blacks incarcerated.[4]

He presented carceral authority as inherently racial, not only in the way it polices populations but also in terms of who gets punished and when. But he also distinguished himself as a youth from the hoods in Baltimore:

> Everyday is an emotional struggle for me on all levels. I am surrounded by individuals, primarily urban youth from Baltimore, who do not value their own lives. Most are members of street gangs, uneducated, poor social skills, and lack personal ambition. Living among these individuals serves as a catalyst for a portion of my stress. It took a while to learn to deal with these negative individuals who want others to share in their negative and counterproductive behaviour. I do my best to circumnavigate their collective insanity.[5]

Here, what is important is that inmates create distinctions among themselves, namely between those who wanted to uplift themselves and those who were so deeply involved in violence that they could not envision a life without it. Conflicts between prisoners are often also based on neighborhood gang-rivalries that enter the lives of prisoners and shape their experiences of violence, stress, and anxiety from which they have a difficult time dissociating themselves. Still Andre was able to develop relationship with some of the inmates. He further talks about experiencing constant anxiety, depression, and anxiety but not requesting help from psychiatrists because he thought that the latter were involved in "overmedicating" people. Even in differentiating himself from other Black men, Andre does not consider the state's care as useful and benevolent. He then adds, "Prison is a psychological torture chamber designed to handicap you from believing you are human."[6] Even correctional officers, mostly viewed as the ethnoracial other by the prisoner, were brought into the vortex of prison violence with strong psychological impacts, with some officers eventually even getting incarcerated upon quitting their jobs as correctional officers in maximum-security prisons of Maryland.[7] Others wrote in their letters to APWA about the extreme anxiety experienced by prisoners before their release and their fear of minor violations resulting in reincarceration.[8] But inherently, the psychological pressures many experienced due to incarceration were further enhanced by being in the grey zones of competing prison and gang-based sovereignties, which many traversed for survival. As much as carceral authority reinforced racial distinctions, there were still new opportunities to traverse racial boundaries. But these negotiations led to greater exposure to violence. The reason why I want to consider this type of violence is to throw light on the psycho-social experiences that create the conditions—and even make it necessary—to numb one's mind through psychoactive drugs.

INCARCERATION AND THE GREY ZONES OF RACE

Jacob told me that he had been incarcerated several times—he even lost count of the number of times he had been incarcerated in the 1990s. For Jacob, those who developed networks by crossing neighborhood-level and racial divisions were specifically prone to violence. They treaded the "grey" zones of divisions that could expose them to new forms of violence. New prison entrants were pulled into the vortex of this violence. Jacob once told me, "I had been able to get work in the prison as a painter and was be able to move from one part of the prison to another for painting work. I did this mainly for members of BGF."

He described how in the process of working for the gang, he had earned the anger of another gang. Jacob's position of cooperating with the Black gangs while being white antagonized Dead Man Incorporated (DMI) members. I came to understand his position as similar to what has been referred to in the literature as a "snitch." While such inmates tend to be viewed as deceptive and the weakest members, some have argued that inmate-snitches are the most aggressive and feared individuals. However, I understood Jacob's position as that of strength but also of immense vulnerability because of his ability to relate with white inmates while also being perceived as being deceptive due to the ease of traversing racial divisions and greater access.[9] He described, "A minority gang called the Crips once attacked me when I was in the shower. When I tried to fight back, the security found me fighting and placed me in the infirmary."

Jacob would give this example to talk about how his experience in the prison made him learn how to fight. His description of the movement of objects in the prison particularly intrigued me. He gave an account of how goods were bought and sold. He continued, "The influential gang members from BGF even had cell phones with them. They used their cellphones if they wanted something to be smuggled into the prison." Thus, the prison's internal economy had constant negotiations taking place between the security personnel and inmates from different gangs. Debts were incurred, and oftentimes these debts were paid off by resorting to violence.

Jacob jumped to another story in which a Black person had been responsible for stealing money from white elderly people. Jacob said that this had happened in front of him. This person had once stolen money from someone who had been close to Jacob. Jacob now anticipated that this person who had robbed was going to end up in a white-dominated prison. The gang, Dead Man Incorporated (DMI), was a white prison gang, and if he were to go to this prison, "The gang members were probably going to skin the person and would hang him on a pole." Thus, while there was a tendency to inflict violence across race, the interconnectedness of the prison and the outside world meant that these scores could easily be settled. Jacob told me about the organization of the prison where he had run contraband as a painter, which enabled him to have access to different groups. It was not as simple as Muslim Brotherhood locked in static relations with the Baltimore Guerilla family. Jacob said, "The two gangs had cordial relations but would use the Dead Man Incorporate to settle their earlier scores. It was through the DMI that revenge was taken."

This was an important point, as it showed how gang members used people from other gangs as proxies. This helped complicate the straightforward division between gangs based on race and showed that the arrangement was much more fluid than I had initially imagined. However, this still showed the predominance of Black gangs in Baltimore prisons, such as the Baltimore Guerilla Family and Muslim Brotherhood, compared to others like Crips and Dead Man Incorporated. The power of the gangs extended beyond the prisons. I will now consider the psychic impacts of the violence inflicted on men during their time in prison. Given these complex relations that prisoners learned to navigate, I ask how some prisoners view dissociating themselves from the violence of prison life as only possible with the help of active reflection or with what they called "slowing down." I now consider the unique pressures of carceral violence for negotiating between racial divisions under state surveillance and the way this provides the impetus to extricate oneself from ongoing gang-rivalries and violence.

SLOWING DOWN

For some men, prisons and the immense violence they experienced allowed them to re-envision lives, and to extricate themselves from the ongoing relations of violence. There is something about the nature of ongoing violence that men stated would take away their ability to reflect. They said that they were born into ongoing rivalries and an endless cycle of rage to avenge the death of a beloved. However, this anger often does not have any end, and these rivalries toward an enemy without a face also extended to prison worlds. One Black male who went to prison for the first time when he was seventeen said,

> I was getting into trouble with my father, I didn't see eye to eye with him, you feeling me? I was getting into fights, and I was hustling, things kind of progressed, I fell in love with a girl, got her pregnant. I was sixteen when I was sent to live with my grandmother. I started robbing because I had to find a way to make ends meet. My mother passed away when I was sixteen. I thought robbing was better than being on the block. When my mother died, I even contemplated suicide. My homeboy and I were doing our thing and got caught. All I had on my mind was how I could earn for my daughter. When I was in the prison, I had the time to *reflect*, and decided to improve the situation with my father, because he had been down the same road. I was born in a project, Lafayette, and everyone there was an addict. My mother was an addict, when you are brought up in such a situation, you have to break the cycle. *God slowed me down, the prison gave me the chance to think about myself.*[10]

The isolation of incarceration intersected with familial obligations and the urge to make up for neglect. While repeat incarcerations have been treated as part of the problem, Black men also talked about incarceration as wisdom, as it helped them learn to navigate difficult power relations without giving into their urges. This does not in any way mean that men view incarceration as beneficial—it serves simply to show that men get the time to reflect on obligations and conflicts that make recovery impossible by being unable to avoid unnecessary conflicts. When I refer to reflection, I do not at all make the case for justifying incarceration and want to stress the permanently damaging impact it has on families for generations. These complicated relationship that inmates learn to navigate are a product of power exerted by prison authorities and the increasing pressure young men came under to comply with gang members they met when they were in the prison. The prison was not an enlightening experience because of its success in disciplining, as much as it was because it helped individuals navigate and specifically reflect on extremely complex web of relations.

Recovery for most Black men, meant learning to inhabit tensions without resorting to violence. Often, family members did not get their relatives bailed out to teach them lessons. These young men thus found a time to reflect upon their mistakes, but often their incarceration also sowed new seeds of distrust. The experience of incarceration was not a singular event but could be considered as one in a series of events, starting with juvenile detention centers. Men are not able to detach themselves of relations of dependence, obligation, and conflict without feeling guilt or severe psychological effects. Substance use thus can not only be understood in relation to the act of consuming drugs but also the product of prison economies that individuals have to navigate. Recently, the work of Orisanmi Burton has eloquently shown how Black men develop relations of solidarity within prisons, going against much of the existing historiography that views Black men in prison as riddled with conflict.[11] Burton talks about hierarchy in the webs of relations among men in prisons and writes,

> Amid the suffocating oppression of prison existence, reciprocal relations and care and community among self-identified Black men constitute an unexamined and under theorized social and political practice.[12]

He shows how instead of Black men being violent with each other, they also share their vulnerabilities with each other, and these relations then offer a kind of praxis. I would add the component of hierarchical relations between white and Black inmates in a complex web of dependence, which is far from stable. What I find particularly useful is Burton's description of the effect of incarceration, in that he argues, "Behind bars for most of their biological children's life, they labored to develop themselves emotionally, intellectually and politically to read, wrote, study and debate," in a way that they would find it extremely hurtful to see their children ending up in prison.[13] Burton thus complicates much of the existing theorization that considers prison experiences as largely static. Other work has shown how women put in efforts to help maintain connections between children and their husbands to give their families a semblance of normalcy.[14] Yet even while being in prison, there are new types of masculine authority experienced by women.[15] Megan Comfort writes about secondary prisonization of women when men are in prisons, yet the concern for Comfort is not so much about the increase in social control over the lives of women by incarcerated men as much as women's stigmatization and loss of privacy as they visit and interact with their partners and spouses.[16] These discussions can be used to consider how familial obligations and experiences of incarceration intersect and help in creating new moral aspirations.

I take from these conversations the point about how gang leaders expand control within and outside of the prison, which is then used to settle existing scores, and that this violence often also becomes a conduit for the state's own disciplinary apparatus, as the state inflicts violence by virtue of its indifference.

For many anthropologists, the interest has been in exploring the way torture or isolation create specific types of irrationalities. For example, according to Rhodes, in prisons, no response to punishment appears to be rational, which offsets the prison's primary task of creating rational subjects. In other words, according to Rhodes, "the prison tends to secrete the very things it tries most to eliminate."[17] Whereas for others like Fassin, the focus has been on how the prison punishes differentially, as he writes,

> There is no equality in the prison system so long as the distribution of sentences is based on the aim of reminding everyone of their place in society. For some, the dreadful prison experience is avoided at all costs. While for others, we impose the supposedly salutary shock of incarceration.[18]

Others have even considered incarceration as a chronic experience, in which social inequalities also become embodied as health inequities.[19] Thus, the prison actually solidifies distinctions of race, which I argue is done by finding collaborators from within inmates as well as by turning a blind eye to gang violence, which the correctional officers often see as a type of punishment inflicted by them but one in which they do not need to participate directly. I draw upon as well as depart from existing work on prisons by making a case for carceral obligations, which shape socialities within the prison but also beyond it. These obligations are shaped by affective experiences of substance use and new demands it places on prisoners for consumption of drugs.

The permanence of neighborhood violence in which men are propelled is also the consequence of their economic conditions. Often, solidarity among young men existed along the lines of neighborhood divisions, and these loyalties extended into prison worlds. Precarious living conditions led to families moving from one project to another, leaving young boys to fend for themselves in new settings. The associations that these young boys fostered with previous neighborhoods made them targets of violence within new neighborhoods. The violence in which young men have been socialized in the ghetto cannot be understood without the new socialities and hostilities created by substance use and unemployment, which, in a curious way, resembles the violence men and women experience under incarceration. Another Black man with vivid memories of the Baltimore prison system stated that the first time he went to the juvenile detention center was when he was thirteen on the charge of possessing a firearm. For him, the decision to "run wild" was not simply a matter of poor upbringing but was shaped by the need to defend oneself and to earn in conditions marked by poverty, where economic opportunities were extremely limited. On top of it, after experiencing incarceration, many carry the carceral habitus outside of prison in a way that continues to affect their sociability with others.

PRISON MENTALITY

This carrying of the carceral habitus outside of prisons often led people to be perceived as aggressive and unable to adjust to life without discipline. One day I was in central Baltimore, finding a place where I could work for a while. When I was trying to lock my bicycle, Jimmy shouted, "Don't worry I will take care of it." I ignored him and continued to lock my bicycle to a pole. This was the first time I met him. He sought an opportunity to initiate a conversation with me. I had seen him on several occasions, but I never had the chance to interact with him. He had seen me before because he stood a few meters away from where I would meet with Jacob for our interviews. This person, Jimmy, as Jacob had called him above, stood up and walked toward me. He was skinny and had a small beard on a slim face with arms full of tattoos. As soon as Jimmy approached me, he immediately began sharing his story with me. He described, "Thirty years ago my sister was beaten up by my brother-in-law and died." He told this to me, expecting me to understand the context of Jimmy's retaliatory actions. He took out a card with his photo to show that he had just completed his parole.[20] In a strange sense of immediacy, he said, "I need fifty dollars to get drug tests before twelve and if I don't get these tests, I will be in the prison again for the next three years."[21] I found his story a little hard to believe and replied, "Let me come get back to you later, I'll see if I can help you." He went back and sat obediently. He said he would be able to return the money in no time if he could get his tests done. I left Starbucks and was on a phone call as I unlocked my bike and walked away.

A few days later, I saw Jimmy coming from in front of my bicycle saying angrily, "I am very upset with you." I went past him, and then I stopped to see what he had to say as I stood a few meters away. He shouted, "You said you had a meeting and that you will give me the money. I kept waiting but you walked away right in front of me." He said this in a way as to assume that I had already committed to giving him the money. Once campus security had been armed and their patrolling had increased in areas further away from the Hopkins premises, what resulted was a greater sense of insecurity. In my next interview with Jacob, I asked him more about Jimmy. He immediately recognized him and warned me, "Stay away from him." Jacob started telling me more about Jimmy, specifically about his habit of fooling other people into giving him money and then disappearing when it was his turn to return. He remarked, "The person still has a *prison mentality*." Jacob suggested that it was important to operate according to a different set of norms and rules once a person was out of prison, which was not the case with Jimmy. The point of comparison was that this person had not left behind the habits required for him to survive in a prison. Commenting on Jimmy's offer to take care of my bicycle, he described,

> What he did was something people in prisons typically do. They accumulate a lot of foodstuffs and then give it to others to put them in the position of an obligation to return and thereby in a state of dependence.[22]

I found Jacob's description very apt at the moment, especially when he gave another example to illustrate how this "prison mentality" was brought by many into the streets. He continued,

> Let me give you an example. If someone had not taken the parking ticket from the booth, what people like Jimmy would do is to stand by the car and tell the owner when he or she returns "oh, I saved you from a fine" and the purpose of this is to show that the owner owed him something for stepping in on time.[23]

Thus, the "prison mentality" would entail putting people in a position of obligation and then putting pressure on these networks for returns. Jacob continued,

> This is the exact kind of predatory behavior present in prison. This person also threatened me, when my position on the footpath began to bother him. Instead of admitting that he had been bullying and threatening me to change my place, he complained to the police that it was me who was threatening him.[24]

In street life, many, like Jimmy, dissociated themselves from the crime. In fact, during my interviews, I felt that there was little discussion about the crimes one had committed. The act itself was usually concealed under a person's present misery. The kinds of crimes could vary from possession of firearms to something like the possession of drugs, but I rarely encountered people referring to each other based on the intensity of crimes they had committed. The only differentiation was based on how much a person brought the prison mentality out into the streets and inadvertently expressed the crime they had committed and the amount of time spent within the prison, as if they embodied the carceral habitus, which they had to unlearn.

In the context of New York, Michael Duneier has shown the complex arrangement that emerges as individuals navigate through street life to occupy certain positions to sell items that they have scavenged or recycled.

The book explores how street life becomes a place for mentorship and guidance, as much as it is one where individuals compete to occupy positions and vie for visibility. The book allows us to think about sidewalks as places of order and enduring social relations.[25] One's position oftentimes was not fixed and whenever a person did claim a spot as his own, this was mainly through interactions with those passing by on the footpath or those entering the restaurants and getting tickets for car parking. One's position became fixed by building relations with pedestrians and these were all mainly brief encounters like exchanging greetings or saying something about one's dog, or sometimes requesting favors. Jacob gave numerous examples of people who he had seen taking hard drugs in front of him on the same street. He differentiated himself from these individuals in many of my conversations with him. This included the so-called 'alcoholics' who slept down the street next to the Subway restaurant. His tone toward the latter involved a kind of moral judgment. These people, according to him, had lost all hopes for improvement in their lives. In other words, the element of striving was missing, even if the struggle was there. Thus, there were differentiations created by individuals like Jacob based on willingness to improve—the "alcoholics" did not have the same willingness to recover as people like him did, as Jacob would say. This is related to the biopolitics of creating an addiction-free population as I will later show, but I want to briefly consider the enduring psychological impacts of incarceration and the difficulties it creates in the process of recovery.

PRISON OF THE MIND

While many were not able to learn attitudes that could help them fully dissociate themselves from their lives in prison, this problem was further compounded because some people suggested that even after coming out of prison, they remained in what they referred to as the "prison of the mind." In the prison, there are competing sovereignties between the state and the gang members. Often, the men I interviewed entered the prison as teenagers but were then re-incarcerated. They referred to their time in the prison as having been "lost time" that they now had to recover. One person told me that he was on a juvenile tier and got into a fight and was sent to the adult prison. Unable to understand the social dynamics of the prison, men often relied upon their relatives already in the prison as a source of knowledge. The psychic effects of incarceration are many. Prisoners carry effects of psychic effects of networks made in prison even outside, as I have shown above. They are also under the pressure to "unlearn" them when they are out. One Black male told,

> I was sentenced twenty years and all were suspended but five and my uncle told me that it meant five years of prison and five years of parole. I had relatives in the prison to guide me.[26]

Often the experience of white men was different in that they were exposed to a different type of violence as a minority in Baltimore prisons. Yet, they shouldered new burdens of managing the delicate balance between gangs by being middle men, as I have shown in the case of Jacob. While most men thought that they could have spent the time in prison on something productive, there were many whose release from the prison led to new types of anxieties which they were not able to easily overcome.

A white ex-gang member shared his experience siding with the prosecution to describe his experience of guilt for having gone against inmates to consider the long-term impacts of incarceration on men, which remain unaccounted for in treatment programs and counselling sessions. The pressure of unmaking carceral selves after imprisonment has severe psychic impacts as it involves breaking the intimacies made. This person came from a wealthy neighborhood in Baltimore county. He said that he did not have a great childhood. He did not get any love from his parents and complained about his mother's substance use problems. His earliest memories of his mother included that "she was running around naked, often too drunk." His earliest memories also included his "grandmother trying to stop her mother." His mother died when he was fifteen, after which he dropped out of school and decided to live the "white boy gangster" life. Where he lived, he had two close friends, both of them Black, with whom he was always watching rap videos. They all got into the same thing together. He lamented that all his friends, including one co-defendant in his trial, had died due to overdose. When he was seventeen, he moved to the city, where, at the age of seventeen, he began to snort heroin, and one year later, he got into "gangster shit and getting high," as he called it. Eventually he began to drive people around and "being used" by dealers. He said,

> They began to pay me for driving. The pay was not good but I was still doing it. They stole my car and crashed it. Still my grandparents had money and were supporting my drug habit.[27]

Now he had completed his recovery and said that his grandmother had decided to forgive him and had agreed to put him back on her will for being sober. He said that it was a good feeling to have a credit card for the first time. When asked about how he felt about being a white kid in Baltimore, he said,

> I was driving around in the hood fearlessly, I was not worried about what might happen to me. When you are doing crack you don't get scared of anything. Once

I was stabbed and got three broken ribs. Once I was attacked when I was in an alley where I had to sell some crack. The witnesses confirmed that I [was] being followed and was attacked.[28]

When he met with the kingpin, he was eighteen and began making $120 a night. He said jokingly, "The kingpin was still a man of God and took the Sunday off." He even had his son sell for him. He continued, "I would begin driving at 5 p.m. [and] would sell drugs all the way to 2 a.m."

He continued,

I had been to prison once. My grandparents said that they would not pick me. My dad finally came to pick me. My best friend's brother who was in the police had told me that when anyone's about to get into trouble, its best to turn oneself in.[29]

The first day, he was jumped on by the DMI for a honeybun. All his commissary was taken away. He reflected that it was important to show that you knew the "dogs" that were respected. When he looked back at his time in prison, he was surprise as to how he even managed to survive. He said, "They just let me live." He described that he was contacted by a detective who asked him to collaborate. He said,

It was my choice, I regret saying yes to them even to this day. It came down to fear. It was a decision that I took that comes to haunt me even to this day. I judge myself every day. I was weak, very weak. I didn't know I was even a man. I thought I was being a man, when I wasn't.[30]

The prosecution asked him to cooperate and tell them everything. While the prosecution provides an aura of autonomy and free choice, prisoners were often manipulated to the advantage of the prosecution as he said, "They know the things in advance and are just trying to see if you are reliable." He decided to work with the prosecution, he added,

Don't ever work with the prosecution. They know you are going to fail. They knew a hundred per cent that I will relapse and will be back in the prison. If I had said no, they would have given me five years and then I would have been out. If I had done that I would have been out already, and also not be as paranoid as I am now.[31]

He said that having an extended sentence would have made his recovery much safer than the psychological pressure caused by siding with the prosecution and the enmity that it created with other inmates. In other words, he said that siding with the prosecution created new forms of guilt—fears of non-compliance—that made the punishment from the state somewhat inevitable. Upon his return to the prison, people in the prison knew he was cooperating. This included the "brothers" as well as members of BGF. Then he shared how he became the centerpiece of the gang rivalry between AB and the BGF.[32] He continued,

> I was talking to someone about it and I knew that the AB dude listened to it. I knew he was going to live off me. He was in Jessup and then came to Jennifer Road. He and another dude had killed a dog. This person began to play the intimidation game on me, asked me for $150 every week in return for a promise of protecting me. I was left in a state of utter fear.[33]

He explained that in the Jennifer Road Detention Center, he was talking to a white guy, when he saw the kingpin across the fence. Even though the lawyer had promised that he would not see him, but he did. The kingpin looked sternly at him and asked, "Why did you raise the statement?" To his surprise, the kingpin smiled and said, "I forgive you." He continues, "People are behind me watching the entire scene and they start coming toward me and he says to them, 'don't touch him I forgive him, let karma do its work.'" After this incident, the person became extremely intimidated and paranoid and thought that he was going to be attacked by other prisoners. The guilt of having sided with the prosecution now haunted him even after he was released, which showed the psychic effects of incarceration,

> I am in my own prison. I am very paranoid, I watch myself in the mirror. I had such a deep regret of having conspired against gang members. I live in the fear of retaliation. The person forgave me for his conscience. I want to tell everyone, don't do it. You will always have to watch your back, you are never free after that.[34]

His use of the "prison of the mind" demonstrated the kind of psychological pressures that shaped the transition from prison worlds to life outside, one that is riddled with ambivalence, fears of not being able to adjust, relapsing and even an eventual return to the prison.

Another person shred,

> People have to make those decisions in the moment, it is because of the government. They take a kid and say fifty years if you don't tell on this guy. I despise the prosecution. The eighteen years old kid may have substance use and the state says, "You will tell us or you are going to die."[35]

Siding with the prosecution means new risks, especially in the case of the return to the prison, which seems to be almost inevitable. At the same time, running contraband for a gang can lead to similar types of violence by other gangs, which shows conflicting sovereignties and their psychic effects that outlast one's time in the prison. He continues,

> Government only says that they will reduce the sentence, but in reality they won't. Kids are going to do the same thing. There is nothing to lean on in the households. When you are cooperating the government loves you, but when you fail to comply, the government can say to the judge that you are a scumbag. I asked my wife whether I should tell on others or not, and she advised me against it. This is a teachable moment. You don't want to watch behind your back all your life. Think about the future when you make a decision. Don't make decisions based on a feeling.[36]

Thus many were pulled into new collaborations with the state which resulted in new anxieties and paranoias even after release from prisons. These psychic effects remind us about what Judith Butler had suggested when she wrote, "power not only acts on a subject but, in a transitive sense, enacts the subject into being."[37] The agency one assumes upon being subjected to power, according to Butler, exceeds the power by which it is enabled. As a result of this carceral power, morally contradicting decisions leave a permanent psychic effect, making it difficult to escape from the "prison of the mind," even when one is outside the physical boundaries of the prison.

HEALING INCARCERATED SELVES

The kind of ethnoracial violence inflicted by correctional officers onto Black inmates requires us to think about how white prisoners are used as conduits by the prison administration. In the process of expanding the disciplinary power of the state, inmates also internalize and reproduce racial difference, the seeds for which are sown by existing gang violence and the state's differential support of one group over the other to mete out punishment through informal means. During my interviews with Jacob, he would often tell me about famous gangs of Baltimore, two of which included the Muslim Brotherhood and Baltimore Guerrilla Family. He told me that he had known about Muslims through his encounter with the Muslim Brotherhood in the central prison. He described,

> Gang members of the Muslim brotherhood converted to Islam during their stay in the prison said the azan (call to prayers) in the prison and greeted each other with *asalam-o-alikum*, but as soon as they were out, they would return to their old habits.[38]

For many Black men, conversion to Islam was in fact viewed as a liberatory experience against the racism of the state. Jacob, however, viewed this differently. He provided a detailed account of the gang with the greater representation in prison and with whom he had worked during his stay. This was the Baltimore Guerilla Family, a gang consisting predominantly of Black inmates, whose members would usually ask him for help when they had to get their work done. He said, "The prison gangs had greater power than the prison security. Members of the BGF would be able to get hookers in their cells without any difficulty."

In creating racial descriptions of the Black Muslim inmate, Jacob was differentiating himself—with a different approach toward the use of religion as an alternative to the carceral authority of the state, compared to Black Muslims I interviewed, as he posited the instrument of the confession as the predominant modality of overcoming past transgressions without the fear of punishment. Here I want to add that just as a racial difference led to certain self-perceptions, there were also new possibilities of healing available to individuals from different faiths and denominations, forms of healing that were understood as alternatives to incarceration where sin was not judged by the state but by God—where the implications for confession were not necessarily punishment from the state. Religion and race bled into each other determining what was available, outside of treatment centers, to enable healing for past traumas and specifically redress past experiences of violence. Jacob shared with me the difficulty of going to church and attending masses due to the coronavirus situation. He could no longer participate in sacraments and penances, which he considered was free psychotherapy. Thus, for many like Jacob, the church not only provided food but also allowed individuals to unburden themselves emotionally through the penance. He mentioned,

> The priest is bound under penalty of death not to reveal what is heard like doctor/client, or lawyer/client privilege. You could go to Penance, say, "I blew up the twin towers." And the priest can't turn you in. He will advise you to do so if you are truly sorry. He can refuse to intercede on your behalf with God. But he can't snitch. Pretty wild, huh? Generally, your penance consists of: don't do it again, maybe volunteer doing something opposite, and prayer and meditation. I always feel better after confession, like a load has been lifted off my shoulders. But in my humble opinion, too many people show for mass, even penance, but don't live the Christian lifestyle, especially here. For example, "I'm so blessed, I just hit a $1,000 scratch-off." I don't think God had anything to do with it. And gambling, or greed, or avarice is one of the seven deadly sins.[39]

The instrument of the confession enabled him to unburden himself and momentarily go beyond the experiences of violence and to atone for his sin. In his description, perhaps unconsciously, he was forging a difference vis-à-vis the Muslim, who was also the racial other. Jacob had known about my Muslim background and frequently mentioned his familiarity with "jailhouse" Islam. He had heard Muslim inmates recite the Quran but noted that they did not pray five times a day. He added, "One would be surprised to know that they had converted mainly for protection." By this, he meant that conversion allowed men to have solidarities that could protect them in prison. Viewing reasons for conversation as selfish, he also used a description of Islam, which anchored a much more generalized fear of the Muslim, as in the statement that one could say to the priest, "you blew up in the twin tower and the priest can't turn you in." In other words, although I was posited as the "true" Muslim to create a distinction with a jailhouse Muslim, the perception of the latter had still seeped into my own characterization.[40] For Jacob, even a Muslim *terrorist/criminal* could through the mediation of the priest, get his or her sins forgiven, however atrocious they might be, a statement directed toward me as the Muslim other.

Jacob mentioned, "I always feel better after a confession like the load has lifted off my shoulders." But this was no longer possible due to the pandemic. Jacob had complained,

> They started offering daily services, but a big part of our service is receiving the second sacrament [which] includes bread and wine that represent the body and blood of Christ. I think most of us know it isn't really that; it is only meant to represent that. So far, they haven't had a "take-out or drive-thru" service, which is honestly a shame. We all take a sip of wine from the same goblet so I don't know how to get around that. I miss the second and third sacraments (confession of sins and the priest asks absolution from God. Kind of like psychotherapy but it's free, I always feel better after Penance).[41]

This is how for Jacob, the Christian body (mostly white), intoxicated and steeped in sin, found peace and meaning, showing the possibility of integrating religious experience in substance use treatment but also how group therapies may be more suited to the Christian ethos of confession, rather than the experiences of other identities.

When I conducted interviews with community members around Masjid-ul-Haq, close to Bolton Hill, I found that gang violence and substance use were considered as the biggest problems engulfing the Black community. Muslim worshippers often referred to "corners" as dangerous places of violence and substance use. One Black imam once said in a Friday sermon, "Substance use leads to violence and this violence results in death. We need to stop people from going to the corners. We need to use our hands to pull this people out of the corners." I found the reference to pulling people with hands striking as it represented both the need for missionary work as well as use of actual labor. There were at least two major incidents of deaths due to drug overdoses and drug-related violence when I was conducting interviews between 2022 and 2023. Though there was an emphasis on the use of physical labor to educate young Black men, the community had not internalized the importance of force—as security discourses would suggest—to pull people out of the problem of substance and in fact even resisted such discourses. Here too, the imam offers an alternative to incarceration, an attempt to use the message of Islam—rather than the force of incarceration—to pull men out of the vortex of gang violence, being mindful of the fact that carceral authority was inherently "white." In the Friday sermon that I attended, another imam talked about the need for resilience against oppression within the Black community instead of giving into desires, citing examples from Quranic stories about Moses and his resolve and patience against persecution by the pharaoh and creating a parallel to the racism of the state. I also understood that among men I interviewed, there was a growing awareness that Black men, among people from other racial backgrounds (sometimes even racial in nature but often presented as an advise for self-betterment), were likely to be more violent only toward Black men, which did not help their cause. One Latino man who had served time said, "I have always seen Black folks committing violence on Black folks in the prison. This is not the case with Latinos. They need to understand that it's only hurting their cause." Such racial perceptions were common, but the reality was much more complicated. What I understood was that among Black prisoners, it was not race as much as neighborhood-level associations, which transmogrified into inter-gang rivalry, sometimes in even more intense forms under carceral settings, shaping their experience of violence. Though some gangs had emerged in the context of providing security to local communities, some of these had turned violent over the years. Different sensibilities about religion as a decarceral force and what it meant to heal were also products of the enormous psychological pressure which was the product of carceral violence, where racial boundaries were not only overcome but also continously reinserted.

CONCLUSION

The purpose of this chapter is to spell out the centrality of the carceral in the experience of substance use and recovery. Instead of viewing the experience of incarceration as a top-down enforcement of power, I have considered both the networks that are available to inmates both within and beyond the prison and the ways in which antagonisms inherent in these relations make recovery difficult for many. To experience the "prison of one's mind," it is necessary to think about how individuals are drawn into new collaborations with the state against other inmates and also have to navigate between existing gang-rivalries in prisons, which often makes them suspect and exposes them to greater violence. Instead of simply thinking about the exchange of drugs in the prison, which is an important aspect of the story, I have considered substance use experiences parallel to experiences of incarceration to think about the enduring psychic pressures and moral ambiguities that make recovery difficult for many. Having considered the context of the prisons, I now turn to courts to ask how courts increasingly incorporate therapeutic aspects that results in a form of therapeutic governance which also punishes drug-users for their infractions, where courts give judgements that further intensify their sufferings through state-sanctioned separations from intimate kin, creating new psychological pressures and promoting fears of a return to prison. I compare my analysis of court sentencing with the actual experiences of couples and partners as they try to undergo treatment while also showing their commitment to their children. The ambivalences and moral paradoxes which are products of carceral authority are erased in the adjudication of cases in courts. I will also consider how seriousness toward medication for opioid use disorders becomes increasingly important as evidence to demonstrate recovery in courts. I use the functioning of courts to explore the move from punishment to rehabilitation, showing the state's turn toward a therapeutic form of justice while retaining punitive attitudes. In doing so, I contend, the state also crucially re-makes familial bonds.

NOTES

1. See Michael H. Agar and R. Owen Murdoch, "Investigating Recent Trends in Heroin Use in Baltimore City: A Pilot "Quantitative" Research Project," *Special Topics of Substance Research, Report 94-1* (1994).
2. Ibid., 5.
3. This archival work was conducted in the digitized American Prison Writing Archive held at Hamilton College.
4. "Coping with Stress in Prison," 7/1/2015. *American Prison Writing Archive.*
5. Ibid.
6. Ibid.
7. "Dear APWA, I am a 36 year old former correctional officer," *American Prison Writing Archive.*
8. "The de-briefing proposal," *American Prison Writing Archive;* "Home: An Essay on Prison Pre-release anxiety and post-traumatic stress disorder," *American Prison Writing Archive.*
9. For more on the power of snitch-inmates, see James W. Marquart and Julian B. Roebuck, "Prison Guards and "Snitches": Deviance within a Total Institution," *The British Journal of Criminology* 25, No. 3 (1985).
10. Interview, Sean.
11. Orisanmi Burton, "Captivity, Kinship & Black Masculine Care Work Under Domestic Warfare," *American Anthropologist* 123, No. 3. (2021).
12. Ibid., 622.
13. Ibid., 628.
14. Gina Clayton, Endria Richardson, Lily Mandlin, and Brittany Farr, *Because She's Powerful: The Political Isolation and Resistance of Women with Incarcerated Loved Ones* (Los Angeles: Essie Justice Group, 2018); Ruth Wilson Gilmore, "Race,

Prisons and War: Scenes from the Gilmore History of US Violence," *Socialist Register* 45 (2009): 73–87. Ruth Wilson Gilmore, *Golden Gulag: Prisons, Surplus, Crisis, and Opposition in Globalizing California* (Berkeley: University of California Press, 2007); Beth Richie, *Arrested Justice: Black Women, Violence, and America's Prison Nation* (New York: NYU Press, 2012).

15. Lotte Siegal in her work on the wives of men incarcerated in Israeli prisons shows how women come to experience social control via their in-laws, sometimes in much more intensified forms. Lotte Segal, *No Place for Grief: Martyrs, Prisoners and Mourning in Contemporary Palestine* (University of Pennsylvania Press, 2016).

16. Megan Comfort, *Doing Time Together: Love and Family in the Shadow of the Prison* (University of Chicago Press, 2009).

17. Lorna Rhodes, *Total Confinement: Madness and Reason in the Maximum Security Prison* (Berkeley: University of California Press, 2004), 29.

18. Didier Fassin, *Prison Worlds: An Ethnography of the Carceral Condition* (Polity, 2015), 153.

19. Carolyn Sufrin, *Jailcare: Finding the Safety Net for Women Behind the Bars* (University of California Press, 2017); Johanna T. Crane and Kelsey Pascoe, "Becoming Institutionalized: Incarceration as a Chronic Health Condition," *Medical Anthropology Quarterly* 35, No. 3 (2021): 307–26. doi: 10.1111/maq.12621

20. While no national figures are available, a recent survey of probation departments in Texas, which has the largest number of probationers of any state, revealed that testing for controlled substances was required of all probationers in 40% of the departments and it was required of the probationers in 60% of departments in the state. The same survey revealed that around 50% of the departments in the state required drug testing once a month; the rest of the departments required testing once every two weeks, once a week, or at the officer's discretion. The Michigan Appellate Court upheld the legality of drug testing as a condition of probation in People v. Roth (1987). Further in Smith v. State of Georgia (1983) the court upheld the use of randomly administered tests, see Rolando V. del Carmen and Jonathan R. Sorensen, "Legal Issues in Drug Testing Probation and Parole Clients and Employees," *US Department of Justice* (1989).

21. Most prisons in the United States have instituted Inmate Work Release Programs which make it possible for participants to maintain regular employment while serving sentences for confinement which facilitates the payment of family support, fines, court costs, taxes and restitution. One requirement of the program is to have a negative urine analysis. If analysis shows the presence of drugs, it is possible to revoke the work release. There is a fee instituted for each day worked. Some have argued that the program has the effect of reducing the propensity of releasees to commit serious crimes. For an example of a work release program visit https://www.aacounty.org/services-and-programs/inmate-work-release-program. For an analysis of the benefits of the work release program see Ann D. Witte, "Work Release in North Carolina. A Program That Works!" *Law and Contemporary Problems* 41, No. 1 (1977): 230–251.

22. Jacob, Interview.

23. Jacob, Interview.
24. Jacob, Interview.
25. see Michael Duneier, *Sidewalk* (Farrar, Straus and Giroux, 2000).
26. Nat, Interview.
27. John, Interview.
28. John, Interview.
29. John, Interview.
30. John, Interview.
31. John, Interview.
32. Aryan Brotherhood is a white supremacist prison gang.
33. John, Interview.
34. John, Interview.
35. Jake, Interview.
36. Jake, Interview.
37. Judith Butler, *The Psychic Life of Power* (Stanford University Press, 1997), 13.
38. Jacob, Interview.
39. Jacob, Interview. Almost 73 percent of substance use treatment centers in the USA include a spirituality-based element, as embodied in the twelve-step programs and fellowship initially popularized by Alcoholics Anonymous, the vast majority of which emphasize reliance on a God or higher power to stay sober. Almost 84 percent of scientific studies show that faith is a positive factor in substance use prevention or recovery, see Brian J. Grim and Melissa E. Grim, "Belief, Behavior, and Belonging: How Faith Is Indispensable in Preventing and Recovering from Substance Abuse," *Journal of Religion & Health* 58, No. 5 (2019): 1713–50.
40. For an overview of how Black Muslim prisoners have been stereotyped in the post 9/11 context, see Kenneth L. Marcus, "Jailhouse Islamophobia: Anti-Muslim Discrimination in American Prisons," *Race and Social Problems* 1, No. 1 (2009).
41. Jacob, Interview.

Chapter 3

Courts, Drug Treatment Programs, and the Re-making of Family

There have historically been stereotypes about racialized minorities, especially Black women, about being burdens on state's benevolence and for acting as fetters on the development of the nuclear family and, by extension, also social evolution, an aspect previously considered by scholars such as Dorothy Roberts.[1] Roberts persuasively shows how the control of reproduction by slaveowners was variously challenged as women tried to remain close to their children, but conversely also when they induced abortions to prevent children from growing up in a world of slave labor. Problems of reproductive control are further exacerbated under conditions of retrenchment in publicly funded reproductive care.[2] I have also considered attempts historically to expose children from Black families to white norms in twentieth-century Baltimore in chapter 1—the understanding of what constitutes a "normal" family is important, and this has implications for the way people are disciplined by courts and treatment centers. This often also plays out in the adjudication of drug-related cases, as I show in the chapter, and in judging intentions to improve and to demonstrate responsibility toward the child due to perceptions about a lack of emotional attachment caused by substance use, ignoring that the bonds between individuals and their intimacies may extend beyond the nuclear family in a way that fictive relations may be even more important than biological relations among families in precarious situations.

Among individuals leaving prisons, violation for parole regulations can result in prolonged incarceration, especially in the context of anxieties that persist even after the completion of lengthy sentences. The punishments imposed for the failure to comply reveal the limits of rehabilitative justice. Courts that adjudicate drug-related crimes increasingly take performance in treatment centers as proof of intentions to recover. This both reveals a transition to a more therapeutically informed approach toward drug-related crimes but also a lingering effect of treating such acts through suspicion.

In 1968, the probation department said that Jacqueline Mills, a mother, had violated her parole by failing to report her treatment for substance use. When the lawyer remarked that the mother had been too detached from her daughter, the judge said, "The child will be much better off than snuggled up to a drug addict . . . the mother did not refrain from drugs as the terms of probation specified . . . the kindest thing in the world is to separate the child from the mother who has already damaged her."[3] The mother, however, in her defense, said, "I stay at home all the time, take care of my other children."[4] The judge responded that he "will consider" based on whether the mother had reported to the Man Alive Program. While the mother was in court, the child remained with the maternal grandmother. Earlier, we have seen how children, especially girls, who did not engage in domestic chores or did not exhibit their skills as successful caretakers were disciplined through social services and in orphan homes. By the 1970s, substance use had become a rampant problem in much of the US. While psychiatric discourses of the 20th century made important strides toward preventative aspects of medicine, this accompanied new forms of intervention into everyday lives, which were often justified, or legitimized, with the help of psychiatric discourses. Fundamentally, psychiatrists or addiction counselors, were brought into an awkward position to sympathize with those with substance use problems while also having to implement parole requirements. Addiction counselors faced new anxieties because they safeguarded their clients from retribution of the state in the case of parole violations, particularly given their interest in de-stigmatizing and de-criminalizing substance use, especially when they had themselves been the victims of substance use. Addiction counselors, in other words, were the benevolent as well as punitive faces of the state. This is also because the administration of methadone in clinics continues to be influenced by a "bureaucratic jungle" of federal and state guidelines, as treatment centers are subjected to considerable oversight from regulatory authorities, shaping the suspicion counselors had toward clients. The same could also be said about judges who were meant to be the guarantors of the law, but were also mindful of the growing drug court movement of the 1980s, especially after 1989, when a chief judge of Florida's judicial circuit set up the first drug court. Through I will not directly consider drug court cases, it is important to be mindful of the increasing shift to adjudicate substance use in drug courts. In 2015, Wes Adams, Anne Arundel's state attorney, calculated the price tag of Anne Arundel's drug court, which he suggested was one-tenth of the cost of keeping defendants in jail.[5] Upon graduating from drug courts, the lucky ones find their jail times waived. This benevolence is especially touted in the way these courts are advertised by the state. The Baltimore City Circuit Court Adult Drug Treatment Court was established in March 1994. Graduation photos often show clients along with their recovery specialists and clinical care coordinators.[6] It would not be inaccurate to suggest that only a small portion of individuals from the population of substance users graduates from the drug court. A graduation typically has thirty to forty graduates. While the attempts have been commendable, the overwhelming majority continue to be tried in criminal courts. In this chapter, I will mainly be relying on case law from district courts and appeals in higher courts to show the inability of courts to absorb the therapeutic aspects of justice and jurisprudence that have been the hallmark of the drug court movement.

Given the host of evidence that the court relies upon to judge intentions behind the crime, whether it was the intention to consume drugs, sell drugs or to commit homicide, the sentencing is inevitably understood by ex-convicts and treatment center clients as arbitrary, which results in individuals using a range of tactics to reduce sentencing, or conversely also playing a role in its extension, when they feel that reduced sentencing can create conditions for another crime, which could result in their return to the prison. There is an increasing frequency of individuals caught on drug-related charges, with judges placing them in institutionalized care rather than in prisons.[7] Thus, one must keep in mind how care and penalty becomes entangled in the court's tackling of substance use cases. In fact, as Rebbeca Tiger has shown, the logic of drug treatment is reversed when the court sanctions it. The court's use of a coercive approach toward treatment fundamentally clashes with the logic of drug treatment, whose purpose is to provide an alternative to incarceration, instead of using rehabilitative sanction to coerce drug users into sobriety. Tiger further shows how these drug courts have increasing power over the lives of parolees.[8] The question Tiger asks is how we got to the stage where we see coerced drug treatment with the threat of incarceration as an "enlightened" and humane approach to drug use. Tiger suggests that there is a shift in the idea of the transformative role courts could play in the lives of addicts by shifting the emphasis from "treatment" to "cure."[9] Tiger shows that the courts may even override the clinical recommendations of treatment programs, while also using medical authority when suited for purposes of expanding their legitimacy.[10] Methadone users in such a case must adhere to strict rules for obtaining the drug, where treatment appears as punitive rather than therapeutic in nature.[11] In fact, as Suzanne Fraser and Kylie Valentine have shown, methadone use is a complicated phenomenon, which allows some addicts freedom while placing others in a "uniquely marginal social location" because they are neither the outlawed heroin addict, nor the docile methadone user.[12]

DRUG COURTS

The first drug court in the United States was established in response to the growing crack problem plaguing cities. Chief Gerald Wetherington, Judge Herbert Klein, State Attorney Janet Reno and Public Defender Bennett Brumer designed the court for non-violent offenders to receive treatment. According to the National Association of Drug Court Professionals, as of December 31, 2013, there were 3,057 drug courts in fifty states. There have been various studies that show that almost 70 percent of users who are sent to prisons rather than drug courts return to drug use. However, there is also competing evidence that shows that the inability to comply with drug treatment while being on parole has resulted in even longer periods of incarceration without the client given any credit for the energy and resources spent on treatment. Moreover, as much as there is proof of reduced recidivism through drug courts, this competing evidence also shows the intense forms of policing and surveillance taking place through treatment centers and courts, resulting in individuals experiencing a loss of autonomy. There is thus a stark difference between the way the state hails the usefulness of drug courts and their therapeutic effects and the actual experiences of those who navigate through multiple carceral regimes, drug courts, prisons, treatment centers and as I will show. Often the stakes for many people with substance use problems are remarkably high, as relapse is taken as a sign of neglect. Among parents, this means being detached from being able to take care of children. While I describe a brief history of the emergence of drug treatment courts, the sources I draw from in the chapter are mainly from appellate courts of Baltimore and Maryland, where actors challenge state decisions of taking away parental rights if they experience problems with substance use. The emergence of drug courts has been a part of recent move toward "rehabilitative justice," a move that has influenced drug, circuit and appellate courts alike to focus on rehabilitation rather than punishment.

In the past, scholars have considered the relationship between drug use and crime,[13] and in the previous chapter, we have considered in detail how scientific discourses have historically treated substance use and crime as indistinguishable or mutually inclusive. Others have considered the role of substance use in straining family relations. particularly when people with problems with substance use problems resort to stealing in low-resource settings, which reveals the limits of care by family members.[14] Among Black families, the family structure is often also multi-generational, as the responsibility for the grandchildren, or even great grandchildren, comes to be shouldered by grandparents.[15] In the absence of parents, children experience new types of social control, and when parental authority is eroded, social control exerted on children may become more intense or even violent. Along with conditions of precarity, what often emerges is a relationship of abuse and intimacy, where the texture of the relations is flattened during adjudication in courts. The ambivalent experiences of domestic relations, of violence and intimacy, are ignored by the state when it decides the best way to provide care for the child. Thus, carceral conditions are not only limited to institutions like prisons but have far-reaching consequences for what happens beyond. Carcerality also has a psychic effect which comes to be borne by children as well as parents, as attempts by parents to be responsible and loving, after lapses, are continuously ignored. Michel Foucault had suggested that the purpose of the prison was to conduct continuous supervision in order to create docile bodies.[16] Beyond his interest in discipline, he also suggested that it was in the state's interest to protect the borders of the nuclear family to ensure that disciplinary power of the state was firmly established over children, with the family serving as a "switch-point" between multiple disciplinary institutions.[17] He also suggested that another important characteristic of the state is to re-create institutions that resemble the dynamics of the family yet are distinguishable from the family in that relations between individuals within these institutes resemble quasi-kinship relations. Yet, what we see in the adjudication of substance use and drug-related crimes by the state is that it is the nuclear family that is treated as the site of pathology. The state, along with its institutions, is involved not so much in the protecting of nuclear family as in "opening" it up for intervention to ensure that violence or neglect inflicted on children can be registered, either in the reports of the social services or the juvenile prison. My concern in this chapter is not so much with the workings of the prison, an aspect I have considered in the last chapter, but to show how actors experience a rupture in relations due to state intervention in the everyday lives of families and create new aspirations for reunion as a result of the state's decision to render parents with substance use problems as incapable of raising children.

The court actually creates the condition for the family to come directly under the gaze of the state to detect any relapses, and while it gives an illusion of independence to ex-convicts, the state intensifies its control over them through parole officers. Minor violations of parole regulations result in stricter sentencing and judgments about the parents' failure to care. While drug courts have been hailed as making a progressive move toward a more humane treatment of substance use, in reality, what we observe is that these courts, often with the help of psychiatric testimonies, even have a coercive and corrosive effect on the lives of people experiencing substance use. In this chapter, I outline some of the disciplinary controls over individuals on parole, whose compliance is continuously being monitored by their parole officers. I ask how compliance is interpreted in subjective ways as the parole officers, judges and clients or parolees employ competing ideas of recovery. As shown in the case above, the definition of being a responsible mother was interpreted differently by the court and the family members. These contestations will help make sense of the impact of incarceration and recovery on social relations. Often, those appealing in court also insist upon being given a fair chance at recovery instead of being further imprisoned. These intentions are judged by the court based on past performances, which show the difficulties experienced by individuals in carving a new life for themselves. In this context of not being able to show compliance to the parole officer, the word "relapse" acquires a new meaning and significance in the lives of individuals with substance abuse. Relapse, in other words, given the close supervision of their lives, can also entail a return to the prison and result in even longer sentences. A relapse can make a difference in being detached indefinitely from intimate kin. In this chapter, my concern is not to describe the evolution of drug courts or their therapeutic aspects, nor is it to show how drug courts have evolved in the past few years in Baltimore, but to show the close policing of the lives of individuals by treatment centers and parole officers. Further, by exploring courtroom dramas, this chapter also explores the ways in which decisions about compliance are handed out somewhat arbitrarily, based on psychiatric evidence, which helps us study the workings of the courtroom ethnographically. Courts favor recovery over punishment in some cases, and punishment over therapy, in other cases. One can take lead from James Nolan, who suggests that the emergence of drug courts has demonstrated the increased judicial activism of courts that has come to characterize the workings of the state. He adds that Supreme and appellate judges go beyond previously respected constitutional constraints to foster arbitrariness all the way to the level of trial courts. James Nolan astutely points out,

> Like the romantic supreme court judges, drug court judges have jettisoned traditional adjudicative constraints, finding them "too confining, boring, unrewarding, insufficiently responsive to social problems."[18]

Nolan reports that one judge contended that it was "okay to be inconsistent," whereas another contended that one "cannot have absolute rules." Yet another judge suggested that "as long as whatever you do is designed to get them off the drugs and put them back out on the street in a position where they can fight using drugs, whatever you do to accomplish that is fine." Others have taken a similar line of inquiry to show the ways in which the practice of courts departs from rules of adjudications. Leslie Paik takes lead from Jeffrey Ulmer to show how relations between judges, prosecutors and defense attorneys shape case outcomes.[19] She shows how non-compliance is socially constructed by drug courts. Paik highlights how attitudes toward the juveniles vary between courts. Judges often treat minor infractions with suspicion, such as non-attendance at school, even when it is taking place due to health reasons. Judges in other courts, use empty warnings more than actual sanctions, and in other cases they even attribute non-compliance to parents' harshness rather than treating it as children's own fault and subsequently give juveniles community service rather than incarcerating them in juvenile halls.

At the same time, rehabilitative justice actually allows for new forms of penalty and control over the lives of individuals experiencing substance use, and as Kaye has shown,

> Disobedience within the drug court ultimately calls forth the uncaring and abusive face of state power in the forms of a warehouse prison that awaits those who fail to reform. While in the program, however, the state offers both an authoritative enactment of a respectful and caring relationship, as well as resources.[20]

Judges themselves also understand the authoritative power they have by virtue of being role models, caring figures yet somewhat distant, in order to be able to penalize when needed. In fact, Kaye goes on to say that while proponents of drug courts place emphasis on incentives, there is far more attention paid to punishment. Kaye points out that even supporters of drug courts have noted that courts seem to pay little attention to rewarding positive behavior among participants and instead focus solely on sanctioning infractions.[21] My concern in drawing upon this insight is not to recapitulate a history of drug courts, nor is it to make sense of the increasing activism of the courts, but simply to show that court decisions may not be as objective and standard as one may presume. In fact, court decisions are based on the judge's impression about the degree of compliance as well as the defendant's will to undergo treatment. While in some cases judges may be forgiving if the person solemnly appeals to undergo treatment. In others case, judges may simply rule out this possibility. I now consider how the state treats substance use as a form of familial disorder and subdue ambivalent feelings and emotional attachments in their decisions in judging against people suffering from substance use, which are then variously contested. Unlike existing work on drug courts, my concern is not so much with the co-imbrication of punishment and care as scholars have already considered, as much as understanding how courts shape kinship and intimate relations in the family. What then are the implications of court's decisions on the everyday life of a family? What are the kinds of aspirations created by drug courts among families to reunite?

"FOSTERING" THE FAMILY

According to the Narcotic Addict Rehabilitation Act of 1966, drug substance use is a disease which should be treated by "providing a better means of dealing with the problem," as mentioned in Maryland's first drug treatment statute.[22] According to the statute, "a court after conviction may suspend the sentencing of any narcotic addict found guilty of violating the provisions of this subheading and commit to any appropriate institute, hospital or other facility in the state for the treatment of narcotics addicts."[23] According to subsection d of section 12, in case the person is deemed unfit for the trial, the defendant is referred to the court for ultimate resumption of the pending criminal proceedings, with the time spent in the facility counted as part of the sentence.[24] In reality, though, the court often constructs convicts as non-compliant, especially because of parole violations, and reincarcerates them. I would like to turn to court cases in which courts debated the restitution of paternal rights to biological parents in the context of substance use and incarceration. In Baltimore and in other parts of the United States, methadone, an opioid agonist, has been propagated for use against opioid dependence. In 1960s, it began to be used widely in the United States as an evidence-based treatment to counter the epidemic of opioid addiction. While its uptake had been slow, nowadays in a city like Baltimore, it would be impossible to find a methadone maintenance center within a few miles' radius.

In some cases, courts went against the wishes of children to reunite with their families. Carol W., a mother, was placed in a drug treatment program, when she found herself unable to find a job and was eventually evicted.[25] Her failure to show up at several appointments resulted in her dismissal from the drug treatment center. Performance in the treatment center was used as incontrovertible legal evidence. The court institutes methadone treatment as the only way to recover, but recovery is not only about taking methadone, but also about active involvement in the program. Her daughter, Latisha, had been living between her father and Carol W. The department claimed that Carol W. was not able to provide care to her daughter and claimed that, in one case, she had struck Latisha with a belt. Shortly afterwards, Carol W. was incarcerated, and her children were placed in foster care. I would like to consider how everyday relationships were modulated by the mother's experience of incarceration. Her children were allowed to visit their mother three times a year, and a case worker noted that in a meeting, Latisha did not "interact well" and her sister did not recognize her mother at all. Upon her release in 2001, Carol W. went to the department and signed a service agreement to get a second chance to be the primary caretaker for her children. She agreed to obtain housing, provide a proof of employment, and show proof of enrollment in a treatment center. One day, when Carol visited her children, the younger daughter refused to recognize her. The caseworker scheduled another visit, but this time Caroll did not show up at all. When the caseworker attempted to contact Carol, she found that her phone was not working. At her trial on March 29, 2001, it was found that Carol had not begun to comply with the conditions of the agreement, nor had she visited her daughters again, which had an "emotionally damaging" impact on Latisha. Then, the court gave Carol another chance for a reunion, in which it ordered for the scheduling of a bonding assessment, but Carol again did not respond. The juvenile court medical office then assessed Latisha and found that Latisha would have liked to live with her biological mother, if she was more responsible. The medical officer recommended Latisha to remain with the foster parent in the long run without terminating Carol's parental rights, given the emotional toll this would take on Latisha. Even with the evidence that the foster mother had once beaten Latisha physically, the recommendation was still made in favor of the foster parent, who had shown an interest in adopting the younger daughter as well. While the social services department had requested the responsibility of long-term care to be assigned to the children's maternal aunt, the court decided in favor of the foster mother, thereby terminating Carol's parental rights. This was then appealed, as the court's decision had not taken into account the emotional toll that termination would have on Latisha.

What we observe in this case is that the court does not provide any consideration to the reasons why Carol had failed to respond to the counsel's call; the court assumed that this was a sign that she was not ready or willing to take up the responsibility of being a parent. The conclusion is no different than the case with which I started the chapter, in that the only evidence for being a responsible parent is understood as compliance in drug treatment, without which the ex-convict's daily struggles are completely ignored. Among some of the clients I interviewed in treatment centers, I learned that they had managed to maintain contact with their children, whereas others had struggled to get out of abusive relationships, with connection with children cut off, but they still strived hard to complete their treatment in order to apply for jobs, which they sought to then use as evidence to contest the denial of their parental rights. Recovery itself was seen as burdensome, which did not leave many with enough time and hence led many to delay reunion until the future, once they were in favorable and more stable conditions, as I show in the case of Mary in chapter 6.

Yet, even as the parent tries to make an effort, as we saw in the case of Carol, substance use itself is taken as grounds to cast doubt on parental love. The court interpreted the relationship between the mother and the child as not being a "normal" one, and thus the ambivalent feelings between the mother and the daughter were dismissed in favor of giving parental rights to the foster mother. Thus, what we observe is that substance use is not merely about a specific type of behavior that risks the lives of children per se but is also a product of the carceral condition, in which the court decides the will to improve and to be compliant. One can therefore not view the effects of substance use in isolation from the way carceral institutions interpret what it means to be addicted. The impact of detachment itself on treatment outcomes is dismissed. Individual experience of substance use continues to be much more nuanced, in that for the daughter, love and responsibility did not map onto each other, whereas for the state, parenthood necessarily entailed responsibility, for which the foremost sign was the ability to undergo recovery. This fact alone could offset the fact that the foster parent, too inflicted corporal punishment, but here it wasn't interpreted as abuse, as it had been in the case of Carol.

Even outside of typical drug courts, evidence provided by treatment programs is central to the adjudication of parental rights. The inability to undergo treatment regularly is conflated with the inability to be a parent, even when many find treatment itself to be an arduous process. I am not at all suggesting that instances of violence and neglect do not occur, but simply that in the adjudication of parental rights, the courts employ evidence about treatment, in a way that has a direct bearing on what a person's legal family would look like. I now consider a separate case in which the defendant's attempts to resume care of the child were viewed as inseparable from compliance with conditions of parole, which prominently entailed the enrolment into a treatment program, but there was also an ambivalence around whether the recovered defendant could still be trusted to take care of the child. I now consider some of these ambivalences by considering both the probationary conditions of completing recovery to signal responsibility to take care of the child and, paradoxically, also the way in which drug treatment too is not considered enough sometimes as methadone use alone does not help overcome perceptions about drug dependence. This perhaps also reveals the arbitrary character of courts, which James Nolan understood to be one of the legacies of the drug court movement.

METHADONE AND THE LIMITS OF RESPONSIBLIZATION

One child was born in April 2012 to SB, an eighteen-year-old former child in need of assistance (CINA), and his father, MW.[26] The father had been convicted in a case of sexual assault in Connecticut. He was later extradited from Maryland to Connecticut and incarcerated there. He had never seen his child. The court took evidence of the child's neglect from the event of the mother leaving the child unattended during a bath and finding her face down in the water, which later led to the child being hospitalized and kept on life support for the next two weeks. The department of social services sought emergency removal of the child from the home, which was granted by a juvenile court. Yet the child was later returned to the mother. The mother then gave birth to twins. Once, when the mother was bathing a brother, the daughter was found to have been left in her car seat unattended with a bottle, which led her to choke. As the mother left for the child, and returned to the kitchen, she found that the brother suffered from severe burns.[27] The child was hospitalized for a month after which the department filed petitions for shelter care for all three children, which the juvenile court granted. After being discharged from the hospital, the brother was placed in a separate foster care, but he eventually joined the rest of the siblings, after all three children were declared to be children in need of assistance (CINA). Meanwhile, the caseworker attempted to locate the father in July of 2014 and found that he was incarcerated in Kentucky. The father then had to negotiate with the parole officer to be able to make it to the hearing after being informed about his children being removed from his partner's protection. A representative from social services then contacted the father's probation officer and shared the father's interest in attending the upcoming hearing. Later, however, the father was incarcerated due to parole violations. He identified an aunt and his brothers as resources for his daughter and shared that he "requested to be sentenced to prison in pursuit of no more probation, which will allow [him] to be relocated back to Baltimore." He also admitted about difficulties he had in trying to reach out to the mother and stated that the mother was "stubborn and withdrawn when [he] asked about H.W.'s whereabouts."[28]

Lee, the case worker, investigated the father's aunt as a possible caretaker for her daughter; however, she declined to be a resource and suggested that she would much rather be a backup plan and thought it would be best for the child to remain with his foster family. However, after hearing the news, Lee sent the father several letters but did not hear from him. This was taken as a sign of neglect, ignoring the attempts by the parent to do whatever he could to provide for her despite his constrained situation. The caseworker opined that removing the child from foster care would only have detrimental effects for him. The father's violation of parole was taken as further evidence of his not being responsible and available. He explained that since he had been in Connecticut, "The majority of [his] situation has been homelessness," and that he had not been able to provide for himself. His parole led to even further instability for him as he was employed for brief periods only. He did send money to his brother, who once babysat his son for "Pampers . . . for food, for a haircut, things like that." After his release, he would no longer be subject to probation conditions. He agreed to participate in a program called "Good Intentions, Bad Choices." He had been referred to programs during his probation, including a drug treatment program, which he had not completed. An important probation condition is, therefore, graduation from a recovery program. Even when the father did have the will to be the son's caretaker, he clearly admitted that he lacked any resources to "transition back to society," indicating the extreme difficulties many faced in getting adjusted to life outside the prison. Care for children was inseparable from various other pressures, such as having a means of income or a roof over the head, which many with experiences of incarceration struggle with. Most notably, the responsibility was judged through the ability to undergo recovery.

However, it is also possible that despite undergoing recovery, viewed as a sign of "responsiblization," a person may still be denied parental rights. Thus, even with a history of neglect, parents do attempt to recreate a lost relationship with their children, as shown above. In unique ways, parents, under incarceration, create new aspirations about parenthood, which although are difficult to actualize, still continue to animate their attempts to regain custody over their children. The primary way to be able to stake a claim to parenthood is to be able to successfully complete a drug treatment program, as I have argued in this chapter. In November of 1991, one appellant and Jacqueline T. had a baby. However, at the time of the birth, both parents were incarcerated. The mother was released before the birth, whereas the father remained incarcerated due to a drug-related first-degree murder. He had been incarcerated since 1974. His time in prison allowed him to earn a substantial sum and to be able to provide for Jacqueline's childcare. He found that his partner was spending the money on buying drugs rather than caring for Kevon. Even though the father had graduated from the drug program, the court observed that he could still not develop close relations with his son, who "did not seem to be becoming more familiar with his father."[29] In 1997, the DSS filed a petition for guardianship, and a hearing was held at the circuit court, which led to the father's termination of parental rights over Kevon, which was later contested by the father.

ASPIRATIONS FOR REUNION

Aspirations to be united with biological kin were effectively erased in court proceedings. There was contestation around "responsibility" for the child, which was tied to being turned into a responsible subject of biopolitical control. In these contestations, there was also an attempt to redeem oneself by undergoing treatment and appearing as responsible parents, based on definitions invoked by the state. At the same time, these court cases show the emotional toll detachment from biological kin plays on family members. Just as the court made a claim about the lack of responsibility, parents conversely made claims about their attempts to complete their treatment, and even as parents attempted to show that they could provide adequate care to their children despite their substance use, it was still possible for courts to use all the evidence they could muster to deny parental rights, especially when biochemical control in the form of methadone use was either missing or violated. In one case, the appellant had gone to North

Carolina for her parent's untimely death without notifying the parole officer about her intention to travel.[30] The mother admitted that she had smoked crack on several occasions when she was in North Carolina. Her inability to provide urine analysis between August and November meant that she was out of surveillance and thus non-compliant – meaning that she had either not taken her methadone or had not abstained from illicit drugs. The court also claimed that she could not provide any documentary evidence for the time she did spend in counselling and treatment. This, combined with her inability to meet with her child, Joshua, led the court to decide that the "permanency plan" for Joshua was adoption. The lack of medical evidence is taken to prove that drug habits had completely taken over the parents existence. The court concluded,

> Parenting is an awesome responsibility, particularly for a special needs child. [Appellant's] desire for drugs consumes her life, leaving no room for the task of providing stability for Joshua. Regrettably, Prince George County's Department of Social Services' request to alter/amend judgment must be granted and the parental rights be terminated. It is unfortunate that the link between Joshua and his siblings never really developed. Any link between Joshua and his father is non-existent. [Appellant] was the last link. She never developed the opportunities for a bond to grow between her and Joshua. *Her substance use became the centerpiece of her existence.* Joshua can wait no longer. It is in his best interests to terminate the rights of his parents.[31]

Substance use is treated as a habit that taints every aspect of a person's existence. This was ascertained through gaps in biochemical control through methadone. The point of using these cases for me is not at all to advocate for children to remain in the custody of parents who are violent; it is instead to show how the evidence gathered by social workers about family relations comes to play a central role in court. The court uses this evidence to make a case against parents based on what it assumes to be the right type of sibling intimacy or what relations between parents and children *ought* to be like.

Further, in almost all cases, piecemeal efforts at reunion with children are not taken as substantial evidence and are thus even downplayed. Even when there is evidence of the appellant providing for children while being incarcerated, as testified by witnesses, caseworkers sometimes still overrule these efforts. In one case, the caseworker suggests, "[I]t was an issue, as he [the parent] was incarcerated for several years; and because of that, he missed time with his children. Had drugs not been an issue, then he wouldn't have been away from his children for two years." Thus, different types of evidence are used to make the case about parental neglect, which does not at all take into account the fact that men and women are themselves making efforts to get adjusted to life outside the prison. *Drugs are viewed as taking up a person's entire existence.*

In other cases, there is some acknowledgement of the efforts made by parents, but again, substance use is taken as grounds to deny parental rights, for which evidentiary knowledge is provided by social workers. Recovery from substance use without any gaps is often the only way to retain parental rights, as in one case the court opined, "At some point the parents may arrest their problem. . . . As far as addictions go, the parents may literally be starting over and they have to make a decision to get better." Each violation is viewed as starting anew. It was important to be drug-free and show evidence of improvement for a substantial amount of time, with each relapse showing their inability to be parents – proving oneself to be compliant to a good parent was tied to being a biochemical subject, each violation not only viewed as a hurdle or obstacle in recovery but also an obstacle in being a parent. The court concluded that it is unclear when, if ever, "the parents will be prepared to handle their parental duties based on their drug addictions, [and] based on their anger management issues."[32] In almost all cases, the intentions of parents were misjudged, with substance use used as grounds to make the judgement about whether parents would be willing to change at all for their children.

Further, if parents appear to be disinterested in their parenting or counselling classes, that too can be taken as evidence for their lack of seriousness toward the child, as in one case the court concluded after cross-examination that the appellant had not been consistent in how long she had been in therapy,

> Indeed, with regard to the condition that she attend parenting classes, Ms. F. even testified that she attended only three classes out of the requisite twelve before making the unilateral decision that they were unnecessary because they taught her "the same exact thing" that she learned in her prior parenting classes. Overall, Ms. F.'s uncooperative attitude signaled to the court that "there [was] not enough evidence of hope" for a change in the future. Ultimately, we see no error in the juvenile court's assessment that this evidence was clear and convincing as to Ms. F.'s unwillingness to alter her previously unfit conduct.[33]

Every instance of lack of compliance provided evidence about the woman's lack of ability to be a mother, a belief further reinforced by any breaks in completing drug treatment. To be drug-free is the only way to be a successful parent, but for many, being drug-free remains an illusory idea which they find difficult to accept and come to terms with.

LIVED EXPERIENCES

I want to compare the treatment of substance use by the courts with actual experiences of families to consider the ways in which they dynamically navigate through risk of incarceration while also ensuring that their children are taken care of. There were violent geographies that had to be traversed by homeless individuals seeking care. I interviewed Sarah, who became homeless in 2019. She described her experience of going through pregnancy while being homeless. Sarah shared that she survived homelessness because of her boyfriend. Both used to ask people for money in order to make ends meet. Below, I provide some snippets from my interview with her.

Khan: If you don't mind me asking, how many months in your pregnancy were you when you became homeless?
Sarah: Almost all of it. I was expecting to deliver in January of 2019.
Khan: Can I please ask what led to you come to out on the streets?
Sarah: My brother sold my parents' house where my boyfriend and I were living.
Khan: Did you ever try contacting your brother?
Sarah: Yes, I have tried to send letters, text messages, but he did not reply at all. He just disappeared. When my brother sold off the property, my boyfriend and I were given one day to vacate the house. We grabbed as much stuff as we could and left. These were mainly toys and clothes we had bought for our children. When we became homeless, I knew I could not drag my children out in this cold, so I immediately contacted social security and applied to find a foster parent.[34]

She told me that the new-born was in the custody of the same foster parent taking care of her older children.

Khan: How many times are you able to meet with your children?
Sarah: I am allowed to meet my children only once a week, but because the foster parent lives a few meters from here it isn't difficult to meet them. The foster parent is super nice and lets me meet more than once. This week was particularly emotional because the foster parent and I went with our son to the park for the first time after he began to walk, I mean . . . Umm the foster parent, my boyfriend, and I.[35]

Sarah would often refer to her boyfriend as her husband to demonstrate stability in her relationship, as I also observed among other couples undergoing recovery. The idea of a moral striving, that is, of being able to reconstitute her life's future trajectory, was not missing, even in this case. In the overall narrative, Sarah's missing out on watching her child grow was a price she was paying for homelessness and her previous problems with substance use. Blood relations had been suspended and new fictive ties had been anchored through foster parenting, yet this did not preclude the struggle for reunion. Street life was a moral struggle, especially as it generated aspirations to give birth to a new life, to separate the baby from oneself indefinitely, and to delay reunion to a distant future.

Sarah continued,

> I was working at a restaurant in a mall in Timonium when we found out that my brother had sold the house. My boyfriend also lost his job. We simply could not make it work once we lost the place to live. He applied for a job at a kitchen in one of the restaurants here, but the owner was not able to offer him a job. There is a guy who has a two-bedroom apartment a few blocks away and is willing to rent one room to us. The only problem is that it is very small. Maybe it would be a good idea to get the place for the time being, and move out as soon as we find a job.[36]

The time that could have been spent with their children was being loaned for a future where a family could be reconstituted.

Sarah shared ecstatically that it was a great moment when her daughter was born. Her boyfriend had taken out his mobile phone to show me his daughter when I told him that his girlfriend had shared with me the good news. The weather began to change. Once the baby had been born, the couple now faced the responsibility of finding a shelter. During the end of April 2021, I met Sarah's boyfriend and asked him if he had any luck finding a job. He replied, "Yes, I did but then this virus happened." The following day, I returned to meet Sarah. I saw her kissing her boyfriend as he left her on her usual spot to run his errands. Sarah said that they now had a room but still needed to be out in the streets to make money to pay their weekly rents. Sarah shared that her partner had gone to meet his mother. She described, "My boyfriend . . . Husband . . . has two other children who are with his mother. The mother already has two of her daughter's children as well so we can't put too much burden on her."[37]

I asked Sarah if there was any limit as to how long the children were going to stay with their foster parents. She replied sternly, "I get what you are trying to say. That is usually for parents who are neglectful of their children or get into drugs. I gave my children myself because we had become homeless." By saying this, Sarah distinguished herself from "neglectful" parents, from whom kids had been taken away by the state due to their neglect. Sarah claimed that she and her husband/boyfriend could get their daughter as soon as their situation improved. When I interviewed Sarah later in 2021, I asked why she was still on the streets. Sarah technically had a roof, but her experiences of earning money for weekly rents were riddled with violence. She replied,

> I got beaten up by a group of guys and they took all my money. This was all the money I had to pay to rent our room for a week. Since we were not able to pay our rent for a week, the landlord asked us to leave. We have our belongings there, but I am still short of $40 to get the place back.[38]

There were a range of dangers the couple were exposed to, given their precarious situation and the lack of stable employment or housing. I asked if she and her partner had been going to treatment.

Khan: Are you going to treatment? Do you have a history of substance use?
Sarah: My boyfriend and I have a history of substance use, but when we were going to have our third child, I warned my boyfriend that either we were going to quit or the relationship was going to end.[39]

Sarah had been "clean" since then, and so was her boyfriend. Sarah pulled out the bottle of methadone to show her striving to become responsible by attending the methadone treatment program and quitting old habits. The reason why I use Sarah's example as a counterpoint to the representations of the "addict" in courts is because the actual experiences of couples in recovery are much more complicated. Being homeless exposed Sarah to a different nature of violence in the streets. The pressure of homelessness also increases exposure to law enforcement. For Sarah, the only place to return was her boyfriend's mother, who was already taking care of his boyfriend's children with a former partner, hence the network of support was already thin. In such a case, Sarah takes on the responsibility of changing habits by enrolling in a methadone maintenance program and receiving counselling along with her partner.

It was common to see how couples were also involved in disciplining each other and keeping them under surveillance, sometimes out of love and care and other times in violent ways, as we will see in a later chapter. The pregnancy certainly enabled the partners to chart a different course for themselves, possibly also because they needed to present themselves as "responsible" individuals in order to live with their children once again. I will now consider how people who experience homelessness draw upon metaphors of medicalization to blur histories of substance use, but also how reliance upon fixed medical templates in their engagement with clinics blurs longer histories of trauma while being on the streets.

CONCLUSION

In this chapter, I have considered how courts come to employ progress in treatment programs as evidence of responsibilization, which has specific implications for whether parental rights are granted or denied. I have considered how gaps in compliance or methadone surveillance are taken as evidence of failure to comply. In the process, courts have also made judgements about parents ability to emotionally connect with children, and this happens even when parents have shown progress in recovery in methadone programs. As much as graduation from methadone programs demonstrates the responsibilization of parents, relapses are still interpreted as the inability to recover but also the inability to be good parents, creating the pressure to start anew, especially as courts view substance use as shaping a parent's entire existence. I have compared this with the attempt by couples to undergo recovery as well as to reunite with children growing up with foster parents. I have considered how couples take children as motivation to recover, even while facing economic pressures, and the risk of homelessness. I have also considered how partners motivate each other to undergo recovery in situations that are otherwise constraining. As much as this serves as a source of encouragement, I will also show how this familial discipline becomes violent and punitive in chapter 6. But before discussing these pressures in the household, it is important to consider pressures to enroll in methadone programs among populations experiencing homelessness, especially under the risks of widespread institutional and public skepticism about drug use. I consider how people often use methadone as proof of their struggles to live drug-free lives, especially in the context of homelessness, where public discourses frequently conflate homelessness with substance use.

NOTES

1. Dorothy Roberts, *Killing the Black Body: Race, Reproduction and the Meaning of Liberty* (Penguin, 1998).
2. Bayla Ostrach, *Health Policy in a Time of Crisis: Abortion, Austerity and Access* (Routledge, 2017).
3. "Court jails baby's mom," (1968, Feb 17). *Afro-American*
4. Ibid.
5. Patrick Madden, "Maryland Turns to Drug Courts in Battle Against Opioid Substance Use," *WAMU 88.5 American University Radio.*
6. Ibid.
7. "Milked of quarter million she earned in 3 years, billie holiday sentenced: Begs U.S. judge to place her in hospital so she can get rid of vicious dope habit," (1947, Jun 07). *Afro-American.*
8. Rebecca Tiger, *Judging Addicts: Drug Courts and Coercion in the Justice System* (New York University Press, 2013).
9. Ibid., 33.
10. Ibid., 76.

11. Ibid.., 84.

12. Ibid., 85; Suzanne Fraser and Kylie Valentine, *Substance and Substitution: Methadone Subjects in Liberal Societies* (Palgrave Macmillan, 2008).

13. D. N. Nurco, T.E. Hanlon, and T.W. Kinlock, "Recent Research on the Relationship Between Illicit Drug Use and Crime, Particularly Stealing," *Behavioural Sciences & the Law* 9 (1991): 221–42.

14. Veena Das and Jonathan M. Ellen, "On the Modalities of the Domestic," *Home Cultures* 5, No. 3 (2015): 349–71. Marina Barnard, *Drug Substance Use and Families* (Jessica Kingsley Publishers, 2007).

15. Linda M. Burton, "Black Grandparents Rearing Children of Drug Addicted Parents: Stressors, Outcomes and Social Service Needs," *The Gerontologist* 32, No. 6 (1992): 744–51.

16. Michel Foucault, *Discipline and Punish: The Birth of the Prison* (Vintage Books, 1995).

17. Michel Foucault, *Psychiatric Power: Lectures at the College de France, 1973-1974* (Picador, 2008).

18. James L. Nolan, *The Therapeutic State: Justifying Government at Century's End* (New York University Press, 1998), 94.

19. Leslie Paik, *Discretionary Justice: Looking Inside a Juvenile Drug Court* (Rutgers University Press, 2011); Jeffrey T. Ulmer, *Social Worlds of Sentencing: Court Communities Under Sentencing Guildelines* (State University of New York Press, 1997).

20. Kerwin Kaye, *Enforcing Freedom: Drug Courts, Therapeutic Communities, and the intimacies of the State* (Columbia University Press, 2019), 95.

21. See also, F.S. Taxman, D. Soule and A. Gelb, "Graduated Sanctions: Stepping into Accountable Systems and Offenders," *The Prison Journal* 79, No. 2 (1999), 185.

22. S. B. Friedman, G. L. Horvat and R.B. Levinson, "Narcotic Addict Rehabilitation Act – its impact on Federal Prisons," *Contemporary Drug Problems* 11, No. 1 (Spring 1982): 101–11.

23. Clark v. the State 348 Md. 722.

24. Ibid.

25. In re ADOPTION/GUARDIANSHIP NOS. T00130003 AND T00130004 IN THE CIRCUIT COURT FOR BALTIMORE CITY. 786 A.2d 803 (2001)141 Md. App. 645.

26. IN RE: ADOPTION/GUARDIANSHIP OF H.W. 189 A.3d 284 (2018) 460 Md. 201.

27. Ibid.

28. Ibid.

29. In RE: ADOPTION/GUARDIANSHIP NO. J970013 IN the CIRCUIT COURT FOR PRINCE GEORGE'S COUNTY. 737 A.2d 604 (1999) 128 Md. App. 242.

30. In re ADOPTION/GUARDIANSHIP OF JOSHUA M. 888 A.2d 1201 (2005)166 Md. App. 341.

31. Ibid.

32. In RE: ADOPTION/GUARDIANSHIP OF DARJAL C. and Khaylelle C. 992 A.2d 503 (2010) 191 Md. App. 505.

33. In RE: ADOPTION/GUARDIANSHIP OF RASHAWN H. and Tyrese H. No. 7, Sept. Term, 2007. 937 A.2d 177 (2007) 402 Md. 477.

34. Sarah, Interview.

35. Sarah, Interview.

36. Sarah, Interview.

37. Early 2021, Stafanie shared with me the news of her mother-in-law's death.

38. Sarah, Interview.

39. Sarah, Interview.

Chapter 4

Medicalizing Homelessness

Men and women who become homeless are increasingly construed as "addicts" and thus put under great pressure to enroll in treatment programs by the state. However, the contingencies of their everyday lives deny them the stability to undertake and complete their programs—many treated recovery as "full-time work," which they could not undertake given the contingencies of life in the streets. In other cases, it was simply the excessive control that many experienced during recovery, especially in the context of homelessness, that resulted in quitting programs midway. Still, homeless people suffering from substance use continue to be viewed as responsible for their own fates, when in reality drug use can be attributed to many factors, some of which are beyond their control, as Phillip Bourgois' interlocutor had said, "If we knew why we were out here, then something could be done. None of us is going to say, 'I want to be a dopefiend all my life.'"[1] Bourgeois and Schonberg came up with the idea of "lumpen abuse," according to which the American public knows that homelessness and drug use are problematic but still remains indifferent and complacent to the everyday suffering generated by structural forces that give rise to violent and destructive subjectivities. They write,

> The lumpen subjectivity of righteous dopefiend that is shared by all the Edgewater homeless embodies the abusive dynamics that permeate all their relationships, including their interactions with individuals, families, institutions, economic forces, labor markets, cultural-ideological values, and ultimately their own selves.[2]

Lumpen abuse is accompanied by symbolic violence, which places the blame for problems squarely on the shoulder of the person suffering from substance use, concealing the structural changes and problems with intimate relations that provide conditions for substance use. Unlike Bourgois, I am not interested in the intersection between homelessness and substance use alone, but people's attempts to successfully complete methadone recovery while being homeless, and thus consider the shift from using illicit drugs to using methadone. People refer to the lack of agency in the decision to start consuming drugs because of the overall constraining situations they are in when they turn to drugs. Many refer to events like death and lack of employment as causes that push them toward substance use. There are, of course, also differences in the treatment of substance use among populations based on the degree to which they internalize and ascribe to the new biopolitics of methadone use. This has been considered in the context of substance use or the use of illicit drugs. The important aspect highlighted by Bourgeois and Schonberg is that while the white addict is portrayed as a "broken down bum," the Black member is referred to as "Black outlaw" who is in control over his life and having fun,[3] thus showing how the agency involved in turning to drugs is distributed differentially, but I would like to expand this to the study of methadone use—namely to the question of who can and cannot make the claim to be a responsible methadone user. I consider the ways in which the homeless pick up the language of medicalization to blur their past experiences of substance use and to demonstrate their responsibilization.

I first explore how people who became homeless discussed methadone maintenance as "medication" as a response strategy to the stigmatization of substance use. Of course, methadone is a form of medication, but linguistically, referring to methadone as "treatment" or as a form of "medication," offers new opportunities to overcome the stigmas of substance use. However, in picking up a medicalized language, there is also a risk that personal experiences may exceed medical templates used by the clinic. I explore perceptions toward the misdiagnosis of mental illness among the homeless, especially as everyday pressures and contingencies are erased. Then I consider longer timelines of trauma and the way these experiences remain unaddressed or even erased due to the violence of street life. I consider the everyday life of surviving in the streets. I proceed by asking how pressures of homelessness create specific types of suicidal ideations, given experiences of abjection and routine violence and public blame, which escape medical attention. I also describe the continuous pressures of demonstrating participation in methadone treatment in street life that those who have become homeless experience. Finally, I ask about how intimacies created in street life offer some degree of respite from daily pressures. In describing the ebbs and flows of everyday life, I ask how homelessness itself is treated as a moral condition, treated interchangeably with substance use, a creates new pressures on men and women to demonstrate the will the recover because of the biopolitics of creating an addiction-free population.

HOMELESSNESS AND ILLNESS

The Chicago-school inspired ethnographies of urban life have motivated many generations of social scientists to study homelessness in urban settings. These scholars have been mainly interested in the impact of de-regulation, dwindling of state services, and neoliberal policies on the emergence of homelessness since the 1980s. Sociologists have shown how instead of life on the streets appearing to be static, people continue to live fairly complex lives that involve a range of negotiations to earn, to find shelter, to eat, and so on.[4] By doing so, sociologists have alerted us to the dynamic quality of street life.[5] Some existing scholarship has focused on uncertainties of streetlife, especially as people are removed from their domestic spaces and families and find themselves without any social networks.[6] Existing scholarship has also considered how homeless individuals find themselves in conditions where others that surround them are much more violent,[7] which means that people are ready to engage in fights over resources much more frequently. What is useful about such scholarship is that it has already explored how populations with problems of substance abuse create specific distinctions among themselves. In some cases, older alcoholics have been described as viewing drug users with a degree of fear because of the latter's habits of stealing.

Moreover, as shown by the foundational work of Baxter and Hopper, it is not as if people who have become homeless already have a mental illness, but that there is something about the toughness of street life that causes people to become mad. In other words, the daily stresses of life on the street can themselves be mentally exhausting and disorienting. Consider the following example provided by Baxter and Hopper,

> A Chinese woman in her early seventies, with no family of friends nearby, had lived alone in an apartment, with no family or friends nearby had lived alone in an apartment until a gang of youths began stalking her at the beginning each month for her social security check. Eventually they took everything she owned . . . She speaks in a whisper or writes messages on scraps of paper for the fear of being overheard by "bad people" like those who destroyed her life.[8]

In fact, Hopper had even suggested that symptoms of mental illness expressed by many homeless can be difficult to distinguish from behaviours that may arise as survival adaptations to homelessness, which is referred to by Hopper as the "more florid street symptomatology."[9] Yet despite all this, there is a great degree to which many employ adaptive strategies, which is a move away from viewing the homeless as static or fixed in time. This also entails developing fictive bonds resembling family relations to make streetlife somewhat bearable, as in the case of people referring to older women as mothers.[10]

On the one hand, there are centrifugal forces the create differentiations among populations, and on the other, there is something about streetlife that is itself viewed as causing illness, perhaps causing many to turn to drugs. Simultaneously, there are pressures to receive some form of medical care as homelessness is conflated with substance use. For example, some rehabilitation centers may create increasing demands upon the homeless to get enrolled in recovery programs. There are some homeless shelters that make it necessary to enroll in treatment, and thus individuals continue to navigate between structured and unstructured lives. I now want to consider, using my conversation with Jacob, how he referred to a combination of structural and personal experiences that led him to drug use, but also ask how methadone use allowed him to present a narrative of medicalization in which he could strategically blur the history of drug use.

METHADONE AS MEDICINE

When I once asked Jacob about what brought him to the streets, he said,

> Everything fell apart when my mother passed away. I used to live with her. She died of multiple sclerosis. Slowly every part of her body stopped working.[11]

He talked about his mother's death and his own illness side by side. He had recently been prescribed medication for depression and anxiety. Jacob said, "But you know medicine is medicine." He told me that he would often appear as if he was under the influence of illicit drugs when he first started using methadone. He said that he would just lie on the footpath with eyes closed and mouth open. After a few seconds, he would try to open his eye. He told me,

> The problem is that when I took the *medicines* that the doctor gave, it felt like I could not do anything. I just felt lazy and tired.[12]

He voiced his complaint about the impact of medication on his body. When he first referred to medicines, I was not sure which ones he was talking about. He said that when he was homeless, on Saturdays, he was not required to go to the clinic, and this meant that there was nothing to prepare for. This was also the case when the doctor prescribed him take-home medication for which he was not required to visit the clinic. At one point, he told me that these medicines mainly included anti-depressants, but he eventually went on to tell me more about his medication. His life was closely entangled with his mother's, and in many ways, he understood his visits to the doctor as his mother's during her last days, when a visit would give her a reason to leave the bed, take a shower, and dress up. He used his own experiences interchangeably with his mother's. Jacob referred to his mother as a partner. To describe his relationship with his mother, he invoked a biological kin with an inflection of conjugality.[13] He said,

> You know it usually happens that when partners are living together, when one person dies, the other follows within a year or two because of the pain.[14]

Like Jacob, many others talked about their turn to drugs in moments of uncontrollable grief. Anthropological work has considered the intersections between homelessness and substance use, specifically the way in which homelessness is attributed to mental illness by the state, as a way to justify the removal of the homeless from public spaces.[15] At the same time, discourses on homelessness often also aim to educate men and women to look within themselves for causes of their substance use,[16] placing the responsibility for becoming homeless solely on individuals.[17] Others have shown how homelessness is conflated with disease categories in a way that the socio-structural determinants are eclipsed.[18] Structural causes of homelessness include the cycle of low-paying jobs and dead-end jobs that fail to provide the means to get off the street and even result in homelessness in the first place.[19] Drawing upon many of these ongoing conversations, I ask how homeless individuals take up medicalized notions of illness to detach themselves from their addictive pasts and to show their commitment to treatment, especially under conditions of intense policing by the state or the wider community. I do not understand medicalization as a way to label and deny the social experiences of those who have become homeless, but as a response strategy to show "responsibility," given the understanding of homelessness as problems of self-control in the age of neoliberalism.

Many people like Jacob continued to experience suspicion from the state, with symptoms of tiredness and sleep deprivation treated as signs of drug use rather than the difficulties of street life. Often Jacob would complain about being awakened from sleep on the sidewalk, "I think I need to start carrying my urinalysis so that I can tell these assholes to keep their mouths shut."

Jacob would refer to personal loss alongside structural transformations to displace his intention to initially turn to illicit drugs in his overall narrative. When I asked him how visits to the hospital could give anyone a reason to feel alive, he described that in the case of his mother, who had been in her 70s, illness often gave a reason to wake up early, to go outside the house, and to have a different day from the usual routine in which she was bedridden. For Jacob, it was after her death that "everything fell apart." His mother did not leave behind any property for him, and his precarious situation was intensified when he lost his job close to her death. In the narrative, Jacob provided a clear "falling apart" moment, which provided a reference point through which other events like the loss of his job could be understood. Jacob had been working at an institute that provided GED training to students. When I wrote about this in my fieldnotes, I realized that the loss of this job echoed broader changes that the city and especially the neighborhoods close to Johns Hopkins had undergone, especially in attempts by development agencies to gentrify and create housing for Hopkins employees and middle-class families.[20] The 2001, East Baltimore Development Initiative (EBDI) promised $36,000 in subsidies for Hopkins families and involved plans to remake eighty-eight acres into an employment center. In development projects in 1950s, over one thousand families were displaced, 90 percent of which were African-American families of low socioeconomic status. In the Middle East Development Program, within six years, less than fifty homes were built, and the vacancy rate doubled. In the EBDI, families were incentivized to relocate in order to get housing aid. Almost 740 families were displaced, mostly Black families without enough money to relocate comfortably. Early initiatives played a role in fostering residential segregation. The death of Martin Luther King sparked riots in Baltimore in 1968. Hopkins reconsidered its future in East Baltimore. The leadership considered relocating to Columbia, but this would have meant a loss of "ready access to clinical material, people with whom it could experiment." In 1970, the hospital's director of planning said the hostile local communities "reminded of past expansion" efforts being resisted. In 2018, the drop in the funding for GED training was part of a broader process of displacement, which prevented many—especially from low-income backgrounds or with criminal records—from envisioning a different life for themselves.

Scholars of neoliberalism have shown that homelessness has come to be increasingly targeted because of the state, especially because the state perceives the homeless as not adequately disciplined in the work ethic of the modern economy. Thus policing and other efforts are meant to discipline homeless individuals to have regimented lifestyles to make their entry into the job market possible. Methadone clinics play precisely this role by re-instituting order in the lives of the homeless. However, as I observed, while temporally the lives of those who had become homeless were not dictated by the same discipline of the market economy, there was a great deal of order as individuals strove to make ends meet as well as strived to regularly visit treatment programs. Life on the streets required a great deal of preparedness to meet contingencies. Often, individuals found it difficult to match the temporal ordering of life on the streets to the discipline required by treatment centers, which they often attributed as the primary cause of their failure in completing recovery.

Jacob continued, "After losing the job, I stopped looking for newer ones because most of my time would be spent taking care of my mother." This was also the time when Jacob had a relapse. Now on the streets, Jacob found the public space increasingly securitized, where he was left to fend for himself. His daggers could be taken as a sign of unregulated aggression, but Jacob mentioned that he would only use them for self-defense. To explain the use of objects for self-defense, Jacob had also drawn upon a generational shift he had experienced. He recalled a time when street life had offered relationships of safety and care for bystanders through notions of mutual trust and protection. According to Jacob, one could no longer find such a sense of security in the context of increased militarization and securitization of public spaces.

He would eventually begin to feel better as his body adjusted to methadone use.[21] The use of medication in Jacob's language slowly began to reveal a history of drug use. Later, I asked him if he could tell me more about his medication. He said that he was on methadone treatment and had to go to the treatment center every day, for which he needed a bus pass. Jacob often drew upon a vocabulary of medicalization to conceal a history of drug and substance use. By showing how he had gone to the methadone treatment program regularly, he reaffirmed his commitment to leave behind his substance use for the life of treatment, which many others had simply refused. What I have found in the literature and discussions on methadone treatment programs is the way they stigmatize drug users, with perceptions toward the drug use among white users different compared to people of color—the former viewed as taking drugs recreationally, whereas the latter viewed as taking them habitually.[22] However, I would argue that people often also refer to their present states as effects of medicalization as they transition from opioids to opioid agonists to overcome the stigma associated with substance use. References to stigma alone remain simplistic ways to define the experiences of substance use and do not allow us to imagine evolving relationships with one's symptoms and conditions. Jacob's language was replete with medical terms, such as "prescription," "treatment center," "clinic," showing that even in a precarious situation, he continued to be a complaint subject, a person in recovery, rather than on drugs.

The description of his condition as medicalized also reminded me of some of the questions in medical anthropology as well as medical sociology, where medicalization refers to the imposition or the use of diagnosis for every sign or medical symptom. Some have even argued that medicalization can offer patients a standing language through which experiences previously inchoate are made intelligible and addressed medically.[23] Others have considered how medicalization denies the social experience of illness by focusing only on its diagnostic reality. According to the latter, medicalization could allow the patient to express his or her problems by using existing linguistic templates. I think that the fact that Jacob had resorted to notions of medicalization, represented the power of clinic and professionalization such that any unusual symptom related to methadone use could itself be rendered as a medical condition.[24] In such a case, one could even deploy symptoms caused by methadone to one's advantage to conceal a history of drug abuse. Some recent work in medical anthropology shows how medical symptoms are vernacularized and circulate in a way that they are used interchangeably with disease categories as in the case of high blood pressure (BP) and hyperglycemia (*sugar*), especially in different parts of South Asia.[25] In cultures of biomedicalization, even normal sensations may be taken as signs of illness.[26] Once symptoms are vernacularized or normalized in everyday life, the medical attention given to them may also decrease. This serves the purpose of showing how the "normal" medical experience is not predetermined but is shaped by interactions in the social world in which the disease is experienced.[27] To assume that normalization of symptoms is complete, in that social actors detect no pathology at all leaves little room for the dynamic nature in which medical symptoms and social life interact. Moreover, frameworks that assume that normalization takes place to an extent that illness can no longer be detected miss the element of moral effort—disciplined, persistent, and ongoing—entailed in the process of addiction recovery.[28] Although some authors writing about social suffering use "repair" as a metaphor to assume that there is a complete normalization of poor health, they represent patients as existing in a state of limbo, as if the element of moral struggle is completely missing. Often, scholars of medicine and its social experiences do not give the word 'repair' its due credit, thus representing illness and its relations to social world as static. My own approach entails that the relation between illness and the social context is much more dynamic: a person experiencing substance use on one day may be fully committed to completing recovery—on another day, due to distress, may be overridden by the desire to numb one's mind from problems of everyday life. However, the use of a medicalizing language was not straightforward; just as Jacob employed a clinical language, he also described his experiences of misdiagnosis—where his experience of homelessness, personal history, and the pressures it created would continually be disregarded in medical evaluation.

MISDIAGNOSING MENTAL ILLNESS

Jacob described that when he was homeless, the doctor's prescription, which he used in order to get a pass for twenty dollars for a month to travel by bus. Three days a week he was able to go with his friend Esther to the treatment center, but the rest of the days he would have to walk and travel by the bus, which would be very difficult because of the distance he had to cover. His daily commute often also came at a price, that is, of not being able to play his melodica and earn his daily pocket money. He could be spending the time playing on the streets and earning a few dollars to get him past the day. In the interviews I conducted in the days to come, I asked him more about his experience of treatment. He said,

> When I was homeless I was treated by a nurse-practitioner who did not understand that what I needed was medicine for my traumatic condition, whereas she kept on medicating me for psychosis.[29]

It may be common for medications for anti-psychosis to be prescribed for those with acute or manic depression or with pain problems, as both may regulate serotonin uptake in the brain and thus improve mood. Jacob understood his condition to be different from the nurse-practitioner's understanding. He continued,

> I feel like I have PTSD because of my persistent anxiety and constant fear of an impending danger, which is due to a history of abuse such as that of being molested as a child. The medicines the nurse is giving, however, is for psychosis, hallucinations, etc. which makes *no* sense. I even told the nurse that I no longer needed this medication, but she only quadrupled the dose from a hundred to four hundred milligrams saying that it will take the edge off. I needed a therapist, not a psychiatrist to understand my issues.[30]

Patients like Jacob resist by clearly differentiating their experiences from psychosis in order for their experiences to be treated as authentic and real. Psychosis is commonly reported by those who have become homeless, and its diagnosis by care-providers may render the patient's experiences as illusory instead of being real and shaped by concrete social circumstances.

Jacob understood his fears well. He knew that his exposure to the dangers of street life and the unpredictability of becoming homeless resonated with earlier experiences in life. The series of contingencies offered by his present life, where one uncertainty led to another, braided with fears such as those of being threatened, molested, or having his safety compromised, manifested in an ever-present state of anxiety, which he expected his nurse-practitioner to address. In other words, he wanted the nurse-practitioner to believe him for what he was saying and not simply discard his fears as symptoms of psychosis. By indicating that what he needed was therapy, he suggested that he needed some resolution for his past experiences as well as his present precarity, which were simply difficult to put into words all at once. Whenever he did attempt to describe his personal life, he feared that his words could be taken as signs of madness. Jacob needed someone to trust his words, even when they were partial or incomplete. I was struck by Jacob's understanding of having been treated wrongly. This was also a product of having an insurance that did not allow him to receive quality care. My interactions with him left a deep impact on me and demonstrated both how people could have their conditions stigmatized even when they tried to responsibly undergo recovery and also how much bureaucratic processes through which care was delivered reduced the emotional and affective space to address a person's social experiences.[31]

Jacob was often denied medication, which he thought he could have used to calm his nerves. For instance, he thought he wasn't given Xanax at times because the doctor thought that Jacob was going to sell the medicine on the streets. He went beyond the immediacy of the present to understand his symptoms in relation to his past, which he rarely recalled, except when specifically prompted. Jacob did not distinguish his medical reality from his social one; both, in fact, were the same for him. His injuries and bruises were not accidents but continuously reminded him of the violence he had to experience as a matter of routine. It wasn't as if his past was always available for articulation. Instead, it was the weight of his present, the sum-total of the bruises of his past, which manifested in the sheer bogginess of his condition, physically as well as perhaps psychologically. Jacob and I both excavated his past in our conversations. He would often introduce me to his friends by saying that I was like his therapist, as a gesture of gratitude for helping him untie so many knots from his past. Our conversations were mutually constitutive; as I made sense of his experience, he too learned and became alive to his past and present. Part of this intelligibility for Jacob was possible as in the articulation of his experiences, Jacob drew upon connections between the part of the body affected and the event that had caused it.

He told me that his insurance could not get him a better psychiatrist who would understand his entire medical history, which is why he appreciated my attempt at documenting it. We were not only documenting Jacob's medical history, but also writing and making intelligible for both the narrator and the listener his past life. Jacob's goal was still to describe a history that could fit the standardized template in which interaction between a doctor and a patient takes place. He wanted our interviews to help him learn how to fit important biographical elements into his medical experiences without the former taking away from the latter. He once commented about my work, "Maybe it might be helpful because our conversations will help me talk about my condition without me having to ramble about it." I now consider the templates in which Jacob would try to fit his experiences to be medically legible and the ways in which his complicated personal experiences defied any linearity.

TIMELINES OF TRAUMA

Jacob and I once sat in his backyard in 2021, after he had found a place to live. He got me a notebook and a pen. He gave them to me even though I had carried a notebook of my own. Jacob opened the first page and made a timeline and said, "I am writing about the first traumatic event I experienced. You should continue writing other events on the timeline by using numbers. You can write the description by using numbers in later pages."[32] He started the timeline from his birth in 1965. The first event was being attacked by a Siberian Husky. This is what he wrote:

> *# 1 Siberian Husky Attacked, 6 Week In-Patient Hospital Stay @ St. Joseph Hospital 30 stitches in his face and head. Through Night Terrors from PTSD. I was sent to psych Dr. XYZ, who prescribed 1, 10 mg Valium (Diazepam) EACH NIGHT + OINTMENT FOR ABOUT 6 MONTHS.*

Jacob said, "At the time they did not have PTSD and did not know what was wrong with me. But that's what I had, I had PTSD."[33] Jacob was right, in fact, as PTSD emerged as a diagnostic category only after the Vietnam War. He continued, "He also gave me drugs for my head. When I wasn't feeling alright, I could take a pill, and I learned this at a very early age."[34] My description in the diary did not follow the same medicalized description that Jacob himself had wanted me to follow. I did not restrict myself to events, visits, or duration of visits to the hospital and began scribbling everything he mentioned as a collaborative exercise. When he graduated from secondary school, he had an age difference with all the boys.

Jacob described, "I hadn't hit puberty and that's when the pedophiles came." This happened from his sixth grade to about the freshman year of high school in 1978. He began telling me about his brother and his friends, and I was already clenching my teeth, hoping that it would not be his own brother. But Jacob told me exactly what I wanted him not to say:

> My brother and his friends were the kind of people who could not get dates and this was a group of two to five boys. They outnumbered me but they did it anyway. *I was raped for years.*[35]

By that time, he still had not made it clear that he had been sexually abused by his own brother. The brother was still somewhat concealed by an emphasis on friends. I had a tear in my left eye. I felt like I had to let him speak. Maybe he understood that I was shaken. We continued to talk for some time without naming the brother. It was as if we were in a kind of a shared agreement in terms of words that could have been left unspoken. It was implicit that we both understood that it was his *own* brother. Jacob continued, "By 1978/9 when my mom would be away. Shit would happen. The older brother would say he could take care of me. Whenever my parents were going away, it would only bring horror. I could not express what was happening to me because I knew all my father was going to say was 'oh that's nothing, it's just what boys do,' and my mother would have begun to blame herself. Besides, my father always favored my elder brother. My older brother was named after my father. Dad would be happy to have a manly son. Jeff junior (elder brother) was supposed to do everything. He probably didn't want to have me. I never tried to compete with my brother because that would piss him off even further. But he was never the kind of kid who could play baseball or football and never had any girlfriends, and all the anger for this would come out on me. I knew I couldn't compete with him in the classroom. . . . The pedophiles continued until I hit puberty. In 1978, in my freshman year of high school, it was two on one (my brother, his friend and me). I beat them up. I literally tortured them and kicked my brother's butt and knee and punched him in his throat and smashed his face on the floor. The friend backed away and I did the same thing with him. I knocked him out. I had lost control of my emotions. I had to stop them from ever doing it again. I broke their noses and lips. I broke every single finger on my brother's hands and then I screamed at him . . . *Yes, Jeff Junior raped me for many years* but then he became completely forgetful of this period out as if it never happened. I wanted to remind him that when I was a kid, I kicked his ass. But we both have a different mentality. When I was finally done with many years of being raped, I had to come to terms with the fact that I could be very violent. I realized that I only got satisfaction after taking revenge from my brother and his friends. After I *maimed* them, I realized that I had this switch and when it turns on, I won't stop. People have to pull me off the other guy. Sure, someone else can call 911 but I can cripple a person in a minute. Once I was surrounded by four Black men and they thought they were in control. You know it hurts me to live with this capability, but I think at some level we all are capable of it. I still think that I do things a bit extreme. If the fight is one on one, I would fight fair but if it is three on one, there is no fair play."

I was no longer able to add dates to it to simple timeline, given the texture of his experiences. The third traumatic event pointed out by Jacob was when he began to have nervous breakdowns. This was around 1977, when his parents were not willing to send him away for college. He continued,

> I mean my home was the place where I was raped for years. I wanted to get away from here. I finally snapped one day. I had an argument with my father. My father would always be working or sleeping. I had an argument with him after which I punched through a window, and began crying and ran outside

> to the lawn. I kept crying while lying on the grass. All I had done was to ask my father if he loved me. He didn't reply and I did this. All I needed was for him to say "I love you." After this happened, he took me to an ER, where a psychiatrist came in. I was sixteen at that time. I had a full load of course work at school. When the psychiatrist asked me about what had happened, I did not tell him anything about sexual abuse. I did not tell him anything about the fact that my brother had ruined my life. The psychiatrist asked me, "Why don't you take a break? Why don't we admit you?" When I was admitted to the hospital, three other women in the ward were schizophrenic and one of them I remember clearly had huddled in a chair like a ball and there was another one who kept dancing and singing. The adolescents in the ward were only troublemakers. We could simply not compare our conditions with the schizophrenic women. One of the troublemakers was a girl who had run away from home and another one was a child who had put a bowling alley on fire. The psychiatrists promised my parents that whatever happened, Jacob would stay in the ward . . . When I met the out-patient psychiatrist, they did not know about my PTSD at that time. I had not told them about the dog bite or sexual abuse. You know I never abused a kid, I broke the chain.[36]

Jacob already looked at psychiatric institutions with suspicion, given his own experience of being kept in a psychiatric ward as a child. Jacob's experience of child abuse as a cause of trauma remained unaddressed, and the newer pressures of homelessness further intensified and made past and present traumas indistinguishable.

The story about the past unfolded alongside his everyday squabbles with his roommate. I want to now move from the backstory to the present reality (by this time, he had found a place). Before this specific interview in 2021, he did not pick my call but wrote an email in which he told that he was having severe headaches and that he had begun to slowly put some food in his system. His anxiety and weakness were also improving. He mentioned that his entire apartment needed a thorough cleaning, and since his roommate was not helping at all, he had finally given up on his dejection and depression. Jacob described, "I gave in to depression and anxiety." He also mentioned that he was slowly getting better and was able to get things in order. When we met, I asked him why he was feeling unwell. He went into great detail to tell me how he had very sharp senses because he had lived all his life in the suburbs and was not used to city life. Alluding to his experiences as a rescue driver in San Diego, he talked about his appreciation for calmness. People who drowned were taking risks with Mother Nature, he added. He continued, "You don't take risks with mother nature." He thought he developed acute senses due to being close to water. The ongoing construction work close to his home bothered him because the noises did not have symmetry. As a musician, he said that he knew that there was no rhythm in the sound of construction. For this reason, he had not been able to sleep at all. Whenever he did sleep, he would wake up frightened by the loud noise of construction work. His experience of having been a rescue driver and musician converged when he talked about his exaggerated startle response, acute anxiety, and PTSD.[37] By sharing his experience as a rescue diver and as a musician, he provided an extended explanation for how his appreciation for rhythms and symmetry had contributed to his present condition, in which he could no longer tolerate noise. I was amazed to find out how much such a history could complicate the way we think about something such as anxiety or depression. He was responding differently to the thuds from nearby or the sound of fire ambulances, whose sirens alerted him about something bad happening. This fear could still be placed in a longer personal history of how one oriented oneself in time and space, where sleeping was not simply about numbing one's senses but tuning one's mind to the rhythm of city life, which his experience of homelessness and its uncertainties had now taken away from him. All this showed the promise of ethnographic knowledge in eliciting deeper histories of trauma and abuse, which were effectively erased by treatment centers, which in the biopolitics of creating an addiction-free population, were only concerned about making compliant subjects.

STREET VIOLENCE

Jacob had often complained about what he termed "reverse racism," in which he was targeted specifically because he was white, within predominantly Black neighborhoods. I want to remain mindful here about not talking about Jacob's position of victimhood by trivializing or silencing the racializing of Black populations by what is construed to be a predominantly white state authority—my goal is simply to capture his fears and anxiety about traversing predominantly Black spaces shaped by racialized perceptions and forms of prejudices often created by carceral authority as I have considered in chapter 2. In chapter 2, I have already considered carceral structures and policing reify racial distinctions, which also shaped Jacob's behavior toward racial difference given histories of gang violence within prisons, which Jacob had also experienced during his time in prison. Jacob thought that he was especially prone to attacks because he carried with him his take-home methadone. On several occasions, Jacob had been mugged. During 2021, Jacob began to have convulsions in public places. After regaining consciousness, he would find that his belongings, including his methadone, would be stolen. This is why Jacob preferred to receive his treatment at the center so he did not have to carry methadone, which would expose him to greater violence on the streets. This prejudice and sense of victimization were also a product of

Jacob's memories of prison, in which he collaborated with and against Black gang members and was punished as a result.

Race becomes entrenched in everyday interactions, which is in some ways reinforced by carceral institutes. Yet I also want to be attentive to how racial categories become unsettled in everyday life. This, however, does not rule out the possibility of being marked permanently by racial difference as a consequence of disciplinary regimes existing in the form of prisons. Institutions of the state create and reify racial divisions as part of policing and disciplinary practices, but thinking about race simply in terms of binary divisions of whiteness and Blackness belies how, in reality, racial difference continues to bleed into many other categories, such as religion, ethnicity, or sexuality, to re-erect and reanimate original fault lines.[38] Jacob's story tells us not only about an individual himself but also about how the racial biases implicit in his words had been a consequence of his past experiences with incarceration and medical care, as well as what this showed about the complexity of the situation in which he had to navigate Black spaces, often as a friend but other times as an accomplice to projects of racialization that inevitably shaped his views.

In addition to having violent clashes with Black men on the streets, especially given Jacob's own history of incarceration and having been involved in gang violence, not having a shelter had created new pressures on movement, adding additional stress. Finding a porch to sleep on when it rained, adjusting time to wake up before the residents could detect his presence and making arrangements to warm himself in the cold were all pressures that made individuals like Jacob much more susceptible to a relapse. Yet these experiences were increasingly ignored, and relapse would continue to be penalized as I will show in the next chapter. Even in traversing racial boundaries and developing hostilities, there were pressures to develop intimacies to support one another and their drug habits and dependencies. These included providing Naloxone for those who had overdosed. These experiences were as much a part of becoming homeless.

When Jacob was homeless, he told that he would often ask people about weather forecast,

> I would have to carry my umbrella the next day. When it rained, I would need to make arrangements like going to McDonald's and buying a coffee every hour for shelter.[39]

Changing weather, especially winters, brought in a new set of anxieties ranging, from ways to protect oneself against the harsh weather, as well as fears about whether one was going to survive at all. When the weather would get colder, Jacob would need to worry about putting on multiple layers of clothing on him. Jacob shared how normal fatigue and sleeplessness had been during his time on the streets, especially when he would not be able to find a porch to sleep. He told me that weekends were particularly bad because he would have to wait for people to return from the bars so that he could sleep on their porches without being caught. He said he had several porches to choose from. The ideal porch would have the lowest visibility from the road and have furniture which could be used to sleep. He said he would alternate between multiple houses so that he would not gain anyone's attention. He even said he had been caught several times, but agreed that some people were kind enough to let him stay, whereas others would ask him to leave, which he did not disagree with because it was their private property he was trespassing. He said "early birds" were a big problem as these people would take their dogs out for a walk, and thereby sleeping on their porches meant being careful about waking up and leaving on time.

He said that there was a time when he thought he wasn't going to make it alive. He said, "I thought I wasn't going to make it through the winter." He had said this in a rather matter-of-fact manner, with little fear or surprise. Some homeless men I met had even gotten frostbites in the winters and received amputations, but still gathered a few bucks to help them get a shelter. Jacob continued, "By February, the weather would get much colder and I thought that I would just get pneumonia and hypothermia and die." Unlike others who had used hospital emergencies for overnight stays, Jacob had refrained from ending up in the hospital, possibly also because of his problem with benzodiazepines, which I will discuss later.

All these pressures of figuring out what to eat, how to sleep, and meeting with acquaintances for support clashed with his visit to the treatment center. Even the ability to find a shelter clashed with making it to the treatment center.

He said,

> There is a housing option but for that, I would have to get a purple line and walk one mile and try to get in the line between seven and nine in the morning. Even if I made it at seven, people who were employed would usually cut the line and get the place first. This would mean that I could never be sure about getting a place and the timing clashed with my methadone program which runs from five-thirty to ten in the morning.[40]

His attendance at the methadone program clashed with his ability to find housing. The visits to the treatment center could even be blamed for Jacob's inability to find a shelter and work. Treatment centers in Baltimore had begun to increasingly provide housing; however, there were many that did not, and long queues meant that some had to make it to their programs without having stable housing arrangements. During my early morning visits to treatment centers, I would often find some of my interlocutors walking to the centers for their methadone. When the weather was about to change, Jacob *had* to find a place to stay. This winter could even have cost Jacob his life.

He launched into a conversation about his medications, which included methadone, for which he had to go to the Maryland Avenue, as well as Prozac and Xanax, for which he went to another clinic a few blocks, where he was being treated by a nurse-practitioner. Jacob suggested that together all the medications could help alleviate the pain in his broken tooth and the knee and would let him sleep at night, but they also had side-effects like short-term memory loss, which he now attributed to forgetting things he had already told me about. When he talked about medication, he referred to both methadone and his depression/anxiety pills. He grouped the two in the same category to blur his past experiences of substance use.

Life for someone homeless would be turned upside down as soon as a rain forecast was available. I wanted to know how he would prepare for the rain. He said it would never be safe to predict the weather by looking at the clouds. Jacob had learned that clouds could deceive. He had learned to differentiate between dark cover and rain clouds and would also use a sense of distance to figure out when it would rain, but he would still not rely solely on his judgment. He would always use someone's cell phone to predict the weather.

Whenever there would be a forecast for rain, Jacob would immediately try to cut branches from the tree with his pocket-knife. He would collect as many of them as he could so that he could be protected from the cold and wet concrete while sleeping at night. He would lay the branches on the ground and then lay his cardboard over them. This would make sure his cardboard did not get wet. He would then try to get garbage bags, cut them up and wear them, one to cover his legs and the other over his upper body. This would protect him from getting wet. He told me that because sleep deprivation did not let him stay awake, whenever he would sleep on the sidewalk, people would pester him with questions about whether he had taken drugs. He said it was not his duty to keep on explaining to people why he wanted to sleep and that he was tired of providing explanations.

SUICIDAL IDEATIONS

Street life created new intimacies and new competitions. Sometimes new forms of care emerged toward those who would suffer from withdrawals or who had overdosed. Despite generous attempts to help others, this could still result in making one's condition worse, especially given the fear many face in reporting overdoses to emergence services. Jacob would once even share that he suffered from suicidal ideations several times. He said, "I would tell people, if I found a place to live, I would still come to play the melodica whenever I can. Or maybe I would have killed myself by jumping off from a building. . . . If the latter is the case, please put flowers on the sidewalk in my memory."[41] These feelings were animated by problems in finding shelter in his position as a white, educated male, which I understood as a problem of privilege turned inward. He complained angrily, "Being white, educated, male and independent meant that I would always be the lowest in every list for housing."[42]

These voices are important to recover to understand the material conditions that foster a deep-seated animosity toward others, based on religion, race, or sexuality. They also prompt us to think about situations of the undoing of privilege or privilege turning inward where one's racial marker, which would otherwise provide privileged access to networks and power, is no longer able to do so. One must also bear in mind that these feelings are also fostered by ethnoracial aspects of carceral authority and race-based solidarities that emerge as a result. Prison authorities foster white authority and supremacy. Jacob also found himself disappointed due to recent visits to the substance use treatment program. He described the drug market I mentioned earlier, but this time he also mentioned the violent fights that took place in the area. He was mainly talking about 2018, when things were probably different compared to 2020, when I visited the treatment center with him. In 2018, the open-air drug market existed outside the methadone treatment center much more prominently, and gang violence was also much more intense. The dealers had disappeared due to police crackdowns, but Jacob commented, "Addicts are all over the place trying to find suppliers." This also led to an increasing incidence of violence, according to Jacob. He said, "They even tried to infiltrate the treatment center. There is a lot of fighting every day."

Jacob once recalled that he used to say to people about his experience of abjection, of feeling stuck, his experience of being routinely questioned, and his inability to care for other homeless people struggling with their symptoms,

> Please don't pray for me, people usually say I'll pray for you. But praying has only made it worse, I respect that you believe in God, so do I, but I am requesting you not to pray for me. If you want to pray, pray for someone else.[43]

He would often also add humor in narrating his experiences. He said that he would frequently talk about jumping from the top of the building on St. Paul, "I told people that I would take my jacket off before jumping so that I can at least break some bones." During his time without a roof, Jacob also suffered from the pain of trying to help others—especially those who had overdosed—and making things worse, instead of easy, for them. Jacob talked about problems with extending life when it was full of miseries. He gave the example of Naloxone that he had given to a few heroin users, which worsened symptoms. This left him questioning whether he should have helped others at all. Naloxone can have several adverse effects. While it may reduce acute symptoms in conditions of withdrawal, it can also make symptoms worse. He told me that now he no longer felt that he had to help others, especially when extending one's life only meant making their miseries worse. Jacob said that no matter how hard he tried to stop himself from protecting others, his good side would always come out. He would always end up saving others, but this was not always successful. He said that at one point he had given up on waiting for housing. He could not afford to give up on a day's earnings by waiting in a queue to get a shelter. He said it was better for him to come outside to play the piano.

He said that even the people who do get housing were usually "drug addicts" and not like him on treatment programs, which made staying in such places even more dangerous. He preferred staying out and playing music. But as the weather began to change, Jacob was no longer motivated to find housing. There was nothing to look forward to now. Jacob said that had reached a dead-end. Jacob would eventually get a roof over his head, but this also came with new stresses, as I will discuss later.

HOMELESS INTIMACIES

Jacob said that he appreciated when people would stop to talk to him. He greatly appreciated this and said, "People gave me a reason to live, especially when I did not have any family or relatives to rely on." I had once seen Jacob sitting with a woman in front of Insomnia cookies. I wanted to ask if the woman he was with was Esther (the woman he had mentioned earlier). He said, "It wasn't Esther, it was Mia." He said she had been with him in the program and was "psychotic." Mia, he claimed, had recently gotten a disability check, and Jacob said she had been telling everyone she had a thousand-dollar check. Jacob said, "I am spending time with Mia to make sure she does not get robbed, which could happen in a heart-beat."

Jacob had a great sense of responsibility to help others and frequently did what he could, but also always differentiated himself from the rest, who supposedly were not trying as hard. Two of the three people, Jacob had called "alcoholics" were Rose and Tay. I had once seen Rose kiss Tay by holding the latter's head in her hands with an almost motherly touch. I found the sight touching as it showed how interactions and the social reality of those who had become homeless was based on care as much as competition, jealousy, and hatred. Rose was a white middle-aged woman who I had seen dragging herself on the street as if in a state of permanent exhaustion. Tay, on the other hand, was a Black man with mental health problems, as Jacob once told me. There were varying thresholds of love and hatred, and while street violence was configured along the lines of racial difference through ethnoracial aspects of carceral authority, it was also about love and care for each other irrespective of racial difference. Sarah, as I showed earlier, had gone through her pregnancy on the streets and lost her share of her parents' property when her brother sold it off without her approval and disappeared. She had two children in foster care and was in the final days of pregnancy in the extreme winters of Baltimore. Street life was about abandonment, as in the case of Jacob, that is, in the absence of blood relatives, as kinship relations were suspended *elsewhere*, as in places like foster homes.[44] The possibility of reunion was deferred to a future when stability could be secured. Sarah, whose case I described in chapter 3, had applied for accommodation and awaited government assistance to get a shelter by the end of 2019. She was hopeful that she was going to get it, but the final days of her pregnancy in the extreme winters were particularly difficult. I had seen Sarah's glowing face and constant smile turning pale, with her flu and a piece of tissue paper stuck in her nose becoming part of her daily appearance as she struggled to make enough money to pay her weekly rents. What had been an energetic hello had slowly changed into a quiet "hanging in there." Being without shelter was viewed as exhausting, there were new intimacies and relationships formed, but these pressures coincided with the regulation of bodies by methadone treatment centers, which created strict forms of surveillance. Many ascribed to this new form of regulation, whereas many others continued to treat it as too regulated and out of sync with the uncertainties of street life.

TREATMENT AS WORK

Part of Jacob's daily routine, of course, included visiting a treatment center, but going for treatment often also meant not being able to make money by playing the melodica, as I have shown above. In 2018, he had been demanding the center to provide take-home medications for four days of the week. He did not push the management because he needed a reason to get ready and go somewhere. The reason why he did not like to go to the center was not only due to the difficulty of commute but also the violence he had to experience during his visits to treatment centers. In addition to the experience of violence, among my interlocutors, there was an understanding that treatment was like "full-time work," which prevented individuals from completing recovery, especially when they were also under the pressure to make enough to buy food for themselves and to sustain their drug habit. Brooklyn, a white woman in her 20s, shared why she wasn't able to continue after a few failed attempts, "Treatment is like work, except that you aren't paid." Brooklyn often engaged in sex work to make ends meet. There was another grievance that the complex experiences and violence experienced by many in households and on the streets, which had caused substance use in the first place, could not simply be "fixed" with treatment. As Brooklyn said, "Medications only numb our pain, but it only gets worse," showing the ambivalent position she held about medication compared to illicit drugs and lack of trust in recovery without adequate psycho-social and emotional support. To understand the delivery of substance use treatment, one must therefore not only focus on care provided in treatment centers but also the psycho-social experiences of clients and the violence of street life, which many have to endure, an aspect I would like to turn to in the next chapter.[45] Brooklyn presented a different type of biopolitical subject than Jacob. While Jacob had been struggling to remain compliant, Brooklyn had simply given up because she thought it was impossible to follow the regimented lifestyle required by treatment while struggling to make enough money to make ends meet. She had given up on treatment. There were thus different subjectivities—one of the compliant and the other of the non-compliant subject—but compliance too could not be taken for granted, as there were different ways in which clients risked non-compliance given the lures of illegal drug markets, as I will explore next.

CONCLUSION

This chapter has considered the ways in which methadone clinics attempt to regulate the bodies of those who have become homeless, and in doing so, create new subjectivities of regulated and unregulated bodies, as I will further consider in the next chapter. While these are new types of control exerted by methadone treatment centers, there are also ways in which it allows clients to use the language of medicalization to blur the history of substance use. However, the medicalization of homeless is an ambiguous process, even as it provides an opportunity to de-stigmatize histories of drug use, it also involves perceptions toward over-medication and misdiagnosis, as homelessness is conflated with the presence of symptoms of paranoia and psychosis, which renders the symptoms caused by broader structural conditions unreal and detached from social situations. I have also considered the ways in which medicalization of homelessness requires individuals to present the traumatic experiences in specific narrative forms when the complexity of social experience denies them such standard forms of expression. Finally, I have considered how the biopolitics of methadone use creates multiple subjectivities among compliant and non-compliant subjects as some remain enrolled in programs, whereas others find treatment centers too ordered and structured compared to the contingencies offered by street life. I now want to consider how intersections between the treatment center and open-drug market create new pressures for recovery and often also create conditions for relapse.

NOTES

1. Phillippe Bourgois and Jaffrey Schonberg, *Righteous Dopefiend* (Berkeley: University of California Press, 2009).
2. Ibid., 19.
3. Ibid., 87.
4. Michael Duneier, *Sidewalk* (Farrar, Straus and Giroux, 2000).
5. Irene Glasser and Rae Bridgman, *Braving the Street: The Anthropology of Homelessness* (Berghahn, 1999), 60
6. James Spradley, *You Owe Yourself a Drunk: An Ethnography of Urban Nomads* (Boston: Little Brown, 1970), 254.
7. David Levinson, "Skid Row in Transition." *Urban Anthropology* 3, No. 1 (1974): 79–93.
8. Ellen Baxter and Kim Hopper, "Private Lives/Public Spaces: Homeless Adults on the Streets of New York City," (1981), 43.
9. K. Hopper, "More than Passing Strange: Homelessness and Mental Illness in New York City," *American Ethnologist* 15, No. 1 (1988), 158. doi: 10.1525/ae.1988.15.1.02a00100
10. J.R. Wolch and S. Rowe, "On the Streets: Mobility Paths of the Urban Homeless," *City & Society* 6 (1992): 127. doi: 10.1525/city.1992.6.2.115
11. Jacob, Interview.
12. Jacob, Interview.
13. The relationship between conjugal and biological kin has been central for both psychoanalysis and anthropologists studying kinship. In Freud's oedipal complex, he talks about sexual attraction to the mother and competition with a primal father figure, showing an inflection of conjugality on biological relations. Anthropologists who have considered the Oedipal complex in their fieldwork of "primitive cultures" prominently include Bronislaw Malinowski among others. However, Claude Levi-Strauss considers the movement from nature to culture as the prohibition of incest through the creation of relations of exchange with other social groups, that is, a separation between conjugality from biological relations. See Claude Levi-Strauss, *Elementary Structures of Kinship* (Beacon Press, 1969); George W. Stocking, Jr., ed. History of anthropology, Volume 4. *Malinowski, Rivers, Benedict and others: Essays on culture and personality* (Madison: University of Wisconsin Press, 1986).
14. Jacob, Interview.
15. A. Mathieu, "The Medicalization of Homelessness and the Theater of Repression," *Medical Anthropology Quarterly* 7 (1993): 170–184. doi: 10.1525/maq.1993.7.2.02a00030

16. Vincent Lyon-Callo, *Inequality, Poverty, and Neoliberal Governance: Activist Ethnography in the Homeless Sheltering Industry* (University of Toronto Press, 2008).

17. Erin Dej, "Psychocentrism and Homelessness: The Pathologization/Responsibilization Paradox," *Studies in Social Justice* 10 (2016): 117–135. doi: 10.26522/ssj.v10i1.1349.

18. Jason Adam Wasserman and Jeffrey Michael Claire, *At Home on the Street: People, Poverty and a Hidden Culture of Homelessness* (Lynne Rienner Publishers, 2009).

19. David A. Snow, Susan G. Baker, Leon Anderson, and Michaei Martin, "The Myth of Pervasive Mental Illness Among the Homeless," *Social Problems* 33, No. 5 (1896).

20. See Steve Hendrix. "Johns Hopkins Hospital Inspires Mistrust and Fear in Parts of East Baltimore." *The Washington Post*, WP Company (2 Feb., 2017), https://www.washingtonpost.com/local/Jacobs-hopkins-hospital-inspires-mistrust-and-fear-in-parts-of-east-baltimore/2017/01/25/a4f402c2-bbf3-11e6-91ee-1adddfe36cbe.

21. Methadone treatment centers provide medication-based therapy for individuals dependent on opioid-based substances such as prescription painkillers or heroin.

22. Sonia Mendoza, Allysa Staphanie Rivera and Helena Bjerring Hansen, "Re-Racialization of Substance Use and the Redistribution of Blame in the White Opioid Epidemic," *Medical Anthropology Quarterly* 33, No. 2 (2019): 242–62.

23. Orkideh Behrouzan, "Medicalization as a Way of Life: The Iran-Iraq War and Considerations of Psychiatry and Anthropology," *Medical Anthropology Theory,* 2 No. 3 (2015).

24. Arthur Kleinman, "Culture, Bereavement and Psychiatry," *The Lancet,* 379, No. 9816 (2012): P608-9.

25. Veena Das, *Affliction: Health, Disease, Poverty* (Fordham University Press, 2014).

26. Duana Fullwiley, *The Enculturated Gene: Sickle Cell Health Politics and Biological Difference in West Africa* (Princeton University Press, 2011); Cameron Hay, "Reading Sensations: Understanding the Process of Distinguishing "Fine" from "Sick," *Transcultural Psychiatry* 45 (2008): 198–229. S.M.H Offersen, et al., "Am I Fine? Exploring Everyday Life & Ambiguities and Potentialities of Embodied Sensations in a Danish Middle-Class Community," *Medical Anthropology Theory* 3, No. 3 (2016): 23–45.

27. Georges Canguilhem, *The Normal and the Pathological* (New York: Zone Books, 1991).

28. For more on normalization and moral struggles involved in the illness experience see S.E. Estroff, W.S. Lachicotte, L.C. Illingworth, and A. Jacobston, "Everybody's Got a Little Mental Illness: Accounts of Illness and Self among People with Severe, Persistent Mental Illnesses," *Medical Anthropology Quarterly* 5 (1991): 331–69; Cheryl Mattingly, *Moral Laboratories: Family Peril and the Struggle for a Good Life* (Berkeley: University of California Press, 2014). Morgan M. Philbin, "'What I got to go through': Normalization and HIV-Positive Adolescents," *Medical Anthropology* 33, No. 4 (2004): 288–302. Y.J. Yu, "Subjectivity, Hygiene, and STI

Prevention: A Normalization Paradox in the Cleanliness Practices of Female Sex Workers in Post-Socialist China," *Medical Anthropology Quarterly* 27 (2013): 360.

29. Jacob, Interview.

30. Jacob, Interview.

31. Arthur Kleinman, *Moral Education of a Husband and a Doctor* (Penguin Random House, 2019).

32. Jacob, Interview.

33. For more on how PTSD emerged as a diagnostic framework after the Vietnam War in the 1970s, see Allan Young, *Harmony of Illusions: Inventing Post-Traumatic Stress Disorder* (Princeton University Press, 1996).

34. For a discussion on how culture mediates the perceptions about the pharmacological efficacy of medications, see Daniel Moerman, *Meaning, Medicine and the 'Placebo Effect'* (Cambridge University Press, 2002).

35. Jacob, Interview.

36. Jacob, Interview. One can understand the role of psychiatry as part of a broader genealogy of the emergence of the state and medical institutions and their use by families to discipline disorderly members by requesting the state to intervene on their behalf. One example of this is provided by *lettre de catchet*, letters written to the state, to request confinement which could take place in a hospital without a trial in late 18th century France. See Arlette Farge, *Disorderly families: Infamous Letters from the Bastille Archives* (University of Minnesota Press. 2017).

37. Some scholars have considered the relationship between childhood trauma and exaggerated startle response among adults by understanding personal history through childhood trauma questionnaires and current symptoms through PTSD Symptom Scale and Beck Depression Inventory, see Tanja Jovanovic et al. "Childhood Abuse is Associated with Increased Startle Reactivity in Adulthood," *Depress. Anxiety* 26, No. 11 (2009): 1018–26.

38. For more on an intersectional approach to race, see Ann Stoler, *Race and the Education of Desire: Foucault's History of Sexuality and the Colonial Order of Things* (Duke University Press, 1995); Kimberle W. Crenshaw "Race, Reform and Retrenchment: Transformation and Legitimation in Anti-Discrimination Law," in *Critical Race Theory: The Key Writings That Formed the Movement,* eds. Crenshaw et al. (The New Press, 1995). Kimberle W. Crenshaw, "Demarginalizing the Intersection of Race and Sex: A Black Feminist Critique of Antidiscrimination Doctrine, Feminist Theory and Antiracist Policies" *The University of Chicago Legal Forum* 1, No. 8 (1989).

39. Jacob, Interview.

40. Jacob, Interview.

41. Jacob, Interview.

42. Jacob, Interview.

43. Jacob, Interview.

44. Anthropologists have considered the question of adoption in which the child navigates between biological and foster parents. Among the Tonga "the adoptee's continuing relationship with his natural parents may range from infrequent to daily contact." On New Hebrides, young children are informed about the adoptive

relationship, but they are never forced to live with either. On the Mahili Atoll to the east of Tahiti, both parents have obligations to the child, but the child's first obligation is to the adoptive parents. See KL Morton. "Tongan adoption." (1976), 64–80; R. Tonkinson, "Adoption and Sister Exchange in a New Hebredean Community," (1976), 228–46; C.C. Brooks. "Adoption on Manihi Atoll, Tuamoto Archipelago," (1976) 51–64 & Signe Howell, "Adoption of the Unrelated Child: Some Challenges to the Anthropological Study of Kinship," *Annual Review of Anthropology* 38 (2009): 148–66.

45. Social scientists have given attention to how sites of care can be engulfed in great violence. In conflicts, sometimes hospitals and humanitarian organizations are no longer seen as neutral places involved in providing care but becomes sites specifically targeted by insurgent attacks as in Iraq, Afghanistan and Sierra Leone. Other problems considered in the literature include difficulties of commute to access care during conflict because of restrictions created by landmines and checkpoints, see Jennifer Terry, *Attachments to War: Biomedical Logics and Violence in the Twenty-First-Century-America* (Duke University Press, 2017); Mariane C. Ferme, *Out of War: Violence, Trauma, and the Political Imagination in Sierra Leone* (University of California Press, 2018); Catherine Lutz and Andrea Mazzarino, *War and Health: The Medical Consequences of the Wars in Iraq and Afghanistan* (New York University Press, 2019).

Chapter 5

Treatment Centers and the Drug Market

Due to the ravaging impacts of heroin substance use, as early as in 1963, an American doctor named Vincent Dole was given a grant by the New York City Health Research Council to find a treatment for opioid substance use. He understood the need for a pharmacological intervention and began experimenting with a variety of combinations. Here, what was of great clinical significance was the ability to remove drug cravings and prevent the onset of withdrawal symptoms.[1] The medication used would be none other than methadone. Drug use was viewed as a chronic condition that needed to be managed as continued studies "indicated that the effects of methadone were corrective but not curative, hence the assumption was that treatment would, like the disease, be chronic, long-term, even indefinite."[2] The perception of drug dependence as chronic creates new challenges for both clients as well as addiction counselors, where the former try to remain compliant despite the lures of the drug market, whereas counselors try to detect infractions in expected behavior through routine urine tests. By the 1970s, there had been a rapid expansion of methadone treatment in much of the United States, yet this expansion was without medical competence, and because methadone was not fully integrated into rehabilitative services, its true promise was not realized. This was followed by a regulatory push back by Drug Enforcement Authority (DEA) which established strict standards for the treatment of narcotic addiction with methadone. The oversight of the DEA effectively removed methadone from the reach of physicians, which resulted in a closed system of methadone delivery.[3] These regulations included emphasis on admission criteria, setting dose limits, controlling take-home doses, and limitations on the duration of treatment. Programs could also be cited for infractions, such as the inability to measure temperatures upon admission. One of the enduring legacies of this strict regulatory oversight, by extension, has been the strict controls exerted on clients to show their compliance.

Given the history of strict regulatory checks and the abuse of methadone without medical oversight, it is important to consider the social meanings of methadone, especially as it facilitates the recovery of clients but also opens new avenues of misuse as an illicit drug itself, as its social meanings are re-signified,[4] especially as it is bought illegally in open-drug markets where its use is complimented with other prescription drugs. This creates new problems and challenges for compliance in drug treatment centers. To understand the problems of compliance with treatment programs, it is important to consider the blurry lines between opioid substitution therapies and illicit drugs in the minds of clients,[5] and the way clients interpret medication use, and whether clients think methadone is efficacious or not in helping them overcome their substance use.[6] I am not denying the usefulness of drug treatment programs and the enormous contribution they have made in enabling people to live dignified and drug-free lives, but simply consider how people variously experiment with methadone and other drugs while risking being non-compliant. Clients try to overcome their withdrawal symptoms by engaging in illegal drug markets while also trying to remain compliant in treatment centers. This creates new vulnerabilities that discourage people from continuing their treatment programs, especially when failure to comply with their programs results in suspension. Kimberly Sue has shown how drug treatment and carceral regimes are closely tied with one another as families send members who have fallen prey to substance use to drug treatment programs situated in prisons.[7] Upon leaving these programs, many find little social support and often return to prison due to relapses. But clients often also look for the next best treatment center with greater flexibility instead of remaining dependent on one, given the proliferation of treatment centers in Baltimore. Previously, scholars have considered the disciplining of substance use.[8] Scholars have previously considered power relations that shape the treatment of clients in treatment centers,[9] whereas others have shown how treatment reveals the contradictions of liberal political practice as it reveals the imbrication of autonomy and coercion,[10] and yet others have considered the ontology and materiality of substances.[11] Particularly, Bourgois has considered how "the contrast between methadone and heroine illustrates how the medical and criminal systems discipline the uses of pleasure" where heroin, being more pleasurable pharmacologically, is considered illegal, whereas methadone is considered medical.[12] Bourgois' fascinating work describes how people turn to methadone when heroin becomes unaffordable. He treats methadone largely as a form of substance use comparable to heroin use. He describes how in methadone maintenance, clients are treated arbitrarily—some days "dirty urine" prevents them from getting methadone. Among others, the methadone doses are not enough to help compensate for withdrawals, whereas for some they are too much—in both cases, methadone eliminates the pleasurable element of drug use and, in doing so, prevents many from functioning normally within social relations, in families, and at work, as they would have with heroin. He also considered how clients use a range of prescription medicines such as Valium or combine methadone with cocaine to increase its effects. Though my argument in this book and specifically this chapter overlaps with his argument, where it departs is that it considers how methadone use is viewed as the best alternative to heroin use, offering many the mantle of respectability that heroin use would not have been able to provide, even when users compliment methadone with benzodiazepines, cocaine, and sometimes heroin. Secondly, the argument is unique in that it considers the client's knowledge of how drugs interact with each other—and how this knowledge is leveraged to remain compliant in drug centers, where instead of viewing the treatment center as having complete power over the clients, I consider how clients exploit regulatory loopholes to their advantage instead of considering methadone maintenance treatment (MMT) through a simplistic picture of the regulation of bodies and populations through biopolitical regimes.

The chapter considers issues of compliance in treatment centers. The treatment center's inability to fully address the clients' experiences of withdrawal results in them engaging in drug markets, where they experiment with a combination of prescription medicines and illicit drugs alongside methadone. I consider this as a form of new pharmaceutical dependence. I then consider how clients combine methadone use with prescription medicine bought in black markets to enhance their experience and make it somewhat comparable to heroin use. Here the close involvement in the drug market not only as a buyer but also as a seller creates new pressures that make recovery difficult, where selling drugs is tied to one's own consumption of prescription medicine. As I show, undergirding the use of multiple drugs is an intimate knowledge about methadone, illegal drugs, and how they affect each other and the body. This often also leads to new secondary forms of substance use with new forms of withdrawal, which clients need to learn to manage because of their engagement in MMT as well as drug markets. This experimentation also makes recovery an ambiguous process where clients also begin to differentiate between those who rely on pills to enhance the effect of methadone and those who return to heroin, where the former often view the latter with suspicion for not fully transitioning from criminal uses of heroine to medical uses of methadone.

To understand the medicalization of substance use, one must go beyond the clinic to the interface between streets, households, and clinics. I will ethnographically describe the transactions taking place in the drug economy right outside of drug treatment centers. I found that these treatment centers were highly securitized spaces, especially in the aftermath of the violent events that had taken place, as I will describe below. Boyd and colleagues (2012) explore the association between the location of methadone treatment centers (MTC) and crime in Baltimore.[13] They argue that the MTCs do not act as a privileged site for crime compared with convenience stores. The article led to a push back against protests over the clustering of MTCs in disadvantaged areas of the city. According to Graham Mooney, the article had serious methodological flaws. Mooney writes,

> Thirteen MTCs in Baltimore were grouped together without taking into account the huge variation in neither the daily number of patients treated in each facility nor the socio-demographic characteristics of the areas surrounding them. The number of patients treated was not compared with the number of customers visiting convenience stores, to the number of people using the hospitals nor to the number of people (permanent residents or ambient population) in residential areas.[14]

According to the Baltimore AIDS Linked to the Intravenous Experience (ALIVE) prospective cohort study, it took nine years of treatment to achieve long-term cessation in about 40 percent of injecting drug users. Using his evidence, Mooney concludes that Boyd and colleagues "avoid the point about why local communities protest the location of the MTCs; it is not the successful patient that matters to them, it is the failures."[15] The unsuccessful patient is the subject of great public controversy as he brings violence to neighorhoods while remaining a marginal figure in the state's biopolitics of an addiction-free population.

THE MARKET FOR RECOVERY

The interesting aspect about clients in MMTs is that they exist in a market as "customers," but still experience new forms of pressure to comply with the ideal subject of methadone-regulated bodies. The presence of multiple MMT centers means that clients are left to their own devices to manage residual effects of treatment, by relying on prescription medicine.[16] There were strict checks and controls by treatment centers on their respective clientele. It took me three years to finally enroll participants, which was delayed by the administration due to safeguards on medical information under Health Insurance Portability and Accountability Act.[17] These guidelines acquired a new salience as HIPAA violations could also result in exposing medical information that could potential risk the life of the client if it got to the wrong person. The HIPAA regulations acquired a new salience in the context of ongoing gang-rivalries. The treatment centers and their substance use counselors were thus mindful of the rivalries and the potential for violence if the client information was leaked, as this could reignite existing enmities. One counselor in an interview in 2022 reflected on strict checks over data via gang-rivalries,

> Its difficult to know who the researcher is [it could be a friend or enemy], which means that the knowledge that you gain may be disclosed to someone else and even be used against the client.[18]

This is why I often recruited participants outside of treatment centers to avoid any unnecessary controversy. My interpretation was that these treatment centers arduously maintained checks over privacy, first due to concerns over safety and security of their clients, but also because they were in intense competition with one another to avoid losing clients and to lure those who were dropping out from their programs. In this chapter, my central concern is to show how the clients' experience of dwindling autonomy makes recovery difficult for many. I also explore the interstices between the clinic and the street to explore the circulation of methadone and illegal drugs. The control of counselors also extended beyond the programs, as counselors could be seen engaging with their clients in a friendly way but also kept a close look to make sure they weren't lured by other counselors because of the presence of almost four treatment centers within a one-mile radius.

While some treatment centers offered housing, others charged clients for housing because insurance plans, including Medicaid and private insurance companies, continue to favor out-patient care over residential care, as I observed in my analysis of databases of treatment centers in Baltimore. Moreover, as Rebecca Lester has shown among patients with eating disorders and psychiatric problems, insurance companies withdraw support for in-patient care when they consider patients to be non-compliant or having borderline symptoms.[19] Residential programs are very important, especially because they provide relief from problems of housing, an aspect which I will discuss in the next chapter. In Baltimore, there are different types of programs, some of which provide residential support whereas, others only provide outpatient treatment. Jacob described his attempts to get enrolled in a treatment program on West Greenmount,

"The problem with the treatment center was that they wanted me to give money for housing as well. Basically, this would have meant absolutely no financial control."

This would have meant living without any money in hand. Thus, clients tried to choose between treatment programs based on which one provided the greatest amount of autonomy while also making sure that this autonomy did not result in their return to their old habits. Literature has been largely silent on the question of autonomy in relation to treatment centers, especially in a context where parole officers are not as closely involved with treatment. One can still take lead from Shana Harris' study in North California, where she shows how therapeutics of buprenorphine govern patients and providers with a desire for freedom and normalcy compared to methadone. She argues that the treatment center's reference to autonomy can be seen as an extension of neoliberal discourses to create self-governing subjects.[20] Instead of a comparison between buprenorphine and methadone, I explore how treatment programs simultaneously create illusions of freedom and autonomy while also introduce new forms of discipline over the lives of the clients.

The decision to change treatment centers was also shaped by inter-racial conflicts, which reanimated prison rivalries. Clients often sought counselors of similar racial backgrounds with whom they could relate in terms of shared experiences. Two of the treatment centers where I conducted interviews were situated only a few meters from each other. Jacob had quit his program on West Greenmount, blaming it on "pedophiles" which I interpreted as a more general anxiousness around being in Black spaces, as I have considered in the previous chapters, as he would often tell me about the Black clients with whom he would get into fights with.[21]

In this chapter, I will show the different uses to which prescription medicine is put in illegal drug economies that flourish outside treatment center and the kind of relatedness and hostilities these create.[22] Through my ethnographic interviews, I gained insights into the intersections between the clinic and the street, which I would not have been able to get by remaining within the confines of the clinic, a problem encountered by many studies based on clinical care. Baltimore had a specific place in the country's substance use treatment landscape. One main characteristic of this landscape was simply the sheer number of treatment centers that had emerged in the city in the past few years. In fact, one of the counselors I had the chance to interview told me, "If someone was not able to successfully recover in Baltimore, they could not recover anywhere in the world."

Like the Black addiction counselor who had himself come from New York for treatment, there were many others who had come from places as far off as Arkansas in attempts to become "clean." Yet as the counselor mentioned, the city was also dangerous in some ways simply because it offered greater opportunities to return to drugs. He argued that one could not successfully complete recovery as long as he or she did not have a will. He himself had relapsed at several points but thought that it was essential to break ties with associations and places that triggered temptation. He used Freud to explain the unconscious temptations which were triggered by spaces and people, which is why he thought it was necessary to change one's surroundings in order to recover. He said, "You are just lying to yourself, if you are going back to the same places and think you can make it unaffected."

Thus, according to this counselor, substance use was not simply the act of consuming drugs but entailed a whole series of affective responses of the body to people and spaces. The competition of treatment centers in the "market" for drug recovery also meant that clients had a wide range of options to choose from based on the treatment center that provided them with the greatest amount of autonomy, but there were still new challenges in getting re-enrolled after violations. The access to pharmaceuticals (or its lack) resulted in new types of violence that I consider below.

OVERPRESCRIPTION

Many scholars, especially investigative journalists, have produced accounts about overprescription and aggressive advertisement as causes of widespread dependence on opioids, as I reviewed in the introduction. I would like to briefly consider something similar in the case of Baltimore to throw light on the new uses to which prescribed drugs are put. In May of 2018, a thirty-two-year-old Tormarco Harris from Baltimore and eight co-conspirators were found to be illegally providing large amounts of addictive prescription drugs in exchange for money to patients. Harris had colluded with Dr. Kofi Shaw Taylor from a wellness center in Glen Burnie and provided patients with unlawful prescriptions for narcotics, including oxycodone, morphine, tramadol, and benzodiazepine. It was found that patients had paid up to $500 for illegal prescriptions. People working at the wellness center in Glen Burnie had even been pressurized to prescribe higher quantities.[23] Later, I will also show how even a few milligrams meant that a legally prescribed drug could be sold for profits in the drug market.

Joao Biehl argues how in the case of Brazil, psychopharmaceuticals became central to the story of how personal lives could "be made and unmade in the moment of socioeconomic transformations" as new types of overprescriptions and psycho-pharmaceutical dependencies were created, also shaping people's experience of abandonment from family and kin in the context of broader social-economic inequalities, loss of employment, and the retrenchment of the state.[24] In Baltimore, the death of Freddie Gray in April of 2015 after sustaining injuries in police custody was a watershed event that displayed the nexus between violent race relations, violence displacement and marginalization of Black households, and abuses of psychopharmaceuticals. The violent unrest that erupted throughout the city, particularly the looting of pharmacies, showed how closely pharmaceutical control and violence were related. I want to briefly discuss how the relationship between pharmaceutical control and violence has persisted at a much granular level.

In April of 2015, Baltimore Police Commissioner Anthony W. Batts said that the police were working with federal counterparts to recover 175,000 units, or "doses" of prescription drugs looted from twenty-seven pharmacies and two methadone clinics when unrest erupted. Batts even said that "there were enough narcotics on the streets of Baltimore to keep it intoxicated for a year."[25] In a more generalized disorder in the context of massive protests against state violence, Jacob merely viewed the attack on pharmacies as deliberate and as an attempt to get more drugs out on the streets, as he said,

> People think about the Freddie Gray riots as racially driven but what they don't understand is that people attacked the pharmacies and their goal was to get prescription medicine on the streets.[26]

He said he interpreted the attack as one on pharmacies to get prescription medicines and circulate them on the streets, and by saying that, as a white male, he disregarded the immense amount of frustration experienced by the Black communities due to histories of policing, medical experimentation, and incarceration. I refer to the contestations and violence around pharmaceuticals as the pharmceuticalization of violence, where restrictions on access create new hostilities depending on who does or does not have access to illegal and medically prescribed medication to sustain one's treatment and/or drug habits. This violence is a product of punishments for the lack of compliance in treatment centers, which also led to clients looking for prescription medicine, illicit drugs and methadone from open-air drug markets. Pharmceuticalization of violence would thus refer to the new risks of state violence and policing, risks of reincarceration, as well as the hostilities of drug markets over delays in payments to sellers. This violence was tied to an invisible drug economy, which, as I will show later, was invisible until I understood the language, signs, and codes through which the drug market operated. The state's infrastructure of indifference led the drug markets to function, except for momentary disruptions and dispersals, as police cars, patrolled the streets outside of the treatment center, or in other moments of crisis.

DRUG EXPERIMENTATION AND VIOLENCE

I visited the place in Central Baltimore where several treatment centers were located one evening and found the place desolate, except for the cars parked and a few people running and cycling. This was very different from the description of the place that Jacob had provided when he discussed his experience of violence. Close to the treatment center where Jacob received his behavioral therapy, there was a shopping center with a normal flow of traffic. The place did not appear to be as dangerous as Jacob described, not at least during daylight. I wondered if there was a social reality of substance use and drug abuse that I simply could not understand and penetrate readily as an outsider. There were almost three treatment centers. One of them mentioned "Bring your life together!" while the other one had a much more sophisticated façade of a research center for behavioral therapy. Before showing the contrasting images of the description Jacob provided and my own experience of the place, I would like to outline a brief history of Jacob's experience in different treatment centers.

When we were returning to Jacob's place, he told me that right outside his treatment program in Central Baltimore, there was another treatment center, and both had the same security. He had previously told me that the treatment program was a dangerous place, but this time he gave me a glimpse of the informal economy of drugs that had sprung up outside the treatment programs. He described,

> You know it is almost like the dealers are openly luring their customers. They say "weed, marijuana, and cocaine." Some dealers have fixed places on the street. Some of the people enrolled in treatment programs also sold their methadone to people for money. They would sell only a few milligrams and keep the rest.[27]

Since Jacob had his personal dealer, he did not have much trouble. He told me about individuals enrolled in the treatment program who navigated between the substance use centers and the drug market outside. One episode he remembered vividly was that of a person he called "Ghost." Jacob described,

> Once he came to the treatment enter, he had not passed the urine test and wasn't given his weekly take-home medication. He was infuriated. He went outside, got his gun, and returned. He shot one of the nurses and then ordered the staff to show him where dispensers for methadone were. He chugged two jars of methadone and held a few people hostage. The police arrived in a few minutes. The police should have simply let him get a hit and pass out in a few minutes. But they shot and killed him.[28]

Jennifer Carroll shows in the context of Ukraine how MAT clinics allowed people to have a semblance of "normal" life despite their inefficiencies, but their abrupt closings had lethal impact on individuals in Crimea and Donbas in 2014 in the context of Russian involvement in the polity.[29] Ghost's experience showed that it was not necessary to close the clinic—in fact, even suspending a person from the clinic for non-compliance could result in violent consequences. In this context, Jacob understood the treatment center as a place of immense violence, and he understood suspension from programs for violations as directly contributing to violence, as he described in the example above. Jacob often referred to the treatment center as a place of danger rather than a place of care. When I accompanied him to his treatment center, he would also tell me about how common it was for clients to carry arms, or at least a dagger which could be placed on the top of a car tire, when the police patrolled the area. He talked about the ease of stabbing and running scot-free, and compared it to the gun fire which could attract everyone's attention, making the dagger the most useful of all arms.

COMPLIANCE AND RACE

There were also racial geographies and racial differences through which Jacob described his efforts at recovery while comparing it with others, mostly Black men. He also talked about the different kind of discipline he found in treatment centers with a predominantly white population compared to those with a Black population, a kind of discipline that he personally did not appreciate, nor found useful for himself. Jacob had spent a considerable amount of time in group therapy both in methadone treatment programs as well as Narcotics Anonymous (NA) sessions. The understanding of different therapeutic communities showed how some settings encouraged talking whereas others were more uni-directional in their approach toward attendees. Already, there has been a history in the United States of creating therapeutic communities centered on making the attendee confront their vulnerabilities through "attack therapy" as in the case of Synanon, which was disbanded in 1991. He differentiated the abstinence-only sessions of the NA in the city and the country which corresponded to Black and white populations, respectively. Whereas the majority of the members in the former were Black, the majority of the clients in the latter were white. In both, he suggested that the support system was completely different. While in the former, the sessions were a lot more conversational, in the latter, it was mainly about the moderator taking charge. The expectation in these sessions was that members of each meeting would be accessible to any person about to relapse. Jacob mentioned that he had collected several numbers to call if he felt like he was going to relapse, but only a handful of people responded. Clients could also sponsor others and in this way, their recovery was gauged through how many people they had referred for NA meetings.[30] Surveillance was thus dispersed in that members of the NA were encouraged to motivate and to keep their fellow NA members under check. This was a different form of discipline than a form of top-down surveillance, with risks of suspension, as in the case of many treatment centers. Here instead the emphasis was on how members could be there for each other in times of need, particularly when someone was about to relapse. Jacob had thus had a fair share of experience with abstinence but eventually failed every time and thus opted for methadone. He still agreed that there were moments when people did come to his help. Jacob gave one example that particularly struck me,

> This is when my mother was still alive. I had some 10 dollars left and I had to go to the gas station. I just really wanted someone to accompany me to the gas station because I thought I was going to relapse. People at the program did come for my help. It is all about how you say you need help. If you really explain your situation, some people are genuinely willing to help.[31]

What struck me about this was how help was sought based on whether a person had enough money to buy drugs at a particular moment in time while being unattended. As mentioned above, people in the NA can be under constant supervision and this can indeed even be welcomed when people realize that they can relapse. Jacob had always sought ways to make himself intelligible to others. It was this anxiety around how best to make his experiences intelligible that shaped Jacob's attitude toward NAs in localities with different racial demographics. In the case of the NA in the city, he remembered that the moderator used to say things like "take the cotton out of your ears and put it in your mouth," to get people to focus on listening rather than talking. Other statements he recalled from his meetings in predominantly Black populations included "you don't know anything" or that "we would have taken your help if we wanted to learn how to relapse." For Jacob, these statements demonstrated a different approach toward recovery which he felt did not work for him (in saying he was also implying that this may have been useful for the typical "Black addict"). This distinction draws on ongoing processes media representations, drug policy and social structures criminalize, demonize the addict as "useless" in public discourses in order to divert attention from exclusionary social causes.[32] Jacob thus created distinctions between himself and the archetypical Black "addict," who he suggested may have needed a much more top-down relation than him, saying, "I have been in treatment for way too long to be treated like this." By suggesting this, Jacob creating distinctions between the white "client" and Black "addict" reserving a place of open-endedness and reflexivity and therapy for himself, while justifying intense discipline for the latter, as to reproduce carceral logics of the state. I now want to consider the ways in which individuals experiment with prescription medicine while remaining compliant. This as I show has to do with an intimate knowledge of drug composition, and how it interacts with methadone or illicit drugs, as clients predict whether or not the interaction will result in "dirty urine" and their suspension from programs or not.

THE NON-COMPLIANT SUBJECT

One white male, Chris, whose first choice of drug was crystal methamphetamine told me that he was prescribed Valium, but he never misused it, unlike his mother who was able to get it prescribed and also misused it. He said, "I take only as I am prescribed, not more nor less. My mother always misuses it. She always uses excess of Valium."[33]

There was a great deal of experimentation with illegal drugs which could affect one's behavior as well as pose new dangers. For instance, one Black teenager from West Baltimore who had a young daughter stopped taking Xanax and opted instead for cocaine and heroin because he did not like his slurry speech and lack of control. Thus, instead of fully quitting drugs, individuals experimented and weighted the effects of one drug over the next and considered which one would help them maintain the greatest semblance of normality in their relations. Anthropologists have made important contributions to explore recreational uses of prescription drugs, including stimulants and sedatives, where users refer to them as if they were illegal drugs.[34] Just as individuals differently perceive the effects of drug on sense perception and their decision-making ability, they also experiment with a combination of illicit drugs, methadone and anti-anxiety pills to achieve the greatest calming effect on their nerves, without facing the risk of non-compliance in treatment centers while also enhancing their "hit."

Jacob told me about the complications that arise with urine analysis in the methadone treatment program if someone had taken drugs. One was required to get regular urine tests to prove that the recipient was taking methadone regularly. This also helped nurses and substance use counselors monitor when the person had consumed an illicit drug.[35] These kinds of tests ensured that the person did not get anyone else's urine for the test because that way traces of methadone in urine would be absent. The requirement was to show methadone in one's urine as well as the lack of any other drug. In either case, the person could be suspended from the program for almost twenty days before he or she could get tested for urine again to prove compliance to be re-enrolled in the program. This may not be the case in all treatment centers, but was the case among some of the clients I interviewed. The treatment center had placed various deterrents on drug abuse to discipline/monitor clients. Any deviation meant that the person was only punishing him or herself, and depriving oneself of methadone, which their bodies were in the process of getting adjusted to. Thus, violations were depicted as doing nothing but causing oneself harm.

Most of the clients' knowledge of drugs included their half-lives and about how long they remained in their bodies and clinically observable. I learned about how much people in treatment programs had attempted to experiment with methadone and illegal drugs simultaneously. Part of the knowledge might perhaps have been the result of clients' interactions with staff in treatment center where they learn about technical details including the chemical composition of methadone and other drugs, but I suggest that this knowledge is also experiential. Jacob said,

> You know the half-life of methadone is a day, and heroin's half-life is only a few hours. If you take 60 ml of methadone you would have to beat the quantity to get the effect of heroin. This is called beating the meth. It can be dangerous because you can keep on taking heroin to get the same effect. The thing is that methadone binds to the receptors in your brain, and then it becomes difficult to get the same impact from heroin until you drastically increase your dose. You know in the treatment center the date on which urine test is taken is random. The idea is to keep the test day a surprise. Sometimes it can be at the beginning of the month and sometimes the end. You do get a sense that you will be tested because there is a person from the lab to take your tests. Sometimes, if you are tested [at the] end of the month you can be tested again [at the] beginning of the following month. We call this the "back to back."[36]

This means that any violation can be punishable. Jacob was also aware about the realities of the drug market as many in recovery, who were poor and desperate, had no choice but to engage as small-time sellers in the absence of other means of livelihood. This was another aspect which created problems in recovering, as pressures, constraints and opportunities of the drug market were often also cited as reasons for relapsing, which included the fear of incarceration and pressures to clear existing dues (if a person had bought drugs from someone on credit). Jacob said,

> You know that the problem is that they say that the medication will solve all the problems. I often ask them about anti-anxiety pills, and they say you should just meditate. They think that if they will give extra medicine you are simply trying to die. You know if I had to die, I could do that at any moment. Why would I wait for them to give me the anti-anxiety pills to die?[37]

Another reason for engaging in the drug market was to make income especially because many clients were unable to find employment, given the increasing impediments on their reentry into formal work force. Visits to the treatment center were taken as opportunities to make income by selling prescription medicines and extra methadone. This were new networks of credit used to secure drugs for supply and sale for profits, however, the inability to return the loans could result in new hostilities in the drug market, possibly with fatal consequences. Jacob said,

> You know if someone has been prescribed Xanax, they can make up to $900 a month by selling them. That's a great amount. The person would have to take some risks such as that of being caught by the police or being robbed, but the thing is that the profit can still outweigh the dangers if you have a family to take care of. See, for these reasons the program does not give us anti-anxiety pills, but one can still buy them outside.[38]

Thus many engaged in drug markets to make profits. The treatment centers too perceived many to be selling extra medication in the market, and thus created limits wherever possible. Just as treatment centers attempted to create compliant subjects, clients tried their best to conceal minor violations. As Steve Farzacca has shown in the case diabetic treatment, the normalizing gaze of the clinic attempts to check whether the patient is in control or not.[39] He shows how patients compared their lab tests with tests at home to ensure that they were fully compliant. When patients made minor infractions, such as eating ice cream, they did their best to bring blood sugar back to normal, even if these attempts were unsuccessful (e.g., eating herbal medicines). The clients' violations and attempts to conceal them demonstrated how the boundaries between illicit drugs, methadone, and other prescription medicines became blurry outside the treatment center where these drugs were often bought and sold.[40]

Jacob had also faced problems several times in getting enrolled in treatment centers. After getting suspended from programs, there was often no choice but to find other programs. In the fall of 2022, Jacob had just changed his program for the third time in four years and said that he was having problems getting accepted because his blood tests did not show traces of heroin. Earlier, Jacob told that he had once purposefully taken heroin to test positive to get enrolled, showing not only how he deflected responsibility onto enrollment procedures rather than his own intentionality, but also the strict checks on enrollment in treatment programs, which excluded those who hadn't recently been on heroin, and instead focused only on those who were transitioning from heroin to methadone. Here too Jacob voiced being discriminated against because he said he wasn't an ordinary "street-junkie." In 2022, Jacob said that he no longer wanted to take heroin just to get enrolled.

POLICING DRUG ECONOMIES

After leaving the program in Greenmount, Jacob came to the one in Central Baltimire (which is when I had begun interviewing him in 2018). He said, "This was the time when there was the crack strip on North Charles right next to the block where my treatment center was located." He continued that it was now being run by a woman. He said, "What she did was whenever she sold something, she would give a signal to someone to rob the customer as soon as the transaction took place."

In this sense selling drugs and violence went hand in hand. Jacob continued,

> The problem was that at one point the crack strip expanded all the way down to the clinic to attract new customers and lure those who had been on the programs back to illicit drugs. There were a few restaurants nearby at that time. There was a coffee shop where the bathroom would be used by people to smoke crack. At one point, there would be lines in front of the toilets just to smoke crack.[41]

This also led to sites of consumption being "burnt down." I noticed that drug economies sprung up in dynamic way after every instance of being policed and ambushed. When I interviewed Jacob in 2021, he told me, "The police knew about the last few stops and were waiting for COVID-19 to end before they could start burning these places down."

When the police began their crackdown of the open-air drug market, these people took to the restaurants for their transactions until they burned every place down. Jacob had visited one coffee shop very often. He said,

> I was homeless at that time, and workers would politely ask me to leave when I was asleep. They would ask me to come back the following day. The McDonald's nearby was almost burnt down. The police conducted raids and emptied places where drugs were being sold, and this eventually led to the 'burning down' of many places.[42]

Initially, the transactions took place in open air and were visible, but later cameras were placed on the corners to monitor the activity of the dealers. After restaurants and surrounding streets had been cleared, the dealers moved to the edges to hide or escape from any police surveillance where policing directly created new "risk environments" where unsafe practices around drug use increased as dealers dispersed from public view.[43] This complicated many of the arguments in favor of the intense policing of drug activities through arbitrary cracking downs.[44] Evidence from Baltimore suggests that arbitrary crackdowns make harm reduction difficult, as users become more likely to ask others for syringes and engage in unsafe practices due to the fear of arrest,[45] with police officers generally often misinformed about the decriminalization of syringe possession, despite the hundreds of possible HIV cases legalized syringe exchange has averted in cities like Baltimore.[46]

Now when Jacob visited the treatment center, there was only one guard for both the treatment centers in the area. He said,

> I know a single guard can't do anything. When he goes inside the treatment center, anything can happen. Drug dealing takes place during different times of the

> day. There were different slots when different categories of people came. The morning is for early birds like me, then between 9 and 10 a.m. there is greater police presence, and finally, at 12, there are crowds in which dealing begins to take place. I know thirty to forty people who visit early morning.[47]

For Jacob, as much as the treatment center was a place of recovery, it was also a site where he was being lured into older habits. He said,

> At noon, the dealers camouflage themselves in crowds outside the centers. These dealers shout when they are in these crowds to attract potential customers. Once a woman was shouting on my face. When I asked her to stop, she started to shout even louder.[48]

What Jacob told next really shook me. He said,

> Now imagine that you are a heroin addict, think about it from the mindset of an addict. You are trying to quit drugs and there are people trying to lure you into buying drugs. You know this is why I think you should come with me to he treatment center. You will see how difficult it is for me to get to the program.[49]

There was something about the way Jacob described the condition of the treatment center that turned his story of abuse to that of victimhood.

His experience of treatment was indistinguishable from the daily experience of violence. There have been some restrictions on take-home flexibilities traditionally and it was only in 2020, that Substance Abuse and Mental Health Services Administration (SAMHSA) created an exception whereby a state could request a blanket exception for all stable patients in an Opioid Treatment Program (OTP) to receive take-home doses. Yet Jacob's attitude toward take-home medication was shaped by dangers of carrying methadone. He said,

> You know these days the treatment center is closed due to the coronavirus but they give meth for a week and there is always a danger of getting robbed. I go inside and they fill the bottle from a dispenser, I drink my meth and leave. After that, I usually sit outside for a smoke and then head back home as soon as possible.

People on the streets also made calculations about when the police could be more intrusive in local drug markets. There are also calculations among clients about when incarceration rates increased or decreased as Jacob said,

> You know there is one block where drug dealing still continues to take place. The police are just waiting for the COVID situation to pass so they can crack

> down on dealers. Prisons are over-crowding and the police have begun to release people with minor offenses.

This interestingly showed how prisons were not places detached from the outside as discussed earlier. In fact, the constitution of the prison was shaped by broader events that influenced the number of people incarcerated over minor offenses, which could potentially also shape how prominently drug dealing appeared on the streets.

Some of the dealers had cars parked in other blocks where they would go to get supplies for their customers. Jacob tried to introduce me to one person returning to his car. Since he was in a hurry, he did not register what Jacob had said. As dealers strolled, they maintained a semblance of ordinary pedestrians. There was nothing strange in the crowd of people. They could not be detected by cyclists and people on cars passing by. It was a world that one had to be introduced to and for which one needed to have adequate grammar. I was introduced to the world as I learned the language in which people interacted. Slowly as Jacob described what was happening, I began to look at people differently. The drug market suddenly became visible. Pedestrians now began to appear either as customers or sellers. Jacob alerted me about the crowd standing right in front of the shop and said,

> You see that crowd, that's the open-air drug market. No, don't look back yet. If the police will come and ask what they all are doing, they will simply say that they were waiting for the shop to open.

I asked Jacob if the police knew what was happening here. He said,

> A hundred percent. Right now in the virus, their only concern to make sure there are no weapons. You know all these dealers still carry weapons, but whenever the police come they simply place their weapons on the wheels of the closest vehicles and stand in front of them. See, I also carry a weapon.

Jacob's weapon, however, was a dagger which he opened right in front of me to demonstrate how it could be kept on top of the tire of the closest car. I was a little intimidated when he had opened the dagger in front of me and pointed it toward me, but I had gotten used to his way of showing otherwise deadly objects and imbuing them with meanings of self-defense, even when their mere possession could scare anyone. The murderers, Jacob told, had never gone to prison because they would just stab and run, and it was difficult to find out who the killer was. A dagger could, in other words, be a lot more lethal than a gun because of the stealth it provided in killing and running scot-free.

Those in the drug markets had known about the times of the day the police would patrol. We had decided to meet again at the treatment center. We wanted to visit the center during early hours to avoid the crowd as well as to avoid having to disperse due to the police. Jacob had mentioned in a message on the day we were supposed to meet,

> Hey buddy, I am down here, have been for 15 min. The police rode through and people scattered. I'm sitting tight, you have nothing to worry about. I imagine in 15 min, they will all come sneaking back. That's pretty common. Walking to the gas station for a coffee. You may want to text before your ride down.

On one Monday, we had planned to meet but weren't able to, and had delayed the meeting to the next day to make sure we avoided the crowd that emerged at around noon. Accompanying Jacob to the treatment center had made me realize that as much as the place was an open-drug market, for many it was also a place to simply hang out, converse and make friends. But as drugs were exchange, there were also moments of dispersals upon the patrolling of the police—many had thus learned to pre-empt police presence and regulate their movements accordingly.

POLYDRUG ABUSE

Jacob complained, "I had been prescribed anti-anxiety pills since I was a kid. This, however, was no longer the case because my counselors in the treatment program thought I was going to sell them which many people did begin to do once they had been insured. I still take Xanax except that I have to turn to my dealers for it." Many make the transition from prescription opiates to heroin due to the latter's ease of access, as has been widely observed among many white users in San Francisco and Philadelphia.[50] Jacob later described what he had heard or experienced about polydrug abuse.[51] He told me that he had learned from many others and his own experience how drugs interacted differently with methadone. He described,

> If you take alcohol, it reduces methadone in your blood. Besides, alcohol does not have any impact on me. Maybe this is because I am Irish and my threshold for getting drunk is different . . . In the case of cocaine, on the other hand, the first shot is really good if you have methadone in your blood, but you can't have the same hit, however many times you try. I tried it once and it was really bad. It really takes you down. The trick is to sleep for a few hours and wake up and try again. I think I have already told you about beating the meth. Third, you can simply take anti-anxiety pills. Do you know the reason why I need anti-anxiety pills? It is because I have these panic attacks which are the worst. It feels like I am going to die. I think about the worst thing when I get a panic attack. I can't

> breathe and my chest becomes heavy. It is really bad, but I still can't get anti-anxiety pills from my program.[52]

This experimentation with polydrug abuse was also shaped by clients' perception that opioids were purposefully smuggled out of the clinic to keep people dependent on them. Among some there was a perception that over-prescription was a form of medical neglect and even represented a form of social iatrogenesis—or the use of medicine to keep people sick, which was viewed in relation to the broader efforts by the state to police poverty.[53] Melody described, "You know these doctors get commissions for prescribing opiates. They know that they are addictive, but for their profits, they continue to overprescribe. They need to hand out a certain number of prescriptions each day. That's why they over-prescribe." According to this impression of clinical iatrogenesis, prisons and health professionals were perceived to be involved by letting prescription medicine and methadone enter drug markets which was not very different from the complicity of correctional officers in prisons who allowed drug transactions to take place behind closed doors. When I once asked Melody, another interlocutor, about what she felt about the open-drug market in the same areas as the treatment center, she replied,

> You know my counselor says that the police have a complete idea about what is happening. They let the drug market exist on purpose so that they can control the population or let people die due to overdose.[54]

Although it might appear as a stretch to think about population control by letting drug markets flourish, I suggest that it does reveal something about the way clients view the participation of the police in the facilitation of the drug trade through lax security or alternatively through shake-ups resulting in incarceration of a few, while leaving the main arteries of the drug ring unobstructed. This also demonstrates how interactions between different forms of institutional neglect from the police as well as healthcare come to be perceived by clients.[55] This reminded me of what Jacob had once said about a policeman who would never say anything to those selling drugs but simply asked them to take their activity elsewhere.

For some clients, the experience of poly-drug use made it appear as if they were still using heroin, even if now they could claim to be somewhat successful in recovery. When I interviewed a couple, they shared that although they had been clean, they were still buying promethazine and clonidine from Lexington (the open-air drug market). Mary, who I will introduce in the next chapter said,

> The two enhanced the effect of the methadone. Basically you get a hit like heroin. And it does not show up in your urine. We told our treatment centre that

> we had taken them. There was no way they could have found out. The fact that we self-reported showed that we were compliant and behaving well.[56]

Confessions were thus made to parole officers as well as counselors in order to gain their trust. Her partner who she referred to as her "husband" shared, "We had been spending up to $600 on buying these and it felt almost like we were doing drugs, it felt like copping, so we decided that we had to stop."[57]

This showed how people compared their experience of methadone with their prior experiences of heroin. They also attempted to combine chemicals to enhance their experience of methadone, but felt that these attempts only resembled the consumption of illicit drugs, though this time without the risk of being considered non-compliant in treatment centers. Drug use was still viewed as a habit—— it was the habit of using pills that made it a form of addiction, not so much the question of what exactly was taken and whether it was lesser in severity compared to heroin. It was this dependence that Mary and her husband came to construe as a problem, which even made methadone somewhat similar in the eyes of clients to heroin, if not taken without regulation. While the ability to abstain from drugs represented the success of recovery, the ability to still be able to purchase benzos and other pills for a better "hit" demonstrated failures and gaps in treatment to many in treatment centers.

WITHDRAWALS

In December of 2020, when I met Jacob, he told me that he had disappeared because he was trying to gather the money required to buy benzodiazepines to prevent an acute withdrawal. He told that he did not have either the supply or the money to prevent acute withdrawals after two days, which he himself admitted could be lethal. He asked people for fifteen dollars with the assurance that he would plan to gradually reduce his tolerance. Already in an extremely precarious situation in a treatment program, his benzo problem remained unaddressed as he continued to buy them from the black market. He found himself locked in dependence, facing an additional pressure to somehow make enough money for his daily fix or else risk having an acute withdrawal.

There were thus secondary dependencies which remained unaccounted for in treatment centers. Mary's husband told me that when he initially enrolled in treatment after having "grown up" in prisons, he had severe withdrawals. While he interpreted the first four days of withdrawals to be a consequence of heroin, he felt sick again after a brief interval of three to four days, which he attributed to fentanyl, which he said was increasingly being mixed with heroin in Baltimore. Like Mary's partner, Jacob too had complained that he was not prepared to suffer the withdrawals. Jacob enrolled in the methadone treatment program at a time when it was not as widespread. He thought there were still problems with the lack of information given by the doctors about the side-effects of methadone and withdrawals of heroin one would experience once enrolled in treatment. He said that these withdrawals included sleepless nights until shivering kicked in. Jacob protested,

> I wasn't ready for any of this. The doctor and the staff in the treatment center never told me anything about withdrawal symptoms. These include severe issues of digestion. You have to go to the toilet very frequently and become very dehydrated. The first week is alright but then the rough patch begins and lasts till about a year. You have trouble even as you tie your laces. You are sweating and have body shakes. I was never told about any of this. Just imagine if you are having such terrible withdrawal symptoms, why would you not return to drugs?[58]

One morning at the end of May 2021, I visited the treatment center in Central Baltimore for a focus group. When I arrived, I saw Jacob sitting with three women on the stairs of a building on the next block. He stood up in recognition and came to meet me. He introduced me to the three women. Two of them were visibly old, while the third one was younger and did not contribute much to our conversation. Jacob introduced me to them. I stood up, and the two women remained seated on the stairs. Jacob said, "You can ask them whatever you like." I told the women that I wanted to get to know them and learn about their experiences with substance use and becoming homeless. One of them, who was a lot more engaging, began narrating,

> Sometimes life is just terrible. We get kicked out of our homes by our own families. My brother had begun to steal and he would put the blame on me. I didn't have anything to do with the stealing. He was also on heroin. I had such a terrible time when I became homeless. Now thankfully I have a home, but the biggest heartbreak was being abandoned by my own family. I had a son and I raised him well. Yes, he made some mistakes and he was living with my parents, but I raised him very well. He died when he was twenty-five, he would have turned thirty-one the day after tomorrow, if he were still alive.[59]

She spoke without looking at me. There was grief in her voice. Meanwhile, there were a few men walking behind me who uttered, "I got loose." I realized that the low volume at which this was uttered was meant to ensure some invisibility while also luring in potential customers. Jacob returned from across the street and said in excitement, "They got footballs [benzodiazepines]."

The women abruptly left the conversation and ran across the road to the dealers. The moment of grief had turned into one of excitement in just a second. Jacob returned, and we went and stood outside the treatment center waiting for his counselor. The treatment centers and open-air drug market presented uncanny sites where care and danger appeared as juxtaposed as clients moved into and outside treatment centers and drug markets.

CONCLUSION

In this chapter, I have considered how treatment centers are perceived as both sites of careof great violence. Specifically, I have considered how the violence of treatment is viewed in direct relation with increasing control treatment centers exert over clients where treatment centers render suspension from programs as a form of self-harm through a denial of much needed methadone to clients. I have also considered how, despite the regulation of bodies in methadone treatment centers, many still try to find ways to compliment methadone use with prescription medicine to enhance their experience of methadone, which shows the neglect of secondary dependencies by treatment centers which many try to fullfill by turning to open-air drug markets, both as consumers but also as sellers, as they are brought into the vortex of the violence of drug markets due to new obligations. Here I have also considered how engagement in treatment centers and drug markets as consumers and sellers creates new exposures to violence but also new vulnerabilities due to potentially lethal withdrawals when access to pharmaceuticals is disrupted. I now consider attempts by intimate kin to both provide care to their loved ones experiencing symptoms of withdrawal, as well as the attempts to discipline recovery and substance use in homes and the violent consequences this has for individuals.

NOTES

1. J.T. Payte, "A Brief History of Methadone in the Treatment of Opioid Dependence: A Personal Perspective," *Journal of Psychoactive Drugs* 23, No. 2 (1991): 103–107. doi: 10.1080/02791072.1991.10472226
2. Ibid.
3. Ibid.
4. Daniel Moerman, *Meaning, Medicine and the 'Placebo Effect'* (Cambridge University Press, 2002); Marcia Meldrum, "'The Long Walk to the Counter': Opioid Pain-Relievers and the Prescription as Stigma," in *Prescribed: Writing, Filling, Using*

and Abusing the Prescription in Modern America, eds. Elizabeth Watkins and Jeremy Greene (Johns Hopkins Press, 2012), 184–206.

5. P. Bourgois, "Disciplining Substance Uses: The Bio-Politics of Methadone and Heroin in the United States," *Culture Medicine and Psychiatry* 24 (2000): 165–195.

6. Daniel Moerman, *Meaning, Medicine and the 'Placebo Effect'* (Cambridge University Press, 2002).

7. Kimberly Sue, *Getting Wrecked: Women, Incarceration, and the American Opioid Crisis* (University of California Press, 2019).

8. P. Bourgois, "Disciplining Substance Uses: The Bio-Politics of Methadone and Heroin in the United States," *Culture Medicine and Psychiatry*, 24 (2000): 165–195; Helen Keane, "Foucault on Methadone: Beyond Biopower," *International Journal of Drug Policy* 20 (2009): 450–452.

9. J. Friedman and M. Alicea, *Surviving Heroin: Interviews with Women in Methadone Clinics* (Florida: University Press of Florida, 2001).

10. M. Bull, *Governing the Heroin Trade: From Treaties to Treatment* (Aldershot: Ashgate, 2008).

11. S. Fraser and K. Valentine, *Substance & Substitution: Methadone Subjects in Liberal Societies* (New York: Palgrave Macmillan, 2008).

12. P. Bourgois, "Disciplining Substance Uses: The Bio-Politics of Methadone and Heroin in the United States," *Culture Medicine and Psychiatry* 24 (2000): 165–195.

13. S. Boyd et al., "Use of a 'microecological technique' to Study Crime Incidents around Methadone Maintenance Treatment Centers." *Substance Use* 107 (2012): 1632–1638.

14. Graham Mooney, "Methadone Treatment Centers and Crime," Letters to the Editor, *Substance use* (2012).

15. See S. Boyd et al. "Use of a 'microecological technique' to Study Crime Incidents Around Methadone Maintenance Treatment Centers," *Substance Use* 107 (2012): 1632–1638; A. K. Walker. "Methadone Clinics Don't Attract Crime, Study Finds: Residents Still Resistant to Clinics in Their Neighborhoods," *Baltimore Sun* (2012); B. L. Genberg et al., "The Effect of Neighborhood Deprivation and Residential Relocation on Long-Term Injection Cessation among Injection Drug Users (IDUs) in Baltimore, Maryland." *Substance Use* 106 (2011): 1966–74; Graham Mooney, "Methadone Treatment Centers and Crime," Letters to the Editor, *Substance Use* (2012).

16. For more on patients as customers see Annemarie Mol, *The Logic of Care: Health and the Problem of Patient Choice* (Routledge, 2008).

17. SJ. Nass, LA Levit, LO Gostin, *Beyond the HIPAA: Privacy Rule: Enhancing Privacy, Improving Health Through Research* (Washington, DC: National Academies Press, 2009).

18. Harris, Interview.

19. Rebecca J. Lester, "Brokering Authenticity: Borderline Personality Disorder and the Ethics of Care in an American Eating Disorder Clinic," *Current Anthropology* 50, No. 3 (2009): 281–302.

20. Shana Harris, "To Be Free and Normal: Substance use, Governance, and the Therapeutics of Buprenorphine." *Medical Anthropology Quarterly* 29, No. 4 (2015): 512–530. doi: 10.1111/maq.12232

21. During my conversations with men with an experience of incarceration, I often heard about the treatment of pedophiles as the lowest class of prisoners, See Durkin and Hundersmarch, "Pedophiles and Child Molesters," in *Extreme Deviance,* eds. Goode and Vail (Sage, 2008).

22. While there have been extensive studies on the agglomeration of drug markets and policing or the economy of drug markets, there has yet to be any systematic analysis of the intersections between treatment centers and drug markets. For studies on policing and drug economies see, J.H. Ratcliffe and T.A. Taniguchi, "Is Crime Higher around Drug-Gang Street Corners? Two Spatial Approaches to the Relationship between Gang Set Spaces and Local Crime Levels," *Crime Patterns and Analysis* 1, No. 1 (2009): 23–46. P. Reuter and R.J. MacCoun, "Street Drug Markets and Inner-City Neighborhoods: Matching Policy to Reality," in *Urban America: Policy Choices for Los Angeles and the Nation,* eds. J. B. Steinberg, D. W. Lyon and M. E. Vaiana (Santa Melody, CA: Rand Corporation, 1995), 227–251.

23. Liz Bowie, "Baltimore Man Convicted of Selling Large Quantities of Prescription Out of Medical Facility," *Baltimore Sun* (May 4, 2018).

24. Joao Biehl, "Life of the Mind: The Interface of Psychopharmaceuticals, Domestic Economies, and Social Abandonment," *American Ethnologist* 31, No. 4 (2004): 476.

25. Justin George and Scott Dance, "Drugs on Baltimore Streets Could Keep It High 'for a year,' Batts Says," *The Baltimore Sun* (June 4, 2015).

26. Jacob, Interview.

27. Jacob, Interview.

28. Jacob, Interview.

29. Jennifer J. Carroll, *Narkomania: Drugs, HIV and Citizenship* (New York: Cornell University Press, 2019).

30. For the structure of Narcotics Anonymous, see Mark Peyrot, "Narcotics Anonymous: Its History, Structure and Approach," *International Journal of the Substance Uses* 20, No. 1 (1985). Public health interventions require certain performances by subjects to demonstrate their obedience to the regime of biopolitics. Here I am reminded of Emma Tarlo's study of forced sterilizations during the emergency period where she uses the concept of co-victimization to refer to people in Delhi being made to get themselves sterilized and sell their certificates to people in the bureaucracy who, in turn, need to show their superiors that they have motivated people to get themselves sterilized to retain their jobs. Victims were not only people who would not have gotten a piece of land if they had not given up their reproductive capacity, but also those who needed to prove that they had motivated others in getting themselves sterilized. See Emma Tarlo, "Body and Space in a time of Crisis: Sterilization and Resettlement During Emergency in India," eds. Veena Das, Arthur Kleinman, Mamphela Ramphele and Pamela Reynolds in *Violence and Subjectivity* (University of California Press, 2000).

31. Jacob, Interview.

32. Merrill Singer and J. Bryan Page, *The Social Value of Drug Addicts: Uses of the Useless* (Routledge, 2016).

33. Chris, interview.

34. G. Quintero, G. and M. Nichter, "Generation RX: Anthropological Research on Pharmaceutical Enhancement, Lifestyle Regulation, Self-Medication and Recreational Drug Use," in *A Companion to Medical Anthropology,* eds. M. Singer and P.I. Erickson (2011). doi: 10.1002/9781444395303.ch17

35. For more on urine surveillance in treatment centers, see Stuart L. Nightingale, William W. Michaux, Penelope C. Piatt, "Clinical Implications of Urine Surveillance in a Methadone Maintenance Program," *International Journals of the Substance Uses* 7, No. 2 (1972): 403–414, Avram Goldstein and Byron W. Brown, Jr. "Urine Testing in Methadone Maintenance Treatment of Heroin Substance use," *JAMA* 214, No. 2 (1970): 311–315.

36. Jacob, Interview.

37. Jacob, Interview.

38. Jacob, Interview.

39. Steve Ferzacca, "Actually, I Don't Feel That Bad": Managing Diabetes and the Clinical Encounter," *Medical Anthropology Quarterly* 14 (2000): 28–50. doi: 10.1525/maq.2000.14.1.28

40. This means that the illicit use of methadone originating from the clinic also continues alongside drugs like heroin. According to a research conducted on illicit use of methadone out of 559 IV users in Montreal, the use of heroin with along with methadone was the highest, compared to methadone use in the cocaine/heroin and cocaine only group. See Pierre Lauzon, et al., "Illicit Use of Methadone among IV Drug Users in Montreal," *Journal of Substance Abuse Treatment* 11, No. 5 (1994): 457–461.

41. Jacob, Interview.

42. Jacob, Interview.

43. T. Rhodes, "Risk Environments and Drug Harms: A Social Science for Harm Reduction Approach," *The International Journal on Drug Policy* 20, No. 3 (2009): 193–201. doi: 10.1016/j.drugpo.2008.10.003

44. Methods of drug market enforcement are diverse and include: sweeps involving the deployment of numerous officers in a defined area for short periods; substantial increases in the number of officers in a given area over an extended period; deployment of undercover officers who act as prospective dealers or drug users, and who perform "buy and busts," or may make "test purchases" of drugs which are later analysed; and surveillance using closed-circuit television and other technologies. David Dixon and Phillip Coffin, "Zero tolerance policing of illegal drug markets," *Drug and Alcohol Review* 18, No. 4 (1999): 477–486. doi: 10.1080/09595239996338; J.A. Greene, "Zero Tolerance: A Case Study of Police Policies and Practices in New York City," *Crime & Delinquency* 45, No. 2 (1999): 171–187. doi: 10.1177/0011128799045002001; T. May, M. Edmunds, and M. Hough, "Street Business: The Links Between Sex and Drug Markets," *Police Research Series Paper* (London: Home Office, 1999), 118; Jessica Jacobson, "Policing Drug Hot-Spots" (1999); Lynn Zimmer, "Proactive Policing Against Street-Level Drug Trafficking,"

American Journal of Police 9 (1990). Drug market approaches often involve traditional policing methods which include the use of "hands on" approaches (e.g., body searches), street-level chases between drug users and police, and physical restraint, see J. Kersten, "Police Powers and Accountability in a Democratic Society: Introductory Report," *European Journal on Criminal Policy and Research* 8 (2000): 237–245. doi: 10.1023/A:1008798412206. Drug market enforcement aims to achieve several goals including disrupting established markets and thereby reducing public disorder as well as interrupting supply and driving up drug prices and increasing the time drug users spend searching for drugs. See J. P. Caulkins, "Local drug markets response to focused police enforcement," *Operations Research* 41, No. 5 (1993): 848–863; M. Hough and M. Natarajan, "Introduction: Illegal Drug Markets, Research and Policy," in *Illegal drug markets: From Research to Policy*, eds. M. Hough and M. Natarajan (Monsey, NJ: Criminal Justice Press, 2000); M.A.R Kleiman, *Against Excess: Drug Policy for Results* (New York: Basic Books, 1992); M. Lee, "London: "Community Damage Limitation" through Policing," in *European Drug Policy and Enforcement,* eds. N. Dorn, J. Jepsen, and E. Savona (Basingstoke: Macmillan, 1996); K. Murji, *Policing Drugs* (Aldershot: Ashgate, 1998). Many studies also critique approaches that prompt drug users to refrain from drug use or enter treatment out of the fear of adverse consequences (e.g., arrest, incarceration) or by making habits difficult to sustain due to rising prices. See D. Weatherburn and B. Lind, "The Impact of Law Enforcement Activity on a Heroin Market," *Substance Use* 92, No. 5 (1997); L. Zimmer, "Proactive Policing Against Street-Level Drug Trafficking," *American Journal of Police* 9, No. 1 (1990): 43–74. While the impact of drug market enforcement on crime and public order has long been investigated, recently there has also been a shift to consider the health and social impacts of these approaches. See S. Burris, K.M. Blankenship and M. Donoghoe, "Addressing the "risk environment" for Injection Drug Users: The Mysterious Case of the Missing Cop," *Milbank Quarterly* 82, No. 1 (2004): 125–156; L. Maher and D. Dixon, "Policing and Public Health: Law Enforcement and Harm Minimization in a Street-Level Drug Market," *British Journal of Criminology* 39, No. 4 (1999): 488–512.

45. N. Flath, K. Tobin, K. King, A. Lee, and C. Latkin, "Enduring Consequences From the War on Drugs: How Policing Practices Impact HIV Risk Among People Who Inject Drugs in Baltimore City," *Substance Use & Misuse* 52, No. 8 (2017): 1003–1010. doi: 10.1080/10826084.2016.1268630; see also D. Broz, N. Carnes, J. Chapin-Bardales, D.C. Des Jarlais, S. Handanagic, C.M. Jones, R.P. McClung and A.K. Asher, "Syringe Services Programs' Role in Ending the HIV Epidemic in the U.S.: Why We Cannot Do It Without Them." *American Journal of Preventive Medicine* 61, No. 1 (2021): S118–S129. doi: 10.1016/j.amepre.2021.05.044

46. M.S. Ruiz, A. O'Rourke, S.T. Allen, D.R. Holtgrave, D. Metzger, J. Benitez, K.A. Brady, C. P. Chaulk and L.S., "Using Interrupted Time Series Analysis to Measure the Impact of Legalized Syringe Exchange on HIV Diagnoses in Baltimore and Philadelphia," *Journal of Acquired Immune Deficiency Syndromes* 82 Suppl 2, No. 2 (2019): S148–S154. doi: 10.1097/QAI.0000000000002176; Leo Beletsky, Grace E. Macalino, Scott Burris, "Atttiudes of Police Officers Towards Syringe Access,

Occupational Needle Sticks, and Drug Use: A Qualitative Study of One City Police Department in the United States," *International Journal of Drug Policy* 16, No. 4 (2005): 267–271.

47. Jacob, Interview.

48. Some scholars have considered how criminal activity disperses due to street-level law enforcement and CCTV surveillance. We will later see how the drug markets concentrate and disperse due to anticipation of police activity. Due to the threat of police action, drug trade and consumption may spread to public toilets, walkways, stairwells, etc. Thus, surveillance leads to the use of less desirable settings putting users in greater risk such as the spread of disease but also the failure to get emergency help in preventing the location from coming under the attention of the law enforcement. This dispersal therefore leads to the drug problem to become more widespread. This leads Maher and Dixon to conclude that that the successes of police crackdowns and their impact on drugs markets may be won at substantial costs, raising doubts about their value. See Lisa Maher and David Dixon, "Policing and Public Health: Law enforcement and Harm minimization in a street-level drug market," *British Journal of Criminology* 39, No. 4 (1999): 488–519.

49. Jacob, Interview.

50. Sarah G. Mars, Philippe Bourgois, George Karadinos, Fernando Montero, Daniel Ciccarone, "'Every 'never' I ever said came true'; Transitions from Opioid Pills to Heroin Injecting,"

51. According to a study, the 2014 Affordable Care Act (ACA) Medicaid expansions led to 19 percent increase in Medicaid-paid prescription relative to states that did not expand. In expansion states, increases in drug utilization were larger in geographical areas with higher uninsured rates prior to the ACA. Moreover, the increases in prescription drug utilization were greater in larger Hispanic and Black populations. See Ausmita Ghosh, Kasoli Simon and Benjamin D. Sommers, "Prescription Drug Use: Evidence from the Affordable Care Act," *National Bureau of Economic Research* (2017). Restrictions in accessing opioids represent a shift toward more rigid standards for prescription due to the development of Prescription Drug Monitoring Programs which allow doctors to know whether patients have been abusing opioids. For changes in standards of prescription i.e., the move from prescribed to over-the-counter (OTC) drugs compared to an opposite move in the case of opioids, see Jeremy Greene and David Herzberg, "Hidden in Plain Sight: Marketing Prescription Drugs to Consumers in Twentieth Century," *American Journal of Public Health* 100, No. 5 (2010): 793–803. An additional challenge has been posed by the emergence of new psychoactive drugs (NPS) since mid-2000s such as fentanyl, which has challenged traditional approaches to drug monitoring, surveillance, control and public health responses. They are considered as alternatives to controlled substances and may be part of established illicit drug use repertoires, be diffused within medical black markets (including counterfeit products) and be more established as illicit drugs in the developed world, see Amy Peacock et al. "New Psychoactive Substances: Challenges for Drug Surveillance, Control and Public Health Responses," *Lancet* 394 (2019): 1668–1684.

52. Jacob, Interview.

53. Emma Varley and Saiba Varma, "Introduction: Medicine's Shadowside: Revisiting Clinical Iatrogenesis," *Anthropology & Medicine* 28, No. 2 (2021): 141–155.

54. Melody, Interview.

55. In the 1970s and 80s, some physicians believed that long term opioids were safe for usage. They gave the patients confidence by giving them the impression that they could be trusted with their prescriptions. Opioid manufacturers such as Purdue Pharma even made the case for chronic opioid therapy until the US Drug Enforcement Authority began to prosecute physicians overprescribing opioids to their patients, see Marcia L. Meldrum, "The Ongoing Opioid Prescription Epidemic: Historical Context," *American Journal of Public Health* 106, No. 8 (2016): 1365–1366.

56. Mary, Interview.

57. Wayne, Interview.

58. Jacob, Interview. For more on the unaddressed side-effects of methadone treatment, see Adam R. Winstock, Toby Lea, and Janie Sheridan, "Patient's Help-Seeking Behavior for Health Problems Associated with Methadone and Buprenorphine Treatment," *Drug and Alcohol Review* 27, No. 4 (2009).

59. Julia, Interview. Scholars have considered the relationship between drug use and crime, see D. N. Nurco, T. E. Hanlon and T. W. Kinlock, "Recent Research on the Relationship between Illicit Drug Use and Crime, Particularly Stealing," *Behavioural Sciences & the Law* 9 (1991): 221–242. Others have considered the role of substance use in straining family relations particularly when addicts resort to stealing in low-resource settings, which reveals the limits of care by family members. For the denial of emotional and monetary support by families of those incarcerated in Baltimore, see Veena Das, Jonathan M. Ellen, "On the Modalities of the Domestic," *Home Cultures* 5, No. 3 (2015): 349–371. For extended families taking care of children of the addicted, see Marina Barnard, *Drug Substance Use and Families* (Jessica Kingsley Publishers, 2006); Linda M. Burton, "Black Grandparents Rearing Children of Drug Addicted Parents: Stressors, Outcomes and Social Service Needs," *The Gerontologist* 32, No. 6 (1992): 744–751.

Chapter 6

Substance Use, Discipline, and Household Disorders

People with substance abuse problems often carry unresolved experiences from their childhoods but also experience new tensions as they live with others in housing provided by treatment centers. Some treatment centers in Baltimore provide methadone treatment but have also supported individual or couple's housing. Drug use and recovery create new therapeutic communities. One example of this is provided by Jarret Zigon, who writes about one of his interlocutors "dying with" his mother, which binds him to the anti-drug war community when he finds that he "has an obligation to disclose and open this community to others and care for them as they arrive."[1] He goes on to write about how the bereaved take the deaths of loved ones as opportunities to plead for abstinence-only ideologies.[2] My own concern is not so much with how families take deaths as events to support abstinence, but to make a case for a therapeutic community in which there is both a form of care for those suffering from withdrawals and violent behaviors and suspicion toward those who not able to fully transition from heroin to methadone use. In drawing the reader's attention to this aspect, my goal is also to reveal the delicate networks of kin relations and the continuous labor they require, through which I also interpret relapses, sustained collective efforts at recovery, and new forms of suspicion toward those deemed as unwilling to heal.[3] An example that comes to mind in this regard is that of Keisha from Meyers' ethnography on recovery in Baltimore, whose drug use, as Meyers argues, was not a repetition of Keisha's mother's substance use, nor was it an escape; instead, Keisha's return to drugs represented pressures of caring for her neglected siblings and a strategy to force her mother to care for them after her own institutionalization.[4] But my concern is not only to consider intimacies and care but also forms of violence inflicted on intimate others in different stages of recovery.

In my interviews, I observed that men and women got into relationships during treatment and referred to each other as husbands and wives to give their relationships a semblance of stability. Men and women created aspirations for conjugality in which they would be able to set up their own houses and make money to have independence. In residences provided by treatment programs, there were several individual rooms, each occupied by a couple. Residents often got into squabbles over limited resources. According to Mary, in the house where she lived before, there would often be disputes over eating each other's food. She did not face the same problem at her current residence. Couples were always competing for limited resources. When I introduced my study to Chris, he promised to refer me to more participants in return for the promise of getting tips for each referral. It turned out that most of the participants I would recruit also shared the same residence as Chris. During my interviews, couples often closed doors to talk more freely, while others referred to their stay in the residence as temporary as they were saving enough money to complete treatment before they could officially enter the job market and get a home of their own. While in some cases housing was provided by the treatment center, in other cases two or more persons in substance use treatment programs were supported by generous individuals who rented clients portions of row houses. Given the fact that a lot of my interlocutors came out of prison after many years, sometimes even decades, they were often isolated from their biological kin and developed fictive bonds with their roommates. In this chapter, I will show how individuals in treatment understand the domestic space and the competition engendered by it as causes of the failure of their treatment. It is my contention that opioid-policy has yet to fully appreciate the dynamics of domestic living arrangements and their implications for success or failure of treatment. By drawing upon my visits to households, I provide an ethnographic perspective on the lives of people in treatment and show some of the challenges they experience due to precarity, fights with roommates and threats of evictions. I consider two modalities of caregiving: one in which intimate kin provide care for withdrawal symptoms, which they view as forms of illness; and the other, which is punitive and may even be violent, where partners police each other's drug habits in ways that result in the unmaking of their own recovery as well as diminishing the self-esteem of intimate partners due to excessive discipline that creates the conditions for relapse. As in the rest of the book, the dialectic between the "client in recovery" and the "drug addict" will remain an important one, as it is often the former's suspicion toward the latter that creates the conditions for hostilities.

Anthropologists have made major strides in exploring the ambivalence in family relations among those experiencing substance use. Yet the gap between anthropological knowledge and policy still remains wide, as causes and experiences of substance use continue to be viewed as individualized, rather than shaped by family and broader social relations. As Angela Garcia has shown, the relations among people suffering from substance use are very complex as they are based on mutual protection and care, especially as children become "natural" drug partners for parents and even shoulder the responsibility of ensuring supply during times of drug-related illnesses, interpreted as a form of "care," which may even result in children being incarcerated.[5] This, according to Garcia, may also be seen as a sort of role-reversal in that the child becomes the primary caretaker, who navigates multiple responsibilities to parents and children and the risks of incarceration.[6] Yet what is ignored in this formulation is that drug-trajectories within families may drastically vary in that one person may opt for treatment, which may result in new forms of discipline in the lives of family members, whose effects are often violent for the family, and may generate the social conditions for a relapse. This is especially the case when one member is in recovery and the other continues to use illicit drugs. As shown by Marcia Meldrum, the reliance on prescription-based drugs also results in increasing disciplinary pressures by intimate partners, resulting in the loss of agency among patients and the loss of self-esteem and self-belief.[7]

There is also a rich diversity of experiences, with some individuals completely detached from their parents while others maintain contact and try to come to terms with their parents' substance use, resulting in a persistent feeling of absence among children.[8] Conversely, it is also possible for parents to display moral striving even after having neglected children, especially in conditions in which their attachment and responsibility are challenged.[9] In other cases, parental attention may be diverted to a sibling who is experiencing illness.[10]

Why is it important to be mindful of multiple competing trajectories of substance use and recovery that generate the impetus for violent forms of discipline and estrangement from the family? One can take a lead from Baltimore-based drama series *The Corner*, in which one can notice how the woman's descent into substance use results in physical violence by her husband, which in turn leads to the wife taking her husband to court. These episodes are common, and partners continue to live with each other, invoking retribution by the state to teach their partners a lesson.[11] One example of this is when the wife reports on her husband when he hides his drugs from her or does not share them equally, where the wife also refuses to bail him out.[12] Even while the wife continues to suffer from substance use, she turns her violence onto her son, who, under conditions of precarity, resorts to selling drugs on the streets, which results in retaliation from the son and even physical violence from him as the mother's authority is resisted. Yet, the mother eventually joins treatment and undergoes recovery, whereas the husband continues to use drugs, showing the multiplicity of treatment and substance use trajectories within the family that become the focal point of conflicts. Yet even as families continue to be riddled by conflict, as Clara Han shows in her study of neoliberal Chile, where women and men are locked in abusive relations yet remain dependent on each other and their parents, acute symptoms provide moments of respite for families to come together or resume normal relations.[13]

The inability to fully acknowledge the complexity of these relations in courts and treatment intensifies social suffering, as shown in earlier chapters. Each social relationship experiences a unique and new set of vulnerabilities when families go through the experience of substance use. As we explore the ways in which illness is experienced in the family, it is also important to be mindful of the changing structures of the family, such as children growing up under the care of grandparents,[14] or when the loss of parental authority within the family results in parents over-exerting themselves, further estranging children from parents.[15] Yet there has been a dearth of anthropological work that explores how substance use shapes social relations at home, with much of the existing work focusing on the experience of treatment.

There are important leads that we can draw from to extend the pressures faced by families in the context of substance use. For example, Bernard and McKeganey have shown how chronically relapsing conditions caused by substance use create new demands for care work.[16] In terms of parental abuse, it is possible that the immediate emotional needs of children are sacrificed to the need to secure the next hit.[17] Even children of parents who are enrolled in methadone treatment are likely to have medical or nutritional needs that may remain untreated for many years. Scholars have also reflected on the ways in which drug use negatively affects the establishment of emotional bonds between parents and children. In fact, physical neglect rarely comes alone but is often accompanied by abuse.[18] As shown by Hein and Honeymoon, maternal aggression is often accompanied by problems of drug use. They suggest that mothers who use drugs are much more likely to impose harsher punishments.[19] Just as networks of care are tested within the family, children and adults, both with substance use problems or indirectly affected by it, seek affection and care elsewhere, such as with other relatives.[20] People with substance use and an experience of homelessness also experience isolated lives as their families break relations with them in case of their stealing habits.

Before I consider the different intimacies and hostilities created by the competing pressures of substance use and recovery. I would like to consider the extent to which, in recent days, knowledge about substance use as inherited has been taken up and internalized in a way that eclipses broader socio-economic determinants and violent personal histories as causes of substance use problems. By describing the use of biological frameworks for substance use, I also make a case for why it is necessary to consider social experiences, even if there has been a push in recent days to consider the biogenetic causes of substance use.

"INHERITING" SUBSTANCE USE

I once met Melody, a middle-aged woman whose boyfriend had served in the military. When I visited the treatment center, I saw her with her boyfriend. I had also seen Sarah and her boyfriend. Two of these couples, whom I had seen going to one of the clinics in central Baltimore early in the morning, demonstrated how much treatment depended on collaborative efforts by couples. When I met Melody, I learned that she needed a few dollars every day for her daily "medication." By this time, I had learned that people who said that they needed to pay for the medication were trying to euphemize their treatment, which continued to be stigmatized. I did not want to rush to any conclusions and listened attentively to what Melody said. Melody said that she visited a psychiatrist as well as a treatment center. Our conversation, which had started with her own medication, later turned to her psychiatric care. Melody, like many other patients, used the language of medicalization to conceal the fact that she had also been enrolled in a drug treatment program. The fact that Melody also visited the psychiatrist next door meant that she could make a claim to being a genuine case of depression or anxiety to avoid gaining any attention to her drug problem. She used the word "medication" strategically to refer to both enrollment in the drug treatment program as well as visiting the psychiatrist. When I inquired Melody if she had trouble accessing psychiatric and addiction treatment as a woman, her response was different from Jacob's, for whom accessing treatment and especially getting enrolled had been difficult, as I have already shown. Melody, on the other hand, was properly screened for environmental factors, such as domestic abuse, and genetic predispositions by her psychiatrist. Melody had somehow internalized that she had a "gene" for depression, which influenced her turn to drugs.[21] She understood herself to be genetically predisposed to anxiety and depression, which, of course, could intersect with other life events. She said, "I probably got it from my father." Melody was particularly close to her father, who had divorced her mother when Melody was sixteen. Melody's father passed away, and after his death, she did not have anyone to stay with and became homeless. She had two half-sisters. She mentioned that she liked the younger one better than the elder one. The elder one too suffered from substance use. The younger one had the burden of taking care of her children as well as the eldest sister. I understood in this interview and in others that experiences of substance use and homelessness were often described either through responsibility to those suffering from substance use or via the burden caused by those with substance use to the caregivers. Close relatives denying help to those suffering from substance use was also a possibility.[22] The biological and fictive relations in biological and stepfamilies, respectively, did not always provide the network of care women and men could draw upon. Melody was in touch with one of her uncles. While there was an idea that one could not rely on stepfamilies, the same could also be the case with biological relatives, with whom some had lost all contact. At the same time, the pressure of being excluded from the kin network was a manifestation of possible contentions that Melody had to navigate between biological and stepfamily. This reliance on the stepfamily also overlapped with her grievance toward the father for having left Melody's biological mother. Her mother had been at a nursing home. Melody had maintained contact but did not meet her often. The references to the methadone treatment center in her description remained elusive. She had been given a cell phone, which she would use for her online counseling sessions, but having to telecommunicate drained her limited internet, which she thought could have been better used on other things.

In recent days, there has been a surge of literature that has shown how genetic factors may contribute to the occurrence of depression and other mental illnesses.[23] Like Melody, I found that many of my interlocutors understood their problems with mental illness as partly a product of their circumstances but also bioloigically inherited. Instead of making a case for how a "gene" exists or doesn't exist which I leave for scientists to deliberate, I am much more interested in how ideas of genetic predisposition gained currency as an explanatory model among people who struggled with substance use in my study. In fact, in 2008, the director of National Institute on Drug Abuse, Nora Valkow, even said that a certain type of dopamine receptor known as D2 might someday be used to predict whether someone will become addicted to alcohol, cocaine or heroin.[24] Many historical and sociological works have shown how scientific discourses have shaped our understanding of the causes of mental illness, as scientific discourses around psychiatric care shifted from psychoanalytical to neurochemical explanations.[25] As Epstein has shown, even scientific discourses can be shaped by grassroot activism, which means that these scientific discourses are not as value-neutral as they appear to be.[26] Although my goal here is not to show the discursive practices that generate scientific discourses so much as to show how these discourses are taken up as a way to explain the existence of substance use problems among individuals. Substance use counselors, who often serve as gatekeepers of scientific knowledge and are in continuous communication with clients, often also use such explanatory factors, which explains why people come to understand their substance use as an inherited problem. Yet the biological cannot be viewed independently of the social in that when people refer to their problems as inherited, they implicitly also refer to the social conditions that generate addictive states among parents as well as children.[27] I argue that this explanatory model is a product of their interactions with psychiatrists, therapists and counselors who serve as gatekeepers of scientific knowledge. My contention is that while some individuals understand their illness as genetically predisposed, they often also draw upon their childhood memories to talk about how it was a social condition—consisting of family disputes, abuse and economic precarity—within their households that led them to substance use. In other words, it was abuse, neglect and violence within the domestic that they interpreted as the cause of their eventual turn to drugs in a way that biological and social explanations for substance use collapsed, and thus participants even understood maintaining distance from close relatives as a way to somehow overcome their problems with substance use. Moving from childhood memories of what it was like to grow up in homes where parents had a drug problem to the tensions existing within households in which people under treatment lived, I ask how notions of care and love were reconfigured such that they represented being able to maintain each other's substance use habits and thus wellbeing in order to avoid withdrawals, and conversely, also ensuring that emotional support was provided to successfully complete recovery. I argue that as much as substance use was something for which members could be excluded from households, addictive states were also a product of reliving horrors of growing up in conditions where members faced competing pressures of treatment and abuse.

One of my interlocutors, Chris, told me about frustratingly about his mother in 2022,

> She basically abandoned me. She was bipolar and had manic depression. I can't stay sober as long as she is around. It is the atmosphere which makes me feel like there will be a relapse. There is always this negativity. She has herself experienced problems of abuse. When her mother died, her stepfather blamed the children for her death, and used to physically beat and sexually abuse them. The only father that she ever knew sexually abused her.[28]

For Chris, it was not as if the mother was responsible for his illness, but she somehow unintentionally brought her children into the vortex of the abusive relationships she had experienced with her stepfather. According to Chris, the mother's own experiences may have also prevented her from giving her children the parental love they deserved. Chris complained,

> In her world. She was the only one. She basically wants me to be her friend, when I am not her friend. I am her son, and that is what I find really problematic.[29]

Yet, Chris also viewed his turn to drugs as arising out of the need to have a calming effect while having a racing mind, which, according to him, was a product of his ADHD. He would say, "I would not have been sitting like this, If I had not taken my Adderall." Thus, Chris showed that one cannot view illness as divorced from its biological and social aspects. The interpretation of hereditary factors also generated social histories of the family and its domestic problems, which were considered as contributing to the turn to drugs. I would now like to consider how many of my interlocutors referred to their troubled childhoods as causes of their illness. Similarly, other homeless individuals in my study also shared that they understood their mental health problems as inherited. Given the biologization of substance use, how then do people experiencing substance use make sense of their problems as hereditary, and what are the ways that, in doing so, they also shed light on their social experiences as evidence for these intergenerational problems?

The story of childhood abuse was common to hear during the study. Some of my interlocutors mentioned that they felt that their parents were more like friends rather than parents, in that they wanted their children to consume drugs with them, while children wanted parents to maintain at least a degree of parent-like behavior. In Jacob's case as well as Mary's, despite the conditions in which they were raised, challenges to parental authority led parents to take their kids to psychiatrists to see if anything was wrong with them. Mary's story was much more violent in that she shared that both her parents were involved in substance use and that there was a lot of violence at home. When she was six, she found out that her parents were involved in substance use. They smoked, and while they were not abusive themselves, Mary said,

> They had other people coming. The drug dealers used to sexually abuse me. I have been raped twice and once the dealer put the marks of burnt cigarettes on my genitals. Whenever I look at them, I remember the violence I have gone through as a child.[30]

Her husband was uneasy as she shared her experience, saying, "it is difficult to see someone you have loved so dearly go through this." The household was not a protected site, and the parents, who had themselves become dependent on their dealers under the influence of drugs, were not able to do much to protect their children. When Mary turned seventeen and graduated from high school, she left her home. Mary's first husband was abusive. She had three daughters with him. Mary had no longer maintained a relationship with her father. While the court allowed that she could meet her children twice a week, she had not been able to do that, as she was concentrating on becoming clean and getting a job so that "she could get her kids back." As mentioned in chapter 2, the wish to reunite with children from former partners, with whom one was in violent and abusive relations, was usually not missing. In fact, individuals like Mary struggled to make sure that they could become independent in order that they could contribute to their children's lives in a meaningful way. The same was the case with Chris, who recently talked to her daughter for the first time on a video call. Mary showed her commitment to her kids by saying,

> I stopped taking drugs before every kid. But after I gave birth, I started again. After Hailey I started again, and then after Kayle, I just moved to Baltimore [from the county]. Ever since, I have been jumping between different programs.[31]

She had been put out of programs for fighting or whenever she relapsed. This also showed the power of the treatment centers to penalize their clients by disregarding whatever minimal amount of effort they had already put in and instead getting them to start from scratch, as I discussed in the analysis of treatment centers in the last chapter. She was also suspended when she violated the curfews, as her movement was often tracked by the treatment center. According to her, the problem with some treatment programs was also that they made going to group meetings compulsory, that too four times a week, which meant that going to a treatment center was like a job. Even while being at home, individuals had to be mindful of any violations. Clients interpreted the treatment center's supervision and monitoring as attempts to reinstitute domesticity in the lives of the clients and to make them realize that they need not always be chasing their next hit. The reason for describing clients' memories of violent familial relations is to show that biological relations had almost lost their signification, and thus the attempt in couple's housing was to recreate intimacy, fidelity and trust that had been violated while growning up in relations of abuse and neglect. While many thought that they may have had a "gene" for substance use, many thought the inheritance was not biological—instead, it was the inheritance of isolation, feelings of being violated, and a lack of security that shaped the experience of substance use, which was not only a reproduction of parental habits but also an attempt to numb painful memories. I want to briefly consider how, despite such painful memories, there were still forms of care and intimacy that mainly involved attending to withdrawal symptoms and overdosing creating new ambivalences and forms of guilt that many found hard to overcome even during recovery.

Substance use also created new forms of intimacy, which was an attempt to make up for the guilt of having lost loved ones to drug use. For instance, Mary shared the guilt she carried after her father, who was living in a hotel then, asked her for beers, benzos and heroin. She told me that the usual dealer was not available, so she tried a new one. She continued,

> I told my dad to be careful. I just got him all the stuff because I did not want him to suffer. I could not see him being sick. My help to him was purely out of care. No one else would have gone to help him. I did. But he died, and I will carry the guilt with me all my life.[32]

Thus, fixing other people's cravings and preventing their withdrawals was also interpreted as a form of care, but this form of care also generated new forms of guilt. My interlocutors also shared instances when they helped others when they had overdosed. For example, Jacob had talked about providing Naloxone to people overdosing on the streets, whereas Wayne had shared that his so-called wife helped him the last time he overdosed, which led him to develop affection toward her. This was a different kind of care than caring for withdrawals in that, in this case, it was about caring for someone under the fear of calling an ambulance. Even though emergency services no longer penalize overdoses as they had in the past, the act of caring for loved ones when they were on the borderline between life and death also created new emotions and intimacies. Yet there are also instances whereby the other, still in recovery or lacking the will to recover, was exposed to new disciplinary pressures and forms of intimate violence, which I will consider now.

RECOVERY, SUSPICION, AND HOUSEHOLDS

I now want to consider how recovery creates different subjectivities—where the "client" in recovery views the "addict" with suspicion and tacitly polices them, resulting in contestations that intensify the suffering for both. In March of 2020, the COVID-19 outbreak stranded everyone at home, and Jacob's program was off, which meant that he would be available to meet at home. We agreed to meet one morning. Jacob's flatmate was still using heroin. She was a middle-aged woman with whom Jacob had frequent squabbles. Both of them received an allowance from an acquaintance, which allowed them to find a place to rent. Whenever Jacob received the money, he got groceries for both himself and Katie. However, his roommate, Katie, would always be wasteful, he claimed. She would frequently get in touch with the donor to ask for more money, which Jacob said could become a burden on him and even mean that his help could be discontinued. Jacob claimed, "My roommate always does expensive groceries. You know she always takes a taxi to go to Giant supermaket."

Compared to this, Jacob would go to the Salvation Army on Greenmount to get cheaper groceries. Jacob said that whenever Katie was away for "work," she would always come back and eat as if she had some kind of an "eating disorder." Jacob described angrily, "And I know what kind of a work she does . . . She prostitutes herself of money." He mentioned that a few days ago she had asked the donor for money to get groceries, and all she got was milk, sugar and a few other items. He complained angrily, "I know she spends the rest of her money on crack." Jacob told me that a few days ago she had asked the donor for some money and said that she was going to get methadone from one of the trucks. Jacob said,

> She has the same insurance as I do, and I know that the trucks she's talking about were there in places like West Baltimore, but I know that they don't exist anymore. Also, methadone is free. There is no way she would have paid for it. The donor asked me about the trucks and whether the insurance required her to pay for her methadone. I told him, "I don't think so."[33]

Katie had recently begun to attend the treatment program with him. When I visited the household, he took me to his room, where he had his piano on one side and a single bed along with a table on the other. He told me that he had been smoking inside the apartment even though he was not allowed to. He showed me the empty bottles of methadone with his name on the label. He checked the dust bin for an empty bottle, and said, "I take the label off before throwing so that no one finds out that it was mine."[34] While the methadone treatment had enabled Jacob to distinguish himself from the rest, he had a sense that being on the treatment had to be concealed in particular ways. Methadone treatment could still provide certain forms of sociability with the wider social world, which many "heroin addicts" simply lacked, as I could also see playing out in Jacob's apartment.

One day in 2021, while walking in central Baltimore, Jacob told me about the issues he was having with his roommate. He recently had a fire in his kitchen, for which he thought his roommate was responsible. He attributed his roommate's irresponsible nature directly to her use of illicit drugs, despite being in a methadone program. Jacob thought she wasn't serious enough. This was a continuous source of frustration for him—as he extended surveillance of her habits outside of the domestic space to learn about her consumption patterns. One day while walking, as we crossed the road to walk to Charles Street, Jacob told me that he had once seen her meet a dealer to buy crack. Jacob continued,

> I saw her right across the street with a dealer outside my treatment center. When she saw me, she acted normally so I asked the dealer how much crack he had sold to the woman when she left. He told that the woman had paid almost a hundred dollars for it.[35]

Among those enrolled in treatment centers, there was competition about who was doing better and those who simply did not have the will to improve. As Jacob was getting his coffee, he said, "I am not saying that I am innocent.

I also buy Xanax but at least I am open about it." This showed that while Jacob was also involved in the drug market, he was particularly skeptical toward Katie, who had still not overcome her heroin problem. The problems of recovery were also shaped by the close proximity of treatment centers and the drug market in Baltimore City. Further, Jacob's suspicion about Katie's lack of effort and will to undergo recovery was a product of the same differentiating forces caused by the biopolitics of recovery that I have tracked throughout the book, and carceral attitudes entailed Jacob policing his roommate to see if she was really committed to the program.

We entered his apartment to go to his terrace and proceeded to the backyard to continue our discussion. We went to his room first, where the smell of cigarette smoke made it difficult for me to stay, and I requested Jacob if we could go outdoors. He wanted me to put the hanging carbon monoxide detector back in its place. When we entered the kitchen which had earlier caught fire out of Katie's carelessness, Jacob claimed, when he had left some oil to heat up. When his flat mate came, frightened that it would catch fire, she threw water on it. Initially, when Jacob messaged and asked if I could get him bleach and some other items to help him clean the kitchen, I thought it might have been a minor fire, but during the visit I saw that all of the walls of the kitchen had turned black. The carbon monoxide detector was lying on the floor. Jacob was thankful that people in the neighborhood did not find out, or they would have reported it. The woman who lived downstairs, whom Jacob had once introduced me to, could have called the fire brigade, and had the landlord found out, the incident could have cost Jacob and Katie their security deposit.

I met Jacob a few days later, in April of 2020, when he continued to complain about his roommate, Katie. Katie had been enrolled in the program, but Jacob thought she was still "dodging." This meant that she was still smoking crack and heroin. In addition to her lack of responsibility, what also frustrated Jacob was the fact that she could make a much stronger claim to the household because she had known the donor before Jacob and had been living in the apartment before Jacob moved in. Jacob complained, "She always acts as if I am the guest and this is her house." Jacob asked me to proceed to the back porch as he said, "Let me get my laptop." As he entered the back porch, he said,

> Whenever I am gone to the bathroom, I always find her inside my room. She acts like she has lost something or has been looking for a pack of cigarettes. You know she could just come and ask me for a cigarette when I am in my room.[36]

This showed that the household could not easily be compartmentalized into one space or another. Ownership of things and space had to be claimed almost violently. In other words, one had to physically guard his or her possessions by carrying them along even while moving around the apartment. This ranged from food items to other personal belongings like laptops, cell phones, and so on. The line between sharing and stealing had also become blurry. Jacob knew that his items could be stolen, but he had to accept this reality.

The roommate's irresponsibility was tied to not being able to follow her program seriously. Jacob said,

> Basically, the problem with my roommate is that she is taking methadone, but she is probably still used to the same hit which is why she might be having a problem. If you take heroin in a syringe or a cigarette you get a hit immediately, which is not the case with meth. Methadone usually takes time to get absorbed in your blood. This is because you drink methadone.[37]

During another visit, he told me that his place was going to be in a mess. He asked me to be quiet, and I nodded. I followed him into the apartment, and he told me that he was going to show me his roommate's clothes that had been lying in the bathtub for over two months now. He had said angrily,

> It is disrespectful to me and to her. At first, I did not want to shower with her clothes because I did not want them to get dirty, but then I realized that I did not care anymore.[38]

We proceeded to the back porch, and he whispered, "She is probably sleeping, she had gone out *to work* last night." Upon inquiring about how the donor had known his roommate, he said, "Maybe she was his mistress, the donor is married. In fact, I do not think my roommate is his mistress. I think his mistress is someone else." We did not know why the donor had been providing for Jacob's roommate, even before Jacob had begun to stay in the apartment. Jacob continued,

> You know the problem is that she plays tricks, and whenever her tricks come, the guys and Katie both smoke crack and then have sex. I don't like it when this happens. You know my room is open and any guy could come in and find my laptop and other belongings lying, pick them and escape, and she would not have a clue. You know I have never been a pimp, and I have never hired a prostitute because I think prostitution is like rape, especially after my experience with being molested.[39]

Jacob further commented on the host of insecurities and new 'dangers' brought by his roommate due to her drug habits. But he was also concerned that because of drug problem, she had started to steal his food, which was another cause of concern and frustration for him.

> I don't know, she just doesn't want to work and takes coke and that is why all my sugar runs out so fast. I get five pounds of sugar and it takes only a day to

> run out of sugar. Maybe she needs the sugar rush when she is on dope. I go out to get food every day. The other day I left some pizza and when I came back, she had left only a single slice, and then I was like how is this even possible, and she said that she did not know who ate the pizza. If she was using the food supplies for her friends, then that is just wrong. She keeps her dishes in her room and never washes them. The other day she brought her dishes out of the room and simply dumped them. You know whenever she goes to do groceries, I know from my calculations that the stuff she gets does not cost more than a few dollars and the rest of the money she spends on drugs.[40]

Just as Jacob's roommate remained a source of frustration, he had to tackle his own benzo dependence. In some of our last few interviews after a gap of several months in 2022, Jacob told me he got really scared of an acute benzodiazepine withdrawal. He shared that his dealer had run out of benzos, and Jacob feared that he was going to have lethal withdrawal symptoms. His economically precarious situation also did not allow him to buy the pills at the time. He requested that his friends make donations to prevent an acute withdrawal. Preventing a potentially lethal withdrawal was linked to his lack of money and his inability to get a prescription. He told me retrospectively, "Acute benzodiazepine withdrawal is worse than heroin! I decided that I was going to try and figure out a taper. I needed every friend I had."[41] He told me about his symptoms, "Imagine, your body is just locked. You are not able to move to body. You have trouble moving your jaw. I have never experienced anything like this." Having considered how Jacob balanced the frustrations of his roommate's inability to recover with his own dependence on prescription medicine, which resulted in his own suffering, I now consider how inability to recover also led to an even more intense form of violence, which led to the undoing of one's own intentions to recover and led to relapses and often even death.

DISCIPLINING SUBSTANCE USE

To fully appreciate the effects of hostilities among individuals in treatment, it is also important to consider how substance use generates intimacies among those who are clean and those who are unable to recover. I had seen Seth a couple of times in Medfield, a small neighborhood, situated right next to Hampden. When I interviewed him in 2020, he said,

> You know I have been living in the apartment for five years, I know someone in the building who has lived here for twenty years. You won't find a place like this in Baltimore with buildings without locks. That is because there is no crime here. There are only two ways of escaping if you did something here. You can

use the woods to get to Cold Spring or use Roland Avenue. In both cases you could easily get caught. That's why it is so peaceful here.[42]

For Seth, North Baltimore was an escape from the life of disorder in the city. Moving to north Baltimore and its quiet neighborhood was an attempt to carve out of new life for himself. He had lost four of his brothers to drug overdose. He continued,

> You know I am the youngest of ten brothers *and four of them died due to drug overdose.* One was twenty-seven when he died. You know I have been there. My brothers were beautiful men if you look at them.[43]

Seth thought he was a rebel because he did not settle for a job, and when I asked him what he exactly meant by being a rebel, he referred to independence and freedom from constraints like loans, indebtedness and poverty, which many Black men around him had experienced. Seth indicated that his decision to live in Medfield was tied to carving a new life for himself, yet he was not able to separate the new set of aspirations from his love for his brothers or his past life. In other words, he was taking death and illness as opportunities—signs of second chance from God—to make new moral projects and to craft new lives for himself that would not be possible otherwise.[44] He thought his brothers were "normal" people. They even had qualities that made them great men. Having been on the path of substance as his brothers, Seth saw his present life of financial independence and thirst for knowledge as a path that was opposite to the mistakes his brothers had made.

On several occasions, I had heard strange noises of screams and thuds from his apartment before our interviews. It was as if a fight had been going on and things were being thrown around. It was evident that in Seth's home, things were not well with his girlfriend. In one interview, he looked nervous. He appeared to be running out of breath. He said,

> My girlfriend has called the police after locking herself up in the room. My girlfriend accuses me of abuse. The police will be there to arrest me. My girlfriend has been coming home late at 2 a.m. and has been smoking crack and heroin at a guy's. I could not take it anymore and wanted her to leave. I have had enough. You know I have had the same kind of a life, but I changed.[45]

During one of my household visits, I saw his girlfriend coming downstairs with her belongings. Seth was also bringing her belongings downstairs and piling them up in front of the main door. Seth had frequently complained about being locked out of his apartment. He once said, "She is high and sleeping so she doesn't know I am at the door." As I observed during a household visit, his girlfriend came and placed her ear on the door of an adjacent apartment possibly to see if Seth was inside. It appeared as if she knew who Seth could possibly rely on in moments like those. Later, I saw two policemen walking downstairs after having cleared the scene. The situation had been cleared, and Seth was now back to his apartment. In my next interview, Seth told me about what had happened in detail,

> My girlfriend is in her 30s but likes to act as if she is in her 20s. She can't stay still. She needs to understand that life can be pretty boring. She just does not want to stay still. She keeps running after dope. Right now she is living with her mother. She has had a difficult life. We had been together for three years. But I don't think it is over. She is going to be back. She will go to different places, see what it is like and then come back. You know there is so much dope in Baltimore. Even in these apartment people make so much money of it.[46]

Drugs had a certain lure and could therefore come in between a relationship. As shown by Seth, drugs did not only mean the act of consumption but a host of other insecurities, possibly fears of promiscuity among partners, which could cause relations to become violent as we saw, but at the same time, the hostilities and intimacies provided relations with an enduring element. This meant that although partners could take breaks and have moments of temporary respite, at the end, partners like Seth did provide some sort of a security for having a shelter over their heads. Seth's recent separation after his partner had gone to live with her mother involved a fair amount of abuse, pain of separation, but also patience for some form of a reunion. He told me that his girlfriend claimed having scratches on her chest, for which she accused Seth. Seth said that he had no idea where she got them from and knew his girlfriend could use them as evidence against him in front of the police.

The lure of drugs and the ability that Seth could provide security and stability to her partner after all of her resources had exhausted, meant that he, in fact, was in the relationship precisely because it was so burdensome. It required endurance and hence helped Seth become a better person, in his own words. Seth described his past relationships and why they could not last compared to the one he was currently in. He said,

> You know my ex . . . she was a great woman. Did not do drugs or anything. Was very kind. But it ended. I love my current girlfriend (referring to his present relationship) *just like my brother*, my brother who died of overdose. Yeah, she reminded me of him. That's why I love her.[47]

What he said really struck me. His reference to conjugality through the frame of reference for solidarity with biological kin was similar but inverse to Jacob's reference to conjugality in referring to his relationship with his mother, as I mentioned in chapter 4. By comparing his girlfriend to his brother, who had died due to overdose, Seth showed how drug abuse moved through kinship relations. It was not simply a case of avoidance, in the sense of quitting drugs and then also avoiding potential partners because of their habits, but seeking partners who resemble in their habits and weaknesses, such as relapsing, to siblings lost to substance use, and then trying to be pillars of support for them, which sometimes even appeared in violent forms (i.e., if Seth did use abuse to discipline his partner, which he disputed). Seth still shared that he would remain committed to the relationship, which he thought was to make up for the time when Seth could not be there for his own brother, possibly due to his own unstable life. His own sobriety was tied to managing his partner's illness. Death due to overdose shaped the decision to enter specific types of relationships. At the same time, there was an element of racial difference. Seth said, "White women can easily get away with drugs. It is not the same for people who are Black." Seth showed that the pressure to quit drugs was disproportionate across racial divide. However, this added more pressure on him as a partner who had been clean to insist his girlfriend to continue the path of recovery. In the absence of any formal control—Seth thought that he had to somehow manage his partner's substance use. Along with this oversight came control over her mobility. His attitude toward his girlfriend's drug problem was a strange transmogrification of an earlier relationship of neglect toward his brothers and making up for it. It was the differential attitudes toward substance use among white and Black individuals that shaped the power Seth exerted over his girlfriend when formal and state-instituted controls failed or weren't as effective among white users.

Next day, when I met Seth, I asked him if his girlfriend had gotten in touch with him. I asked him the question because he had said that his girlfriend was going to be back soon. He replied, "Yes she called me and said that she forgot her blow-dryer and wanted to come and get it." Henceforth, the belongings remaining in Seth's apartment provided an opportunity to meet and to gradually once again embrace a life together as partners. Seth had recently been laid off and had been asking acquaintances for money. He had admitted that he had made mistakes. Yet he was still ready to shoulder the responsibility of a partner. When I once asked if he thought she was going to come back, Seth said, "Where else is she going to go?" Seth knew that, despite the violent nature of their relationship, his girlfriend would trust him to take care of her. Yet he also understood that his care for his girlfriend could become burdensome for her, and hence he was open to a break.

In a later interview, we began to discuss the overall geography of Medfield and its access to other places in Baltimore. Seth said that the place was very well connected through the light rail. I had often seen him emerge from the trees close to our apartment building. At first, I thought that his description of the proximity of our apartment building to the light rail was simply related to the access it provided to other parts in Baltimore, but then I realized that there was something else about the light rail that was important for him. This was linked to his moral striving to remain clean. Seth described,

> I want things to slow down. I still go to the VA for counselling once a week. I need to force myself to stay at home and try to slow things down so that I don't even get close to drugs.[48]

When I asked if he was satisfied with the services he received in the VA, he said, "VA is good for those who went to make use of it. I use the services but for someone like my girlfriend even a good counselor won't be any good."

Two months later, when I met Seth, he had found employment in the VA, like he had once before. His girlfriend had returned to living with him. I had seen him walk with his girlfriend while romantically holding her hand. I reminded myself that one could not divorce such hard-won moments without thinking about the violent relationship they had been a part of, a relationship that became over-burdening because of care and protection from Seth, from which they had sought a break almost aggressively in order to ensure a reunion. The next day, when I met him, he said, "You know I got to take care of her. I have been chosen to take care of her. There is no other way."

A couple of months later, I found that Seth had lost his life to overdose one night while smoking crack with his partner. His neighbor told me,

> [His girlfriend] could have ordered the ambulance earlier, but she didn't. She waited and thought he was going to get better. He died. The woman has his blood on her hands, she is the one who is the real criminal, but now is hanging around freely and this beautiful man is dead.[49]

As I heard from community members, Seth locked in tense relationships, economic precarity and the lure of drugs relapsed, overdosed, and died. Addiction resulted in new forms of policing and violence among partners, but also tested people's own resolve to recover. Just as there were new forms of care introduced by the experience of substance use in the family, there were also moments when these relationships were tested, where the inability to attend to acute symptoms could even result in death, creating new forms of public blame.

CONCLUSION

In this chapter, I have considered the new types of intimacies and hostilities created by the experience of recovery and substance use. It is useful to consider the relation of suspicion between "client" and "addict," which is a product of the heterogenous impact that recovery centers have on the regulation of selves. While some remain compliant, others remain dependent on illicit drugs, continuing to act as roadblocks in the new biopolitics of creating an addiction-free population. One of the consequences of these heterogenous impacts also include new intimacies around providing care to the sick—those suffering from severe withdrawal symptoms— but also new forms of policing others who dodge the regulation of methadone treatment centers as in the case of Katie. However, there are also times when people view disciplining partners as a responsibility due to longer histories of familial neglect. This responsibility also comes at the cost of new psychological pressures and hostilities—physical and emotional—with partners, which even results in the undoing of recovery. In considering these different modalities, my goal has been to highlight what carceral approaches to the substance use look like in domestic spaces and how we can re-envision care and responsibility to those suffering from substance use problems. Ethnography has important value in this regard—it can help us contextualize deep-seated hostilities to devise recovery strategies tailored to individual needs.

NOTES

1. Jarrett Zigon, *A War on People: Drug User Politics and a New Ethics of Community.* (Oakland: University of California Press, 2018), 85.
2. Ibid., 89.
3. Todd Meyers, *The Clinic and Elsewhere: Substance use, Adolescents, and the Afterlife of Therapy* (Seattle: University of Washington Press, 2013).
4. Ibid.
5. Angela Garcia, "The Promise: On the Morality of the Marginal and the Illicit," *Ethos*, 42 (2014): 51–64. doi: 10.1111/etho.12038
6. Ibid.
7. Marcia Meldrum, "'The Long Walk to the Counter': Opioid Pain-Relievers and the Prescription as Stigma," eds. Elizabeth Watkins and Jeremy Greene in *Prescribed: Writing, Filling, Using and Abusing the Prescription in Modern America* (Jacobs Hopkins Press, 2012), 184–206.
8. Phillippe Bourgois and Jaffrey Schonberg, *Righteous Dopefiend* (Berkeley: University of California Press, 2009).
9. Carolyn Rouse. "'If She's a Vegetable, We'll Be Her Garden': Embodiment, Transcendence, and Citations of Competing Cultural Metaphors in the Case of a Dying Child." *American Ethnologist* 31, No. 4 (2004): 514–29. http://www.jstor.org/stable/4098866.
10. M. Bluebond-Langner, *In the Shadow of Illness: Parents and Siblings of the Chronically Ill Child* (Princeton University Press, 1996); L. M. Gerace et al. "Sibling

Perspectives on Schizophrenia and the Family," *Schizophrenia Bulletin* 19, No. 3 (1993): 637–47. doi: 10.1093/schbul/19.3.637

11. Simon and Burns, *The Corner* (HBO, 2003).

12. Families trying to maintain distance from incarcerated members have also been examined by Veena Das and colleagues in the context of prisons in Baltimore. Veena Das, Jonathan M. Ellen, "On the Modalities of the Domestic," *Home Cultures* 5, No. 3 (2015): 349–71.

13. Ibid.

14. M.F. Taylor, D. Coall, R. Marquis et al., "Drug Substance Use Is a Scourge on the Earth and My Grandchildren Are Its Victims: The Tough Love and Resilient Growth Exhibited by Grandparents Raising the Children of Drug-Dependent Mothers," *International Journal of Mental Health Substance Use* 14 (2016): 937–51. doi: 10.1007/s11469-016-9645-7

15. Patricia Fernandez-Kelly, *The Hero's Fight: African Americans in West Baltimore and the Shadow of the State* (Princeton University Press, 2015).

16. Marina Barnard, and Neil McKeganey, "The Impact of Parental Problem Drug Use on Children: What Is the Problem and What Can Be Done to Help?" *Substance Use* (Abingdon, England) 99, No. 5 (2004): 552–9. doi: 10.1111/j.1360-0443.2003.00664.x

17. Neil McKeganey, Marina Barnard, and James McIntosh, "Paying the Price for Their Parents' Substance Use: Meeting the Needs of the Children of Drug-Using Parents," *Drugs: Education, Prevention and Policy* 9, No. 3 (2002): 233–46. doi: 10.1080/09687630210122508; T.L. Hawley, T.G. Halle, R.E. Drasin, and N.G. Thomas, "Children of Addicted Mothers: Effects of the 'crack epidemic' on the Caregiving Environment and the Development of Preschoolers," *American Journal of Orthopsychiatry* 65 (1995): 364–79. Andy Taylor and Brynna Kroll, "Working with Parental Substance Misuse: Dilemmas for Practice," *The British Journal of Social Work* 34, No. 8 (2004): 1115–32. *JSTOR*, http://www.jstor.org/stable/23720534. Accessed 12 Dec. 2022.

18. Kerwin E. MaryLouise, "Collaboration between Child Welfare and Substance-Abuse Fields: Combined Treatment Programs for Mothers," *Journal of Pediatric Psychology* 30, No. 7 (October/November 2005): 581–597. https://doi.org/10.1093/jpepsy/jsi045; K. Connell-Carrick, "A Critical Review of the Empirical Literature: Identifying Correlates of Child Neglect," *Child & Adolescent Social Work Journal* 20, No. 5 (2003): 389–425. doi: 10.1023/A:1026099913845

19. D. Hein and T. Honeyman, "A Closer Look at the Drug Abuse—Maternal Aggression Link," *Journal of Interpersonal Violence* 15 (2000): 503–22.

20. B. Carlini-Marlatt, C. Gazal-Carvalho, N. Gouveia, and M.F. Souza, "Drinking Practices and Other Health-Related Behaviors among Adolescents of Sao Paulo City, Brazil," *Substance Use & Misuse* 38 (2003): 905–32.

21. The idea about psychiatric problems being transmitted genetically has medicalized the issue and has prevented attention to social relations, such as violent domestic relations, which create pressures on mental health. This has also led to the racialization of mental health due to the perception that people from certain backgrounds are

more susceptible to developing mental illness. In the context of colonial psychiatry in Africa, ideas of "detribalization" had salience in psychiatric circles in making the claim about the inability of immigrants to adjust to urban environments. See Mathew Heaton, "Contingencies of Colonial Psychiatry: Migration, Mental Illness, and the Repatriation of Nigerian 'Lunatics,'" *Social History of Medicine* 27, No. 1 (2014): 41–63.

22. For more on finite responsibility under conditions of economic precarity, see Clara Han, *Life in Debt: Times of Care and Violence in Neoliberal Chile* (University of California Press, 2012).

23. C. Epps and E.L. Wright, "The Genetic Basis of Substance Use," in *Perioperative Substance Use*, eds. E. Bryson and E. Frost (New York: Springer, 2012); C.C.Y Wong, J. Mill and C. Fernandes, "Drugs and Substance Use: An Introduction to Epigenetics," *Substance Use* 106 (2011): 480–89. doi: 10.1111/j.1360-0443.2010.03321.x

24. For example, N.D. Volkow et al., "Stimulant-Induced Dopamine Increases Are Markedly Blunted in Active Cocaine Abusers," *Molecular Psychiatry* 19, No. 9 (2014): 1037–43. doi: 10.1038/mp.2014.58

25. Jonathan Sadowsky, *The Empire of Depression: A New History* (Polity, 2020).

26. Steven Epstein, *Impure Science: AIDS, Activism, and the Politics of Knowledge* (Berkeley: University of California Press, 1996).

27. Clara Han and Veena Das, *Living and Dying in the Contemporary World* (University of California Press, 2015).

28. Chris, Interview.

29. Chris, Interview.

30. Mary, Interview.

31. Mary, Interview.

32. Mary, Interview.

33. Jacob, Interview.

34. Jacob, Interview.

35. Jacob, Interview.

36. Jacob, Interview.

37. Jacob, Interview.

38. Jacob, Interview.

39. Jacob, Interview.

40. Jacob, Interview.

41. Jacob, Interview.

42. Seth, Interview.

43. Seth, Interview.

44. Jarrett Zigon, "*HIV is God's Blessing*": *Rehabilitating Morality in Neoliberal Russia* (Berkeley: University of California Press).

45. Seth, Interview.

46. Seth, Interview.

47. Seth, Interview.

48. Seth, Interview.

49. Tom, Interview.

Conclusion

FROM ETHNOGRAPHY TO PRACTICE

Carceral recovery refers to the experience of substance use animated by a punitive attitude by the state, relatives, friends as well as care-providers. My attempt in this book has been to shed light on how a punitive attitude can be counterproductive because it produces the very conditions of substance use that treatment tries to inhibit. Seen in this light, addiction is not the act of consuming drugs; addiction is a social condition marked by punishment, hostilities and violence, which makes recovery impossible for many and makes drug use a means to numb one's mind to the effects of longstanding structural and intimate forms of violence. However well-intentioned policy and public health efforts appear to be, there is always a gap between policy prescriptions and the lived realities of substance use. This point has previously been raised by Lisa Maher based on her work in several countries.[1] Without an understanding of lived realities, it is impossible for public health messaging to have a concrete impact on people's experiences with substance use. Fundamentally, many of the topics raised by the book have already been considered by policymakers. Questions about the role of policing on violence in drug markets, the impact of policing on increasing prices of illicit drugs, the iatrogenic progression of drugs into more compact and dangerous substitutes under conditions of criminalization, as well as the move from using opioid and methamphetamine-based products to drugs like heroin, have all been considered by physicians, economists, policy-makers, sociologists, public health experts and anthropologists. The question then is: what new does this book add to these debates? Anthropology as a discipline has often dealt with total "social facts," which includes an understanding of how social lives are constituted by a range of institutions, events and practices, instead of isolating any single practice or person.[2] While there has been a dearth of ethnographic work influencing drug policy, one promise that an anthropology of drug use offers is that it allows us to consider the social experience within myriad institutions, and the way they create racial difference, and generate the conditions for the intervention of the state in the everyday lives of individuals. To fully capture the social meaning of substance use, it is important to consider that substance use is not simply the experience of taking drugs, or the fact that people trade drugs as atomistic individuals, but that substance use is a *social* experience. While it may at first appear as if making a case for substance use as a social experience may be cliché, there has still been a failure for drug policy to catch up with realities detailed in this ethnography. Anthropological evidence is necessary as it shows us that substance use creates specific types of relatedness and intimacies that are necessary to understand aspirations to live addiction-free lives and the inability to move beyond existing patterns of substance use and relapses. Ambivalence is central to the experience of individuals experiencing substance use. Why after all is ambivalence such an important analytic? The reason is simply that while individuals may be stereotypically viewed as having lost the ability to live, this may be far from true, as neglect and abuse are closely entangled with new forms of care by families and the state in the new biopolitics of creating an addiction-free population.

The intervention in the everyday lives of Baltimoreans is not a recent phenomenon. It has in fact persisted and throws light on much longer histories of public health efforts to which social services, medical and legal institutes contributed. Foucault had once referred the movement from the externalization of lepers to the internalization of plague victims within society to demonstrate difficulties as well as opportunities for public health in its management and control of populations.[3] A similar move took place in Baltimore, especially with the establishment of the Colored Asylum, in which initially only girls were admitted, after which both boys and girls were admitted until the 1920s, when the last person reached the age of majority and graduated. For girls, graduation from these institutes meant being able to successfully take care of domestic chores, whereas for boys, this meant learning skills to be employed as manual laborers. Pathologies were detected not just in an individual but within the household, where signs of parental neglect were construed almost racially, even if the racial otherization is difficult to detect in some medical sources of the early 20th century. The management of youth is an important aspect in the history of substance use in Baltimore. The humanitarianism and so-called good will of medical institutions gave way to racial biases, for which grounds had already been established with theories of substance use and pathology relying on hereditary explanations, especially with the work of Hurd, as I discussed in chapter 1. While the work of Meyer played an important role in going beyond the hereditary basis of mental disorder and vice, which Meyerian psychiatry would have been well-suited to resist, there would only be a continuation of many of the ongoing processes of policing domestic lives. The growing emphasis on the social environment and the lack of adaptation as the cause of substance use, or mental illness more generally, meant that now the individual and the social relations around him or her could provide the impetus for intervention in the domestic lives of the poor.

The effect of child welfare on Black families has already been discussed by scholars like Dorothy Roberts.[4] My concern in the book has been to highlight, with the help of ethnography, the ways in which the poor are constructed as unable to provide for their children within courts, ignoring the efforts that are made to demonstrate "responsibility," for which I turn to the story of Sarah and her partner. While it may appear that people battling with substance use may be neglected in courts, which treat "responsibility" as the ability to show up to court hearings and visit children under the supervision of the social security, the reality indeed is much more different. Parents like Mary strive to undergo recovery and get a job before they can enter the lives of children in any meaningful way.

Foucault's important insights in *Psychiatric Power* about the emergence of psychiatry in relation to the nuclear family are not an exact parallel but help us understand how the state enters the family when substance use is constructed as a public health problem, especially with a preventative aim in order to break the cycle of substance use and poverty.[5] Thus, it is important to be mindful of the ways in which medical discourses help legitimize the intervention in domestic lives among children and youth who are viewed as neglected. This preventative logic is also used to legitimize state-led violence. In this context, it is not a coincidence that medical intervention gives way to policing, especially as racial boundaries, at least in scientific discourse, became much more fixed by the turn of the twentieth century.

Thus the historical context helps contextualize many of the medico-moral arguments about the need for the poor family to be helped. This book has been written with the intention that the failures or gaps in the country's opioid-policy may be addressed with the help of ethnographic data. The gap that I situate for future policy debates is to address the grey zones between prisons, medical institutions, households and sidewalks, where individuals experience a range of disciplinary pressures. The chain of events, though by no means typical, is often as follows: a young boy first experiences prison in his early teens, leaves the prison, and given the instability of the domestic situation, finds himself doing the same things that initially took him to prison. Now as a juvenile, he is still treated with tenderness, but as soon as he turns seventeen, he is shifted to another detention center, in which he is often the youngest. He becomes part of gang violence and slowly learns a way to stay out of it to make it out of the prison alive. He promises the court that he will join recovery, be a better person, try to find a job and take care of his family. Once he is out, he finds himself under the supervision of a parole officer and the treatment center. Under conditions of household precarity, any violations of the treatment protocols result in his being suspended from treatment. Frustrated, he gives up his attempt to heal and often "relapses." There are often two probabilities: that he will either end up in prison or remain the determined to continue his path of recovery. Yet all this is only part of the story; another part is the domestic conflicts that he experiences with family, friends and others about being betrayed, as time in prison creates pressures on families to provide for them monetarily, a demand which families are not able to fulfill because of their own precarity and desperation. There are other realities of domestic abuse that further intensify their suffering, with these longer histories often erased in the treatment provided to individuals. Of course, the chain of events may be different based on the person, yet the effects of participation are the same for almost everyone who has a problem with substance use, experienced incarceration and now is seeking to complete recovery.

The failure of much of drug policy is that it has been almost silent on the question of household pressures that shape substance use outcomes. Instead, it has continued to focus on the criminalization of drug use and possession. Specifically, it has been quiet on the ways in which the intervention into domestic spaces has been "colored," as Dorothy Roberts reminds us.[6] This is what sets Baltimore apart from other American cities that do not share the same racial demographics and do not have a similar history of an expansive and interventionist public health system. The history of policing the youth is thus important as a predecessor to the expansion of carceral politics in twentieth-century Baltimore. Anthropologists have recently made important moves toward expanding our understanding of prisons as sites of complex networks of intimacies and care. I use the concept of carceral obligations to show how prison worlds extend beyond the prison into domestic spaces and neighborhood life as existing obligations and enmities are settled in violent ways. Prisons are also sites where collisions with the state create psychological stresses that exceed an individual's time in the prison. The book provides a move to consider the new forms of intimacies that are formed in the prison and the ways in which incarceration is understood as an opportunities for the cultivation of wisdom by some, especially given the complicated webs of relations individuals are made to traverse within and across racial boundaries. Yet the story does not end there. In fact, as individuals come out of prison, they are completely unprepared for lives on the streets and carry various kinds of pressure to make ends meet. Street life re-activates many of the rivalries made in prison, but this is also a period in which individuals are under increasing pressure to live drug-free lives in the new biopolitics of medication for opioid use disorders (MOUD).

I argue that individuals who become homeless are put under pressure to live "medicalized" lives, which means that there is a need to constantly prove to state authorities and bystanders their struggles to live drug-free lives, even when the experience between medication and drug substance use may not be substantially different for many.

How then do we understand these experiences as products of longer racial histories or medical discourses that shape epidemiology and public health in Baltimore? This book has shown how the relationship between clinics and black markets has been established through the increasing surveillance of narcotics. The intervention that I hope this book has made is to focus on a motley arrangement or a political pharmacology of narcotics, painkillers, opioid agonists, and anti-anxiety pills and their trade in the illegal drug markets. I hope to have ethnographically captured how the lack of access to medication as well as the lack of economic stability allow individuals to turn to the informal drug economy. A close study of the political pharmacology of drug use would entail not only the way prescription and illicit drugs change hands but also the social life of these drugs and the new types of relatedness to which they give birth.

The way the opioid epidemic and incarceration have impacted social behaviors requires a lot more work than has been done in the past. Instead of simply viewing individuals as "dangerous," it is important to consider how surveillance and policing sow the seeds of disorder within families and suspicion toward medical institutes and public health initiatives. There are a few areas where interventions are urgently required to reduce drug-related violence. This includes first and foremost introducing those dependent on drugs to evidence-based treatment, along with counselling and economic support. Without counseling, consisting of psycho-social support, treatment is likely to fail. The purpose behind describing what the domestic space looks like for a family experiencing dependence on drugs is to precisely show the pressures on social relations and the difficulties these create for those in recovery. My household visits helped to provide encouragement to individuals to engage with other members to find solutions such as the equitable distribution of resources, which was a major cause of disputes and a lack of psycho-social wellbeing. Providing safety nets to the poor and homeless and residential support can have positive impacts on recovery. Outpatient services have played a positive role, but it is urgent to expand counselling services to the doorstep without individuals experiencing the risk of criminalization for relapsing.

Even though the narcotics have been criminalized, the state is often lax in controlling the exchange of opioids, both within the city and the prisons. It is important to disaggregate crimes by distinguishing danger from drug possession, because as long as this does not happen, a humane approach to substance use will remain absent. Epidemiological approaches continue to focus on overdoses and drug-related crimes instead of usage. The epidemiological and legal focus on death stabilizes the category of homicide, which eludes prevention in favor of a focus on the loss of life. Methodologically, this leads to drug use and its lethal consequences being treated as a legal matter rather than a question about ensuring the wellbeing of individuals by avoiding the criminalization of drug use and providing the support necessary to complete treatment. At the same time, there is a need to fully institute evidence-based treatment in prisons to prevent the smuggling of more lethal drugs into prisons. Individuals experiencing re-incarceration continue to employ relationships in prisons to secure narcotics and opioids. The movement of drugs continues to flow through webs of these relationships, in which correctional officers often also collaborate, which is why it is urgent to create more robust forms of surveillance and outpatient treatment with counseling at the doorsteps to reduce the risk of overdosing and reduce re-incarceration for the possession of drugs. I have shown how we also need new sociological frameworks to understand the movement of drugs, a departure from viewing carceral institutions as closed. This would entail considering a broader picture that encapsulates prisons and households. Such a perspective will not only make for a robust form of surveillance but also help consider at a granular level the psycho-social pressures experienced by individuals as they come out of prison, readjust to social relations, and start treatment in addiction treatment centers. Sociological and anthropological perspectives are also required to understand the impact substance use has on social behavior within the household and beyond. Instead of "criminalizing" substance use, it is better to refer to substance use as shaped by social determinants like excessive policing, racialization, displacement and poverty. Moreover, it is also useful to consider the pressures placed by substance use on social relations, as people vie for drugs and experience fissures in relations with intimate kin when drug use places a strain on meagre household resources. I have used the concept of pharmaceuticalization of violence to anthropologically consider when domestic relations and those with the wider community are marked by suspicion and danger due to competition for access to opioids and narcotics, as violence is shaped by access to or restrictions on the use of pharmaceuticals. At the same time, it is urgent for physicians to fully understand patient histories to provide access to opioids under supervision and empower patients to regulate their dosage where necessary. If individuals continue to negotiate access to opioids in black markets the way they do now, the lack of medical oversight will make consequences such as overdose and substance use an ever-present risk.

Jacob's experiences and those of others I interviewed show that homelessness is a looming possibility. Homelessness exposed individuals to constant stress about making ends meet and travelling to the treatment center for medication while experiencing dangers of street life, such as gang violence. Jacob's experiences showed how clients too pick up the language of patienthood to erase longer histories of drug-abuse. The stance toward medicalization was not straightforward. Jacob knew about his mental illness and tried to express the histories of childhood and street violence that were erased in this clinical encounter, especially when he was treated for psychosis when in reality he was demanding treatment for his anxiety. He resisted the diagnosis of psychosis by insisting on the need for therapy so that the treatment fully incorporated his past experiences. At the same time, he showed how one's plotline of illness is entangled with that of an intimate other, as in the case of his mother's illness and death, providing a standing language for his own experience of substance use.

Moreover, even as Medications for opioid use disorders (MOUD) have become common in Baltimore and these centers vie for greater prominence by promising recovery, there are novel issues faced by prospective clients. First, even though psychiatric care is often provided to those in MAT, there are often competing ideas about mental illness as inherited genetically or caused by social experiences. The use of genetic explanations blur the etiologies of mental illness and substance use. Patients often also resist this blurring of etiologies by urging a shift to how the state is complicit in expanding the market for illicit drugs and opioids and letting people die. While MAT has been expanded, which is a welcome move, the models that they use are still punitive in nature and assume that the patient is necessarily also an ex-convict and thus in need for punishment for his or her lack of compliance. Failure to pass urine tests can result in suspension from a program for up to a month, which creates pressure for complete abstinence, creating further withdrawals and possibilities of relapse and making the likelihood of re-entry into the program increasingly difficult. In such a case, individuals are much more likely to turn to the illegal drug economy to buy methadone in combination with narcotics and opioids, which creates further risks and makes relapse and return to narcotics much more likely. There is an urgent need to educate clients about withdrawal symptoms they are like to experience as they shift from heroin to methadone and provide social support to make the transition possible. At the same time, it is necessary to incorporate faith-based sessions beyond the prison that do not discriminate yet are also receptive to different racial and religious experiences to provide motivation to individuals to successfully complete their programs. Providing opioids and methadone under surveillance of medical professionals is much better than letting individuals access them in black markets. I have also shown through Jacob's experiences how treatment centers are increasingly considered places of gang violence and drug trade, which is why it is necessary to provide safe spaces for individuals to interact without the risk of experiencing street violence.

Further, medical professionals should urgently consider that those engaging in the drug trade and having a history of incarceration continue to experience racial violence on the streets. It is urgent that physicians, nurses and correctional officers, instead of fostering differences, also work toward building bridges across gang-based divisions so that conflicts in prison do not translate into violence outside, or vice versa. When Jacob described that stealing outside the prison could have consequences in terms of how the person was treated when inside the prison, he demonstrated that many of the individuals with records of incarceration and involvement in drug economies were constantly vulnerable to threats while on the streets. Currently, the prison system only furthers racial distinctions and rivalries between gangs, which I have demonstrated through Jacob's role in moving contraband during his time in the prison. Jacob also threw light on how his perception of those in the prison continued to color attitudes toward them when they were out on the streets. Under strict parole regulations, any physical altercation can result in the person's re-incarceration, which becomes even more likely as prison-rivalries extend outside.

Finally, it is urgent to integrate anthropological knowledge as part of drug treatment and therapy. This means understanding the exact pressure points in relationships, fictive and non-fictive, that prevent positive treatment outcomes. Often, Jacob would share the extreme depression he would experience when he was living with Katie. Moreover, it is urgent to integrate an assessment of kin relations to understand trajectories of drug abuse as well as the success or failure of treatment. Relations in which patients lack autonomy, are infantilized, or are considered criminals are not likely to result in positive treatment outcomes. It is necessary to foster relationships around the patient in which the patient is not infantilized. It is important to provide relationships that provide a source of encouragement, even when the possibility of a relapse is latent. There are relations of conjugality that provide encouragement to successfully undertake treatment, as in the case of Sarah and her boyfriend. There is another dimension to consider, that is, the person's substance use trajectories in their own words, to understand how their own memories and past traumas impact their psycho-social wellbeing and result in their turn to narcotics or opioids. When a person has been divorced from kin due to the burden he or she placed on household resources, it is important to provide social support accompanied by counselling to reintroduce them to their families and restore trust. If they continue to be in their families and treatment places an economic burden, it is essential to provide economic support to the family, which also includes providing the encouragement to start and successfully complete treatment. Positive treatment outcomes can only be ensured when we fully understand the social experience of substance use and place it in relation to broader socioeconomic structures that enable and disrupt specific addictive states. This will concomitantly also entail re-thinking the way we approach substance use—changing the language of punishment to one of empathy, from failure to success, from discipline and constraint to empowerment.

NOTES

1. Lisa Maher, "Don't Leave Us This Way: Ethnography and Injecting Drug Use in the Age of AIDS," *International Journal of Drug Policy* 13, No. 4 (2002): 311–25.
2. Marcel Mauss, *The Gift: Forms and Functions of Exchange in Archaic Societies* (London: Cohen & West, 1966).
3. Michel Foucault, *Discipline and Punish: The Birth of the Prison* (Vintage Books, 1995).
4. Dorothy Roberts, *Shattered Bonds: The Color of Child Welfare* (Civitas Books, 2002).
5. Michel Foucault, *Psychiatric Power: Lectures at the College de France, 1973-1974* (Picador, 2008).
6. Dorothy Roberts, *Shattered Bonds: The Color of Child Welfare* (Civitas Books, 2002).

Bibliography

Adams, Walter, Norbert Glasser, & Leonidas H. Berry, "The narcotic problem in an urban community." *Journal of the National Medical Association* 45, no. 1 (1953): 52.

Agar, Michael H., & R. Owen Murdoch, "Investigating recent trends in heroin use in Baltimore city: A pilot "quantitative" research project." *Special Topics of Substance Research, Report 94-1* (1994).

Anslinger, H. J., "Narcotic substance use as seen by the law-enforcement officer." *Federal Probation* 21, no. 2 (June 1957): 34–41.

Ball, J. C., L. Rosen, E. G. Friedman, & D. N. Nurco, "The impact of heroin substance use on criminality." *Committee on Problems of Drug Dependence* (1981).

Baltimore, MD., Ordinance 692 (May 15, 1911).

Barnard, Marina, *Drug Substance use and families* (Jessica Kingsley Publishers, 2007).

Barnard, Marina, & Neil McKeganey, "The impact of parental problem drug use on children: What is the problem and what can be done to help?" *Substance Use* (Abingdon, England) 99, no. 5 (2004): 552–559. doi: 10.1111/j.1360-0443.2003.00664.x.

Baxter, Ellen, & Kim Hopper, "Private lives/public spaces: Homeless adults on the streets of New York city." (1981), 43.

Behrouzan, Orkideh, "Medicalization as a way of life: The Iran-Iraq war and considerations of psychiatry and anthropology." *Medical Anthropology Theory* 2, no. 3 (2015): 40–60.

Beletsky, Leo, Grace E. Macalino, & Scott Burris, "Atttiudes of police officers towards syringe access, occupational needle sticks, and drug use: A qualitative study of one city police department in the United States." *International Journal of Drug Policy* 16, no. 4 (2005): 267–271.

Bett, W. R., "William Steward Halsted (1852-1922) Cocaine Pioneer and addict." *British Journal of Substance Use to Alcohol & Other Drugs* 49 (1952): 53–59. doi: 10.1111/j.1360-0443.1952.tb04225.x.

Biehl, Joao, "Life of the mind: The interface of psychopharmaceuticals, domestic economies, and social abandonment." *American Ethnologist* 31, no. 4 (2004): 476.

Bluebond-Langner, M., *In the shadow of illness: Parents and siblings of the chronically ill child* (Princeton University Press, 1996); Gerace, Laina M., Dorothy Camilleri, & Lioness Ayres, "Sibling perspectives on schizophrenia and the family." *Schizophrenia Bulletin* 19, no. 3 (1993): 637–647. doi: 10.1093/schbul/19.3.637.

Bluemel, C. S., "Morphine habit." *The Journal of Nervous and Mental Disease* 51, no. 1 (1920): 105–106.

Boas, Franz, "The mind of primitive man." *The Journal of American Folklore* 14, no. 52 (1901): 1–11.

Bonnycastle, D. D., & C. W. Delia, "Effect of hepatectomy upon the analgetic action of 1 methadone." *Proceedings of the Society for Experimental Biology and Medicine* 74, no. 3 (1950): 589–591. doi: 10.3181/00379727-74-17983.

Bor, Jonathan, "Blacks' mistrust of doctors slows AIDS treatment." *Baltimore Sun* (1990).

Bourgois, P., "Disciplining substance uses: The bio-politics of methadone and heroin in the United States." *Culture Medicine and Psychiatry* 24 (2000): 165–195.

Bourgois, Phillippe, & Jaffrey Schonberg, *Righteous Dopefiend* (Berkeley: University of California Press, 2009).

Bowlby, Jacob, "The Adolf Meyer lecture: Childhood mourning and its implications for psychiatry." *American Journal of Psychiatry* 11, no. 6 (1961): 481–498.

Boyd, Susan J., Li Juan Fang, Deborah R. Medoff, Lisa B. Dixon, & David A. Gorelick, "Use of a 'microecological technique' to study crime incidents around methadone maintenance treatment centers." *Substance Use* 107 (2012): 1632–1638.

Broadwater, Luke, & Ian Dunkun, "'Neighborhoods are crying out': Baltimore has highest homicide rates in US big cities." *Baltimore Sun* (September 2018).

Brooks, C. C., "Adoption on Manihi Atoll, Tuamoto archipelago," (1976) 51–64 & Signe Howell, "Adoption of the unrelated child: Some challenges to the anthropological study of kinship." *Annual Review of Anthropology* 38 (2009): 148–166.

Broz, D., N. Carnes, J. Chapin-Bardales, D. C. Des Jarlais, S. Handanagic, C. M. Jones, R. P. McClung, & A. K. Asher, "Syringe services programs' role in ending the HIV epidemic in the U.S.: Why we cannot do it without them." *American Journal of Preventive Medicine* 61, no. 1 (2021): S118–S129. doi: 10.1016/j.amepre.2021.05.044.

Bull, M., *Governing the heroin trade: From treaties to treatment* (Aldershot: Ashgate, 2008).

Burris, S., K. M. Blankenship, & M. Donoghoe, "Addressing the "risk environment" for injection drug users: The mysterious case of the missing cop." *Milbank Quarterly* 82, no. 1 (2004): 125–156.

Burton, Linda M., "Black grandparents rearing children of drug addicted parents: Stressors, outcomes and social service needs." *The Gerontologist* 32, no. 6 (1992): 744–751.

Burton, Orisanmi, "Captivity, kinship & black masculine care work under domestic warfare." *American Anthropologist* 123, no. 3 (2021): 621–632.

Butler, Judith, *The psychic life of power* (Stanford, CA: Stanford University Press, 1997).

Canguilhem, Georges, *The normal and the pathological* (New York: Zone Books, 1991).

Carlini-Marlatt, B., C. Gazal-Carvalho, N. Gouveia, & M. F. Souza, "Drinking practices and other health-related behaviors among adolescents of Sao Paulo City, Brazil." *Sub Use Mis* 38 (2003): 905–932.

Carroll, Jennifer J., *Narkomania: Drugs, HIV and citizenship* (New York: Cornell University Press, 2019).

Cassino, Frank, "Control of narcotic substance use." *American Journal of Psychotherapy* 7, no. 1 (1953): 164.

Caulkins, J. P., "Local drug markets response to focused police enforcement." *Operations Research* 41, no. 5 (1993): 848–863.

Clark v. the State 348 Md. 722.

Clayton, Gina, Endria Richardson, Lily Mandlin, & Brittany Farr, *Because she's powerful: The political isolation and resistance of women with incarcerated loved ones* (Los Angeles: Essie Justice Group, 2018).

Cobun, Heather, "Woman enters plea for selling fake drugs to undercover deputy." *Baltimore Sun* (August 19, 2014).

Cohen, M. Bernard, & Ruth E. Fairbank, "Statistical contributions from the mental hygiene study of the eastern health district of Baltimore." *Human Biology* 11, no. 1 (February 1939): 112.

Cole, Jonathan O., "Report on the treatment of drug substance use." (1966). https://www.ojp.gov/pdffiles1/Digitization/135534NCJRS.pdf#page=144.

Comfort, Megan, *Doing time together: Love and family in the shadow of the prison* (Chicago, IL: University of Chicago Press, 2009).

Connell-Carrick, K., "A critical review of the empirical literature: Identifying correlates of child neglect." *Child & Adolescent Social Work Journal* 20, no. 5 (2003): 389–425. doi: 10.1023/A:1026099913845.

"Coping with Stress in Prison," 7/1/2015. *American Prison Writing Archive.*

"Court jails baby's mom," (1968, February 17). *Afro-American.*

Courtwright, David T., *Dark paradise: A history of opiate substance use in America* (Cambridge, MA: Harvard University Press, 2001), p. 123.

Crane, Johanna T., & Kelsey Pascoe, "Becoming institutionalized: Incarceration as a chronic health condition." *Medical Anthropology Quarterly* 35, no. 3 (2021): 307–326. doi: 10.1111/maq.12621.

Crenshaw, Kimberle W., "Demarginalizing the intersection of race and sex: A black feminist critique of antidiscrimination doctrine, feminist theory and antiracist policies." *The University of Chicago Legal Forum* 1, no. 8 (1989): 139–167.

Crenshaw, Kimberle W., "Race, reform and retrenchment: Transformation and legitimation in anti-discrimination law." In *Critical race theory: The key writings that formed the movement*, edited by Kimberlé Crenshaw, Neil Gotanda, & Gary Peller (The New Press, 1995).

Das, Santanu, "The Indian sepoy in the first world war." *The British Library* (2014).

Das, Veena, *Affliction: Health, disease, poverty* (New York: Fordham University Press, 2014).

Das, Veena, & Jonathan M. Ellen, "On the modalities of the domestic." *Home Cultures* 5, no. 3 (2015): 349–371.

David, Phil, "Prison exterminator, two others admit to role in smuggling drugs in Jessup prison." *Baltimore Sun* (September 18, 2019).

David Simon & Ed Burns, *The corner* (HBO, 2003).

"Dear APWA, I am a 36 year old former correctional officer," *American Prison Writing Archive*.

Dej, Erin, "Psychocentrism and homelessness: The pathologization/responsibilization paradox." *Studies in Social Justice* 10 (2016): 117–135. doi: 10.26522/ssj.v10i1.1349.

del Carmen, Rolando V., & Jonathan R. Sorensen, "Legal issues in drug testing probation and parole clients and employees." *US Department of Justice* (1989).

Dixon, David, & Phillip Coffin, "Zero tolerance policing of illegal drug markets." *Drug and Alcohol Review* 18, no. 4 (1999): 477–486. doi: 10.1080/09595239996338.

Donovan, Edward J., "Two years of the presidency of the New York Academy of Medicine." Address of the Retiring President, *Bulletin New York Academy Medicine* 33, no. 4 (1957): 230.

"Dope habit widespread, judge says: No section of the city free of drugs." *The Sun* (October 14, 1951), p. 30.

Drucker, Ernest, *A plague of prisons: The epidemiology of mass incarceration in America* (New York: The New Press, 2013).

Duneier, Michael, *Sidewalk* (New York: Farrar, Straus and Giroux, 2000).

Durkin, Keith F., & Steven Hundersmarch, "Pedophiles and child molesters." In *Extreme deviance*, edited by Erich Goode & D. Angus Vail (Sage, 2008).

"Epilepsy, and certain types of epileptiform attacks." *JAMA* 75, no. 14 (1920): 932–933. doi: 10.1001/jama.1920.02620400026008.

Epps, C., & E. L. Wright, "The genetic basis of substance use." In *Perioperative substance use*, edited by E. Bryson & E. Frost (New York, NY: Springer, 2012). doi: 10.1007/978-1-4614-0170-4_2.

Epstein, Steven, *Impure science: AIDS, activism, and the politics of knowledge* (Berkeley, CA: University of California Press, 1996).

Estroff, S. E., W. S. Lachicotte, L. C. Illingworth, & A. Jacobston, "Everybody's got a little mental illness: Accounts of illness and self among people with severe, persistent mental illnesses." *Medical Anthropology Quarterly* 5 (1991): 331–369.

Farge, Arlette, *Disorderly families: Infamous letters from the Bastille Archives* (Minneapolis: University of Minnesota Press, 2017).

Farmer, Paul, "An anthropology of structural violence." *Current Anthropology* 45, no. 3 (2004): 305–325.

Farmer, Paul, "Social inequalities and emerging infectious diseases." *Emerging Infectious Diseases* 2, no. 4 (1996): 259–269. doi: 10.3201/eid0204.960402.

Fassin, Didier, *Prison worlds: An ethnography of the carceral condition* (New York: Polity, 2015).

Ferme, Mariane C., *Out of war: Violence, trauma, and the political imagination in Sierra Leone* (Berkeley: University of California Press, 2018).

Fernandez-Kelly, Patricia, *The hero's fight: African Americans in west Baltimore and the shadow of the state* (New Jersey: Princeton University Press, 2015).

Ferzacca, Steve, "Actually, i don't feel that bad: Managing diabetes and the clinical encounter." *Medical Anthropology Quarterly* 14 (2000): 28–50. doi: 10.1525/maq.2000.14.1.28.

Flath, N., K. Tobin, K. King, A. Lee, & C. Latkin, "Enduring consequences from the war on drugs: How policing practices impact HIV risk among people who inject drugs in Baltimore city." *Substance Use & Misuse* 52, no. 8 (2017): 1003–1010. doi: 10.1080/10826084.2016.1268630.

Foucault, M., *Abnormal: Lectures at the College de France, 1974–1975* (New York: Picador, 2003), p. 21.

Foucault, Michel, *Discipline and punish: The birth of the prison* (New York: Vintage Books, 1995).

Foucault, Michel, *Psychiatric power: Lectures at the College de France, 1973–1974* (New York: Picador, 2008).

Fraser, Suzanne, & Kylie Valentine, *Substance and substitution: Methadone subjects in liberal societies* (New York: Palgrave Macmillan, 2008).

Friedman, J., & M. Alicea, *Surviving heroin: Interviews with women in methadone clinics* (Florida: University Press of Florida, 2001).

Friedman, S. B., G. L. Horvat, & R. B. Levinson, "Narcotic addict rehabilitation act—Its impact on federal prisons." *Contemporary Drug Problems* 11, no. 1 (Spring 1982): 101–111.

Fullwiley, Duana, *The enculturated gene: Sickle cell health politics and biological difference in West Africa* (New Jersey: Princeton University Press, 2011).

Garcia, Angela, *The pastoral clinic: Substance use and dispossession along the Rio Grande* (Berkeley: University of California Press, 2010).

Garcia, Angela, "The promise: On the morality of the marginal and the illicit." *Ethos* 42 (2014): 51–64. doi: 10.1111/etho.12038.

Genberg, Becky L., Stephen J. Gange, Vivian F. Go, David D. Celentano, Gregory D. Kirk, Carl A. Latkin, & Shruti H. Mehta, "The effect of neighborhood deprivation and residential relocation on long-term injection cessation among injection drug users (IDUs) in Baltimore, Maryland." *Substance Use* 106 (2011): 1966–1974.

George, Justin, & Scott Dance, "Drugs on Baltimore streets could keep it high 'for a year,' Batts says." *The Baltimore Sun* (June 4, 2015).

Ghosh, Ausmita, Kasoli Simon, & Benjamin D. Sommers, "Prescription drug use: Evidence from the affordable care act." *National Bureau of Economic Research* (2017).

Gilmore, Ruth Wilson, *Golden Gulag: Prisons, surplus, crisis, and opposition in globalizing California* (Berkeley: University of California Press, 2007).

Gilmore, Ruth Wilson, "Race, prisons and war: Scenes from the Gilmore history of US violence." *Socialist Register* 45 (2009): 73–87.

Glasser, Irene, & Rae Bridgman, *Braving the street: The anthropology of homelessness* (New York: Berghahn, 1999), p. 60.

Goffman, Erving, "On the characteristics of total institutions." In *Asylums: Essays on the social situation of mental patients and other inmates* (1962), pp. 1–124.

Goldstein, Avram, & Byron W. Brown, Jr. "Urine testing in methadone maintenance treatment of heroin substance use." *JAMA* 214, no. 2 (1970): 311–315.

Goldstein, Kurt, *The organism* (New York: Zone Book, 2000).

Greene, J. A., "Zero tolerance: A case study of police policies and practices in New York city." *Crime & Delinquency* 45, no. 2 (1999): 171–187. doi: 10.1177/0011128799045002001.

Greene, Jeremy, & David Herzberg, "Hidden in plain sight: Marketing prescription drugs to consumers in twentieth century." *American Journal of Public Health* 100, no. 5 (2010): 793–803.

Grim, Brian J., & Melissa E. Grim, "Belief, behavior, and belonging: How faith is indispensable in preventing and recovering from substance abuse." *Journal of Religious Health* 58, no. 5 (2019): 1713–1750.

Groark, Kevin, "Freud among the Boasians: Psychoanalytic influence and ambivalence in American anthropology." *Current Anthropology* 60, no. 4 (2019): 559–588.

Guenther, Anthony L., "Compensations in a total institution: The forms and functions of contraband." *Crime & Delinquency* (1975).

Han, Clara, *Life in debt: Times of care and violence in neoliberal Chile* (University of California Press, 2012).

Han, Clara, & Veena Das, *Living and dying in the contemporary world* (Berkeley: University of California Press, 2015).

Harm Reduction/Clean needles, AIDS Posters & Stories of Public Health. https://www.nlm.nih.gov/exhibition/aids-posters/digitalgallery_theme_6.html.

Harris, Louis S., "Impact of heroin substance use upon criminality (from problems of drug dependence)." Proceedings of the 41st annual scientific meeting (1979). https://www.ojp.gov/ncjrs/virtual-library/abstracts/impact-heroin-substance use-upon-criminality-problems-drug-dependence.

Harris, Shana, "To be free and normal: Substance use, governance, and the therapeutics of buprenorphine." *Medical Anthropology Quarterly* 29, no. 4 (2015): 512–530. doi: 10.1111/maq.12232.

Hawley, T. L., T. G. Halle, R. E. Drasin, & N. G. Thomas, "Children of addicted mothers: Effects of the 'crack epidemic' on the caregiving environment and the development of preschoolers." *American Journal of Orthopsychiatry* 65 (1995): 364–379.

Hay, Cameron, "Reading sensations: Understanding the process of distinguishing "fine" from "sick."" *Transcultural Psychiatry* 45 (2008): 198–229.

Heaton, Mathew, "Contingencies of colonial psychiatry: Migration, mental illness, and the repatriation of Nigerian 'lunatics.'" *Social History of Medicine* 27, no. 1 (2014): 41–63.

Hein, D., & T. Honeyman, "A closer look at the drug abuse - Maternal aggression link." *Journal of Interpersonal Violence* 15 (2000): 503–522.

Henderson, D. K., "The treatment of drug substance use." *Glasgow Medical Journal* 85, no. 3 (March 1916): 190–202.

Hendrix, Steve, "Johns Hopkins hospital inspires mistrust and fear in parts of east Baltimore." *The Washington Post*, WP Company (February 2, 2017). https://www

.washingtonpost.com/local/Jacobs-hopkins-hospital-inspires-mistrust-and-fear-in-parts-of-east-baltimore/2017/01/25/a4f402c2-bbf3-11e6-91ee-1adddfe36cbe.
Herzberg, David, *White market drugs: Big pharma and the hidden history of substance use in America* (Illinois: The University of Chicago Press, 2020).
Hopper, Kim, "More than passing strange: Homelessness and mental illness in New York City." *American Ethnologist* 15, no. 1 (1988): 158. doi: 10.1525/ae.1988.15.1.02a00100.
Hough, M., & M. Natarajan, "Introduction: Illegal drug markets, research and policy." In *Illegal drug markets: From research to policy*, edited by M. Hough & M. Natarajan (Monsey, NJ: Criminal Justice Press, 2000).
Hurd, Henry M., "A case of inebriety with insanity: With remarks." (1889).
Hurd, Henry M., "How can psychiatry assist preventive medicine?" *American Journal of Public Hygiene* 18, no. 3 (1908): 273–278.
Hurd, Henry M., "Imbecility with insanity." *American Journal of Psychiatry* 45, no. 2 (1888): 263.
Hurd, Henry M., "Paranoia." *Journal of Insanity* (April 1886).
Hurd, Henry M., "Some mental disorders of childhood and Youth" (1894), p. 282.
Hurd, Henry M., "The data of recovery from insanity." *American Journal of Psychiatry* 43, no. 2 (1886): 246.
Hurd, Henry M., "The hereditary influence of alcoholic indulgence upon the production of insanity." *Sanitary Convention* (Michigan, 1883).
Hurd, Henry M., "The teaching of psychiatry." *American Journal of Insanity* LVI, no. 2 (1899): 220.
Hurd, Henry M., *The institutional care of the insane in United States and Canada 1843–1927* (1916), p. 511.
Hurd, Henry M., "The treatment of periodic insanity." *American Journal of Psychiatry* 39, no. 2 (1882): 179.
"Images from the history of public health service." https://www.nlm.nih.gov/exhibition/phs_history/images.dir/134.gif.
In re adoption/guardianship Nos. T00130003 and T00130004 in the circuit court for Baltimore city. 786 A.2D 803 (2001)141 MD. APP. 645.
In re adoption/guardianship of Joshua M. 888 A.2D 1201 (2005)166 MD. APP. 341.
In re: adoption/guardianship No. J970013 in the circuit court for prince George's county. 737 A.2D 604 (1999) 128 MD. APP. 242.
In re: adoption/guardianship of Darjal C. and Khaylelle C. 992 A.2d 503 (2010) 191 Md. App. 505.
In re: adoption/guardianship of H.W. 189 A.3d 284 (2018) 460 Md. 201.
In re: adoption/guardianship of Rashawn H. and Tyrese H. No. 7, Sept. Term, 2007. 937 A.2d 177 (2007) 402 Md. 477.
Isbell, H., S. Altschul, C. H. Kornetsky, A. J. Eisenman, H. G. Flanary, & H. F. Fraser, "Chronic barbiturate intoxication: An experimental study." *Archives of Neurology and Psychiatry* 64, no. 1 (1950): 1–28. doi: 10.1001/archneurpsyc.1950.02310250007001.
JHH Patient Records, Admissions and Discharges – December 1913–September 1914.

JHH Patient Records, Admissions and Discharges – February 4, 1918–September 1918 (308346).

JHH Patient Records, Admissions and Discharges – February 4, 1918–September 1918.

JHH Patient Records, Admissions and Discharges – October 4, 1899–November 29, 1900 (113540).

JHH Patient Records, Admissions and Discharges – September 1, 1920–May 6, 1921 (113543).

Johns Hopkins Hospital, Colored Orphan Asylum Logbook, 1875–1923.

Jovanovic, Tanja, Nineequa Q. Blanding, Seth D. Norrholm, Erica Duncan, Bekh Bradley, & Kerry J. Ressler, "Childhood abuse is associated with increased startle reactivity in adulthood." *Depress. Anxiety* 26, no. 11 (2009): 1018–1026.

Kaye, Kerwin, *Enforcing freedom: Drug courts, therapeutic communities, and the intimacies of the state* (New York: Columbia University Press, 2019), p. 95.

Keane, Helen, "Foucault on methadone: Beyond biopower." *International Journal of Drug Policy* 20 (2009): 450–452.

Keefe, Patrick Radden, *Empire of pain: The secret history of the Sackler dynasty* (New York: Doubleday, 2021).

Keller, Mary Grace, "Baltimore man charged with giving drugs to inmates who overdosed at Carroll County Detention Center." *Baltimore Sun* (March 10, 2020).

Kelvey, Jon, "Mount Airy woman charged with attempting to smuggle drugs into jail." *Baltimore Sun* (June 30, 2018).

Kelvey, Jon, "Sexy letters vs. jailhouse censors." *Baltimore Sun* (November 21, 2019).

Kersten, J., "Police powers and accountability in a democratic society: Introductory report." *European Journal on Criminal Policy and Research* 8 (2000): 237–245. doi: 10.1023/A:1008798412206.

Kleiman, M. A. R., *Against excess: Drug policy for results* (New York: Basic Books, 1992); Lee, M., "London: "Community damage limitation" through policing." In *European drug policy and enforcement*, edited by N. Dorn, J. Jepsen, & E. Savona (Basingstoke: Macmillan, 1996).

Klein, Ira, "Plague, policy and popular unrest in British India." *Modern Asian Studies* 22, no. 4 (1988): 723–755. doi: 10.1017/S0026749X00015729.

Kleinman, Arthur, "Culture, bereavement and psychiatry." *The Lancet* 379, no. 9816 (2012): P608-9.

Kleinman, Arthur, *Moral education of a husband and a doctor* (New York: Penguin Random House, 2019).

Kleinman, Arthur, Veena Das, & Margaret Lock, *Social suffering* (Berkeley: University of California Press, 1997).

Knight, Kelly Ray, *Addicted, pregnant, poor* (Durham: Duke University Press, 2015).

Kolb, Lawrence, & A. G. Du Mez, "The prevalence and trend of drug substance use in the United States and factors influencing it." *Public Health Reports* (1896–1970) 39, no. 21 (May 23, 1924): 1179–1204.

Kolb, Lawrence, "Pleasure and deterioration from narcotics substance use." United States Public Health Service Hygienic Laboratory, Washington, DC, Reprint No. 211, the National Committee for Mental Hygiene, Inc., New York City (1925).

Lauzon, Pierre, Jean Vincelette, Julie Bruneau, François Lamothe, Nathalie Lachance, Michel Brabant, & Julio Soto, "Illicit use of methadone among IV drug users in Montreal." *Journal of Substance Abuse Treatment* 11, no. 5 (1994): 457–461.

Lester, Rebecca J., "Brokering authenticity: Borderline personality disorder and the ethics of care in an American eating disorder clinic." *Current Anthropology* 50, no. 3 (2009): 281–302.

Levinson, David, "Skid row in transition." *Urban Anthropology* 3, no. 1 (1974): 79–93.

Levi-Strauss, Claude, *Elementary structures of kinship* (Boston, MA: Beacon Press, 1969).

Lindner, Robert, *The fifty-minute hour* (New York: The Other Press, 2013).

Linker, Beth, *War's waste: Rehabilitation in world war I America* (Illinois: University of Chicago Press, 2011).

Liz, Bowie, "Baltimore man convicted of selling large quantities of prescription out of medical facility." *Baltimore Sun* (May 4, 2018).

Lutz, Catherine, & Andrea Mazzarino, *War and health: The medical consequences of the wars in Iraq and Afghanistan* (New York: New York University Press, 2019).

Lynton, S. J., "OEO turns town narcotics plan: Refuses to give funds for substance use treatment." *The Sun* (July 1, 1967).

Lyon-Callo, Vincent, *Inequality, poverty, and neoliberal governance: Activist ethnography in the homeless sheltering industry* (Toronto: University of Toronto Press, 2008).

Macy, Beth, *Dopesick: Dealers, doctors, and the drug company that addicted America* (Boston, MA: Little, Brown & Co., 2018).

Madden, Mary, "Braving homelessness on the ethnographic street with Irene Glasser and Rae Bridgman." *Critique of Anthropology* 23, no. 3 (2003): 289–304. doi: 10.1177/0308275X030233003.

Madden, Patrick, "Maryland turns to drug courts in battle against opioid substance use." *WAMU 88.5 American University Radio.*

Maher, L., & D. Dixon, "Policing and public health: Law enforcement and harm minimization in a street-level drug market." *British Journal of Criminology* 39, no. 4 (1999): 488–512.

Maher, Lisa, "Don't leave us this way: Ethnography and injecting drug use in the age of AIDS." *International Journal of Drug Policy* 13, no. 4 (2002): 311–325.

Maher, Lisa, & David Dixon, "Policing and public health: Law enforcement and harm minimization in a street-level drug market." *British Journal of Criminology* 39, no. 4 (1999): 488–519.

Maldrum, Marcia L., "The prescription as stigma: Opioid pain relievers and the long walk to the pharmacy counter." In *Prescribed*, edited by Elizabeth Watkins and Jeremy Greene (Baltimore: The Johns Hopkins University Press, 2012).

Marcus, Kenneth L., "Jailhouse islamophobia: Anti-Muslim discrimination in American prisons." *Race and Social Problems* 1, no. 1 (2009): 36–44.

Marquart, James W., & Julian B. Roebuck, "Prison guards and "snitches": Deviance within a total institution." *The British Journal of Criminology* 25, no. 3 (1985): 217–233.

Mars, Sarah G., Philippe Bourgois, George Karadinos, Fernando Montero, & Daniel Ciccarone, "'Every 'never' I ever said came true'; Transitions from opioid pills to heroin injecting." *International Journal of Drug Policy* 25, no. 2 (2014): 257–266.

MaryLouise, Kerwin E. "Collaboration between child welfare and substance-abuse fields: Combined treatment programs for mothers." *Journal of Pediatric Psychology* 30, no. 7 (October/November 2005): 581–597. doi: 10.1093/jpepsy/jsi045.

Mathieu, A., "The medicalization of homelessness and the theater of repression." *Medical Anthropology Quarterly* 7 (1993): 170–184. doi: 10.1525/maq.1993.7.2.02a00030.

Mattingly, Cheryl, *Moral laboratories: Family peril and the struggle for a good life* (Berkeley: University of California Press, 2014).

Mauss, Marcel, *The gift: Forms and functions of exchange in archaic societies* (London: Cohen & West, 1966).

May, T., M. Edmunds, & M. Hough, "Street business: The links between sex and drug markets." In *Police research series paper* (London: Home Office, 1999), p. 118; Jessica Jacobson, "Policing drug hot-spots" (1999).

Mcauliffe, W. E., *A test of Lindesmith's theory of opiate substance use* (Dissertations & Theses at Johns Hopkins University, 1973).

McGehan, F. P., "Baltimore's drug scene-I: Silent disease infects rich, poor." *The Sun* (1969, June 24).

McKeganey, Neil, Marina Barnard, & James McIntosh, "Paying the price for their parents' substance use: Meeting the needs of the children of drug-using parents." *Drugs: Education, Prevention and Policy* 9, no. 3 (2002): 233–246. doi: 10.1080/09687630210122508.

Meier, Barry, *Pain killer: An empire of deceit and the origin of America's opioid epidemic* (Penguin Random House, 2018), p. 19.

Meldrum, Marcia, "'The long walk to the counter': Opioid pain-relievers and the prescription as stigma." In *Prescribed: Writing, filling, using and abusing the prescription in modern America*, edited by Elizabeth Watkins and Jeremy Greene (Baltimore: Johns Hopkins Press, 2012), pp. 184–206.

Meldrum, Marcia L., "The ongoing opioid prescription epidemic: Historical context." *American Journal of Public Health* 106, no. 8 (2016): 1365–1366.

Mendieta, Eduardo, "Plantations, ghettos, prisons: US racial geographies." *Philosophy & Geography* 7, no. 1 (2004): 53. doi: 10.1080/1090377042000196010.

Mendoza, Sonia, Allysa Staphanie Rivera, & Helena Bjerring Hansen, "Re-racialization of substance use and the redistribution of blame in the white opioid epidemic." *Medical Anthropology Quarterly* 33, no. 2 (2019): 242–262.

Meyer, Adolf, "An attempt at analysis of the neurotic constitution." *American Journal of Psychology* 14, no. ¾ (1903): 98.

Meyer, Adolf, "Mental and moral health in a constructive school programs." In *Suggestions of modern science concerning education*, edited by Herbert Jennings, Jacob B. Watson, Adolf Meyer, & William Thomas (New York, NY: MacMillan Co, 1917).

Meyer, Adolf, "Presidential address." *American Journal of Psychiatry* 85, no. 1 (1928): 20.

Meyer, Adolf, "The anatomical facts and clinical varieties of traumatic insanity." *American Journal of Insanity* LX, no. 3 (1904): 373–441.

Meyer, Adolf, "The dynamic interpretation of dementia praecox." *American Journal of Psychiatry* 21, no. 3 (1910): 388.

Meyer, Adolf, "The mental hygiene movement." *Canadian Medical Association Journal* 8, no. 7 (1918): 632.

Meyer, Adolf, "The philosophy of occupational therapy." *Archives of Occupational Therapy* 1, no. 1 (February 1922): 1–10.

Meyer, Adolf, "The problems of mental reaction-type, mental causes and diseases." *Psychological Bulletin* 5, no. 8 (1908): 245–261. doi: 10.1037/h0072906.

Meyer, Adolf, "The problems of the physician concerning the criminal insane and borderland cases." *JAMA* LIV, no. 24 (1910): 1930–1935.

Meyer, Adolf, "The role of mental factors in psychiatry." *American Journal of Psychiatry* 65, no. 1 (2006): 46.

Meyer, Adolf, "What do histories of cases of insanity teach us concerning preventative mental hygiene during the years of school life?" *The Psychological Clinic* 2, no. 4 (1908): 89.

Meyers, Todd, *The clinic and elsewhere: Substance use, adolescents, and the afterlife of therapy* (Seattle: University of Washington Press, 2013).

"Milked of quarter million she earned in 3 years, billie holiday sentenced: Begs U.S. judge to place her in hospital so she can get rid of vicious dope habit." (1947, June 7). *Afro-American.*

Moerman, Daniel, *Meaning, medicine and the 'Placebo effect'* (Cambridge: Cambridge University Press, 2002).

Mol, Annemarie, *The logic of care: Health and the problem of patient choice* (Routledge, 2008).

Mooney, Graham, "Methadone treatment centers and crime." Letters to the Editor, *Substance use* (2012).

Moore, Merrill, Alice F. Raymond, & Mildred G. Gray, "Alcoholism and the use of drugs; a review of 841 cases diagnosed "with psychosis due to drugs and other exogenous toxins" or "without psychosis: Drug substance use." *Quarterly Journal of Studies on Alcohol* 2, no. 3 (1941): 496–504.

Morton, K. L., "Tongan adoption." (1976), 64–80; R. Tonkinson, "Adoption and sister exchange in a New Hebredean community." (1976), 228–246.

Murji, K., *Policing drugs* (Aldershot: Ashgate, 1998).

Nass, S. J., L. A. Levit, & L. O. Gostin, *Beyond the HIPAA: Privacy rule: Enhancing privacy, improving health through research* (Washington, DC: National Academies Press, 2009).

National Institute of Drug Abuse, "Maryland: Opioid-involved deaths and related harms."

"NCAIDS Hearing on HIV Disease in African American Communities," Transcript, Baltimore, Maryland.

Nightingale, Stuart L., William W. Michaux, & Penelope C. Piatt, "Clinical implications of urine surveillance in a methadone maintenance program." *International Journals of the Substance Uses* 7, no. 2 (1972): 403–414.

Nitardy, F. W., "Notes on early drug legislation." *Journal of Pharmacological Science* 23 (1934): 1122–1127. doi: 10.1002/jps.3080231113.

Nolan, James L., *The therapeutic state: Justifying government at century's end* (New York: New York University Press, 1998), p. 94.

Nurco, D. N., T. E. Hanlon, & T. W. Kinlock, "Recent research on the relationship between illicit drug use and crime, particularly stealing." *Behavior Science Law* 9 (1991): 221–242.

Offersen, Sara Marie Hebsgaard, Mette Bech Risør, Peter Vedsted, & Rikke Sand Andersen, "Am I fine? Exploring everyday life & ambiguities and potentialities of embodied sensations in a Danish middle-class community." *Medical Anthropology Theory* 3, no. 3 (2016): 23–45.

"Officials Shun AIDS Report," Baltimore Evening Sun (1991). https://collections.nlm.nih.gov/catalog/nlm:nlmuid-101763264X163-doc.

Ostrach, Bayla, *Health policy in a time of crisis: Abortion, austerity and access* (Routledge, 2017).

Owen, Jacob E., "How delinquent are our juveniles?" *The Educational Forum* 21, no. 2 (1957): 203–206. doi: 10.1080/00131725709341085.

Oxenden, McKenna, "Baltimore Guerilla family member gang member sentenced to life in prison." *Baltimore Sun* (June, 2019).

Paik, Leslie, *Discretionary justice: Looking inside a juvenile drug court* (New Jersey: Rutgers University Press, 2011).

Partridge, George E., "A study of 50 cases of psychopathic personality; psychopathic personalities among boys in a training school for delinquents; psychotic reaction in the psychopath." (1932).

Partridge, George E., "Psychopathic personality and personality." *The American Journal of Psychiatry* 6, no. 85 (May 1929): 1053–1055.

Payte, J. T. "A brief history of methadone in the treatment of opioid dependence: A personal perspective." *Journal of Psychoactive Drugs* 23, no. 2 (1991): 103–107. doi: 10.1080/02791072.1991.10472226.

Peacock, Amy, Raimondo Bruno, Natasa Gisev, Louisa Degenhardt, Wayne Hall, Roumen Sedefov, Jason White, Kevin V. Thomas, Michael Farrell, & Paul Griffiths. "New psychoactive substances: Challenges for drug surveillance, control and public health responses." *Lancet* 394 (2019): 1668–1684.

Peard, Julyan G., "Tropical medicine in nineteenth-century Brazil: The case of the 'Escola Tropicalista Bahiana,' 1860–1890." In *Warm climates and western medicine* (Leiden, The Netherlands: Brill, 1996). doi: 10.1163/9789004418448_010.

Perry, Heather R., *Recycling the disabled: Army, medicine and modernity in WWI Germany* (Manchester: Manchester University Press, 2014).

Peyrot, Mark, "Narcotics anonymous: Its history, structure and approach." *International Journal of the Substance Uses* 20, no. 1 (1985): 1509–1522.

Philbin, Morgan M., "What I got to go through": Normalization and HIV-positive adolescents." *Medical Anthropology* 33, no. 4 (2004): 288–302.

Porter, Roy, "The patient's view: Doing medical history from below." *Theory and Society* 14 (1985): 175–198.

Preston, James, "What can be done to improve the living conditions of Baltimore's negro population?" *Baltimore Mun.* 1, no. 1 (March 16, 1917).

"Proceedings of an annual meeting of the National Drug Trade conference held at the Hotel Emerson, Baltimore," January 4 (1918) In Pursuance of a call of the president upon the written request of five delegates.

"Pupils in families with drugs get aid." *The Sun* (1990, December 23).

Quintero, G., & M. Nichter, "Generation RX: Anthropological research on pharmaceutical enhancement, lifestyle regulation, self-medication and recreational drug use." In *A companion to medical anthropology*, edited by M. Singer and P. I. Erickson (2011). doi: 10.1002/9781444395303.ch17.

Rankin, Katherine, "A critical geography of poverty finance." *Third World Quarterly* 3, no. 4 (2013): 547–568.

Rasmussen, Nicholas, "Goofball panic: Barbiturates, "dangerous" and addictive drugs, and the regulation of medicine in postwar America." In *Prescribed*, edited by Elizabeth Watkins and Jeremy Greene (Baltimore: The Johns Hopkins University Press, 2012).

Ratcliffe, J. H., & T. A. Taniguchi, "Is crime higher around drug-gang street corners? Two spatial approaches to the relationship between gang set spaces and local crime levels." *Crime Patterns and Analysis* 1, no. 1 (2009): 23–46.

Rentz, Catherine, "Freddie gray remembered as jokester who struggled to leave drug trade." *Baltimore Sun* (November 2015).

Report of the Superintendent of the Johns Hopkins Hospital (1914).

"Report of the Superintendent of the Johns Hopkins Hospital," (1889).

Reuter, P., & R. J. MacCoun, "Street drug markets and inner-city neighborhoods: Matching policy to reality." In *Urban America: Policy choices for Los Angeles and the nation*, edited by J. B. Steinberg, D. W. Lyon, & M. E. Vaiana (Santa Monica, CA: Rand Corporation, 1995), pp. 227–251.

Reyes, Raquel A. G., "Environmentalist thinking and the question of disease causation in late Spanish Philippines." *Journal of the History of Medicine and Allied Sciences* 69, no. 4 (October 2014): 554–579. doi: 10.1093/jhmas/jrt030.

Rhodes, Lorna A., *Total confinement: Madness and reason in the maximum security prison* (Berkeley: University of California Press, 2004).

Rhodes, T., "Risk environments and drug harms: A social science for harm reduction approach." *The International Journal on Drug Policy* 20, no. 3 (2009): 193–201. doi: 10.1016/j.drugpo.2008.10.003.

Richie, Beth, *Arrested justice: Black women, violence, and America's prison nation* (New York: New York University Press, 2012).

Roberts, Dorothy, *Killing the Black body: Race, reproduction and the meaning of liberty* (New York: Penguin, 1998).

Roberts, Dorothy, *Shattered bonds: The color of child welfare* (New York: Civitas Books, 2002).

Rosenbloom, J. R. "Notes on Jewish drug addicts." *Psychological Reports* 5, no. 3 (1959): 769–772. doi: 10.2466/pr0.1959.5.3.769.

Rouse, Carolyn, "'If she's a vegetable, we'll be her garden': Embodiment, transcendence, and citations of competing cultural metaphors in the case of a dying child."

American Ethnologist 31, no. 4 (2004): 514–529. http://www.jstor.org/stable/4098866.

Ruiz, M. S., A. O'Rourke, S. T. Allen, D. R. Holtgrave, D. Metzger, J. Benitez, K. A. Brady, & C. P. Chaulk. "Using interrupted time series analysis to measure the impact of legalized syringe exchange on HIV diagnoses in Baltimore and Philadelphia." *Journal of Acquired Immune Deficiency Syndromes* 82 Suppl 2, no. 2 (2019): S148–S154. doi: 10.1097/QAI.0000000000002176.

Sadowsky, Jonathan, *The empire of depression: A new history* (New York: Polity, 2020).

Samantha, Samiparna, "Unseen enemy: The English, disease, and medicine in colonial Bengal, 1617–1847." *The Historian* 78, no. 4 (Winter 2016): 792.

Schuldiner, J. A., "Identification of amidone." *Analytical Chemistry* 21, no. 2 (1949): 298–300. doi: 10.1021/ac60026a017.

Segal, Lotte, *No place for grief: Martyrs, prisoners and mourning in contemporary Palestine* (Pennsylvania: University of Pennsylvania Press, 2016).

Seliger, Robert V., & Victoria Cranford, "Psychiatric orientation of the alcoholic criminal." *JAMA* 129, no. 6 (1945): 421–424.

Simon, D., "Politics and drugs: Preventing AIDS by having drug users exchange needles, as has been suggested in Kurt L. Schmoke's Baltimore, May Work but the politicians don't seem to want to find out." *The Sun* (1990, April 15).

Singer, Merrill, & J. Bryan Page, *The social value of drug addicts: Uses of the useless* (Routledge, 2016).

Snow, David A., Susan G. Baker, Leon Anderson, & Michaei Martin, "The myth of pervasive mental illness among the homeless." *Social Problems* 33, no. 5 (1896): 407–423.

Spradley, James, *You owe yourself a drunk: An ethnography of urban nomads* (Boston: Little Brown, 1970), p. 254.

Stinchcomb, Blake Carolyn, "Debate and discussion: Methadone: Treatment, or a worse substance use?" *The Sun* (1976, January 31).

Stocking Jr., George W., ed. "History of anthropology." Volume 4. In *Malinowski, rivers, benedict and others: Essays on culture and personality* (Madison: University of Wisconsin Press, 1986).

Stoler, Ann, *Race and the education of desire: Foucault's history of sexuality and the colonial order of things* (Durham: Duke University Press, 1995).

Sue, Kimberly, *Getting wrecked: Women, incarceration, and the American opioid crisis* (Berkeley: University of California Press, 2019).

Sufrin, Carolyn, *Jailcare: Finding the safety net for women behind the bars* (Berkeley: University of California Press, 2017).

Sullivan, Harry Stack, "Socio-psychiatric research: Its implications for schizophrenia problem and for mental hygiene." New York City. Presented in abstract at the eighty-sixth annual meeting of The American Psychiatric Association, Washington, D. C., May (1930).

Sykes, Gresham M., *Crime and society* (New York: Random House, 1967), pp. 175–176.

Sykes, Gresham M., *The society of captives: A study of a maximum security prison* (New Jersey: Princeton University Press, 1958), pp. 63–83.

Tarlo, Emma, "Body and space in a time of crisis: Sterilization and resettlement during emergency in India." In *Violence and subjectivity*, edited by Veena Das, Arthur Kleinman, Mamphela Ramphele, & Pamela Reynolds (Berkeley: University of California Press, 2000).

Taxman, F. S., D. Soule, & A. Gelb, "Graduated sanctions: Stepping into accountable systems and offenders." *The Prison Journal* 79, no. 2 (1999): 185.

Taylor, Andy, & Brynna Kroll, "Working with parental substance misuse: Dilemmas for practice." *The British Journal of Social Work* 34, no. 8 (2004): 1115–1132. *JSTOR*, http://www.jstor.org/stable/23720534. Accessed 12 December 2022.

Taylor, M. F., D. Coall, & R. Marquis. "Drug substance use is a scourge on the earth and my grandchildren are its victims: The tough love and resilient growth exhibited by grandparents raising the children of drug-dependent mothers." *International Journal of Mental Health Substance Use* 14 (2016): 937–951. doi: 10.1007/s11469-016-9645-7.

Terry, Jennifer, *Attachments to war: Biomedical logics and violence in the twenty-first-century-America* (Durham: Duke University Press, 2017).

"The Black Butterfly: Racial Segregation and Investment Patterns in Baltimore." https://apps.urban.org/features/baltimore-investment-flows/.

"The de-briefing proposal," *American Prison Writing Archive;* "Home: An essay on prison pre-release anxiety and post-traumatic stress disorder," *American Prison Writing Archive.*

The Kansas City Medical Index-Lancet, Volume 7 (1889).

"The Negro tuberculosis problem in Maryland: Whose problem?" *Maryland Association for the Prevention and Relief of Tuberculosis* (1915).

Tiger, Rebecca, *Judging addicts: Drug courts and coercion in the justice system* (New York: New York University Press, 2013).

Ulmer, Jeffrey T. *Social worlds of sentencing: Court communities under sentencing guidelines* (New York: State University of New York Press, 1997).

"U.S. Comm'n on Civil Rights, Understanding Fair Housing 4-5" (Clearinghouse Pub. No. 42, 1973).

Varley, Emma, & Saiba Varma, "Introduction: Medicine's shadowside: revisiting clinical iatrogenesis." *Anthropology & Medicine* 28, no. 2 (2021): 141–155.

Venters, Homer, *Life and death in Rikers Island* (Baltimore: Johns Hopkins University Press, 2019).

Volkow, N. D., D. Tomasi, G. J. Wang, J. Logan, D. L. Alexoff, M. Jayne, J. S. Fowler, C. Wong, P. Yin, & C. Du. "Stimulant-induced dopamine increases are markedly blunted in active cocaine abusers." *Molecular Psychiatry* 19, no. 9 (2014): 1037–1043. doi: 10.1038/mp.2014.58.

Wacquant, Loic, "Creating the neoliberal state: Workfare, prisonfare, and social insecurity." *Sociological Forum* 25, no. 2 (2010): 197–220.

Wacquant, Loic, "Deadly symbiosis: When Ghetto and prison meet and mesh." *Punishment and Society* 3, no. 1 (2001): 95–134.

Wacquant, Loic, "From slavery to mass incarceration," *New Left Review* 13 (2002): 50.

Wacquant, Loic, "From slavery to mass incarceration: Re-thinking the 'race question' in the US." In *Race, law and society,* edited by Ian Haney Lopez (Routledge, 2007).

Wacquant, Loic, "The new 'peculiar institution': On the prison as surrogate ghetto." *Theoretical Criminology* 4, no. 3 (2000): 377–389. doi: 10.1177/13624806000004003007.

Walker, A. K. "Methadone clinics don't attract crime, study finds: Residents still resistant to clinics in their neighborhoods." *Baltimore Sun* (2012).

Wasserman, Jason Adam, & Jeffrey Michael Claire, *At home on the street: People, poverty and a hidden culture of homelessness* (Colorado: Lynne Rienner Publishers, 2009).

Watkins, D., *Cook up: A crack rock memoir* (New York: Grand Central Publishing, 2017).

Weatherburn, D., & B. Lind, "The impact of law enforcement activity on a heroin market." *Substance Use* 92, no. 5 (1997): 557–569.

Weizman, Eyal, *Hollow land: Israel's architecture of occupation* (New York: Verso, 2017).

Werb, Dan, Greg Rowell, Gordon Guyatt, Thomas Kerr, Julio Montaner, & Evan Wood, "Effect of drug law enforcement on drug market violence: A systematic review." *International Journal of Drug Policy* 22, no. 2 (2011): 87–94.

Whitehead, T. L., "Urban low-income African American men, HIV/AIDS, and gender identity." *Medical Anthropology Quarterly* 11 (1997): 411–447. doi: 10.1525/maq.1997.11.4.411.

Winstock, Adam R., Toby Lea, & Janie Sheridan, "Patient's help-seeking behavior for health problems associated with methadone and buprenorphine treatment." *Drug and Alcohol Review* 27, no. 4 (2009): 393–397.

Witte, Ann D., "Work release in North Carolina. A program that works!" *Law and Contemporary Problems* 41, no. 1 (1977): 230–251.

Wolch, J. R., & S. Rowe, "On the streets: Mobility paths of the urban homeless." *City & Society* 6 (1992): 127. doi: 10.1525/city.1992.6.2.115.

Wong, C. C. Y., J. Mill, & C. Fernandes, "Drugs and substance use: An introduction to epigenetics." *Substance Use* 106 (2011): 480–489. doi: 10.1111/j.1360-0443.2010.03321.x.

Young, Allan, *Harmony of illusions: Inventing post-traumatic stress disorder* (New Jersey: Princeton University Press, 1996).

Yu, Y. J., "Subjectivity, hygiene, and STI prevention: A normalization paradox in the cleanliness practices of female sex workers in post-socialist China." *Medical Anthropology Quarterly* 27 (2013): 360.

Zigon, Jarrett, *A war on people: Drug user politics and a new ethics of community* (Oakland: University of California Press, 2018), p. 85.

Zigon, Jarrett, *HIV is god's blessing: Rehabilitating morality in neoliberal Russia* (Berkeley: University of California Press).

Zimmer, L., "Proactive policing against street-level drug trafficking." *American Journal of Police* 9, no. 1 (1990): 43–74.

Index

About the Author

Sanaullah Khan is a medical and psychiatric anthropologist. He received his PhD in anthropology from Johns Hopkins University. He has also received advanced training in history of medicine and a graduate certificate in global health from Johns Hopkins University. He is the co-editor of *Globalization, Displacement and Psychiatry* (2023). In the past, his research on militarization and psychiatric care has appeared in *Critical Military Studies, Asian Anthropology, Journal of South Asian Studies, Medical History, South Asian Development*, and *City & Society*. Previously, he taught medical and cultural anthropology at the University of Delaware and Towson University.

www.ingramcontent.com/pod-product-compliance
Ingram Content Group UK Ltd.
Pitfield, Milton Keynes, MK11 3LW, UK
UKHW012118150926
475560UK00002B/169

9 781666 929096